Transcultural Sound Practices

Transcultural Sound Practices

British Asian Dance Music as Cultural Transformation

Carla J. Maier

BLOOMSBURY ACADEMIC
NEW YORK • LONDON • OXFORD • NEW DELHI • SYDNEY

BLOOMSBURY ACADEMIC
Bloomsbury Publishing Inc
1385 Broadway, New York, NY 10018, USA
50 Bedford Square, London, WC1B 3DP, UK
29 Earlsfort Terrace, Dublin 2, Ireland

BLOOMSBURY, BLOOMSBURY ACADEMIC and the Diana logo
are trademarks of Bloomsbury Publishing Plc

First published in the United States of America 2020
Paperback edition first published 2021

Copyright © Carla J. Maier, 2020

For legal purposes the Acknowledgments on pp. xi–xii constitute
an extension of this copyright page.

Cover design: Louise Dugdale
Cover image © Peter Denton / Getty Images

All rights reserved. No part of this publication may be reproduced or
transmitted in any form or by any means, electronic or mechanical,
including photocopying, recording, or any information storage or retrieval
system, without prior permission in writing from the publishers.

Bloomsbury Publishing Inc does not have any control over, or responsibility for,
any third-party websites referred to or in this book. All internet addresses given
in this book were correct at the time of going to press. The author and publisher
regret any inconvenience caused if addresses have changed or sites have
ceased to exist, but can accept no responsibility for any such changes.

A catalog record for this book is available from the Library of Congress.

ISBN: HB: 978-1-5013-4956-0
PB: 978-1-5013-8598-8
ePDF: 978-1-5013-4958-4
eBook: 978-1-5013-4957-7

Typeset by Integra Software Services Pvt. Ltd.

To find out more about our authors and books visit
www.bloomsbury.com and sign up for our newsletters.

Contents

Preface   vi
Acknowledgements   xi

Introduction   1

Part One   Towards a Cultural Analysis of Sound Practices

1. Renegotiating Culture in the Age of British Asian Dance Music   15
2. The Concept of Transcultural Sound Practices   49

Part Two   Listening to British Asian Dance Music

3. Re-Fusing and Reclaiming UK Bhangra: Apache Indian, *No Reservations* (1992)   89
4. Demystifying Asianness: Asian Dub Foundation, *Community Music* (2000)   105
5. Sonic Fictions, Global Noise: M.I.A., *Arular* (2005) and *Kala* (2007)   121
6. Performativity, Technology and the Body: Nathan 'Flutebox' Lee, *Flutebox* (2011)   143
7. The Sonic Politics of Place: Dusk + Blackdown's *Margins Music* (2008)   159

Part Three   Thinking Sound as Cultural Transformation

8. Conclusion – Transcultural Sound Practices in British Asian Dance Music   179
9. Outlook – On Transcultural Sound Practices beyond Music   191

Notes   195
References   203
Index   216

Preface

It was the sound that completely captured me and sparked my interest in the aesthetics, socialities and cultural politics of South Asian dance music in Britain. When I went for a dance night out to Monday's *Anokha* club night in London with my friend Anne in the late summer of 1997, it was the sound and the special atmosphere that completely fascinated me. There was an excitement, attentiveness and keenness that manifested in the ways people moved around, how they danced, how they gathered around the turntables of the DJs.

To me, the fast-forward beats and sub-bass frequencies, interspersed with melodic samples, were familiar and unfamiliar at the same time. I've been dancing to drum'n'bass music in Berlin and Frankfurt/Main, and felt an immediate connection to the sound and the space through the particular speed, syncopation and intensity of the music. But the sampled sounds were significantly different from what I was used to hear at the drum'n'bass clubs in my home country Germany: Hindi film music vocals, sped up tabla breaks, loops from Indian ragas mixed over broken beats and layered with sustained sub-bass lines – this was new to me.

It seemed also rare to me at the time to see such a great presence of South Asian youths at the turntables, behind the bar and on the dance floor, what I experienced as a very self-confident scene. Young women wearing sneakers and a bindi, some with black cajal or some glitter around the eyes, made me aware of how much London, or this club night in particular, seemed to be a transnational and translocal place in which cultural identities were to be negotiated and reinvented on the dance floor and behind the decks. Again, speaking from my previous experience of growing up in a multicultural city like Frankfurt/Main, in terms of clubs and dance music culture, the presence of Turkish dance music culture, for instance, was quite separated from the distinct German electronic dance music (EDM) scenes, with more shared spaces and practices in the context of (Turkish-German) rap and hip-hop. I felt a commonality in the transcultural mix of people at *Anokha*, and was especially delighted that a good number of women were present on the dance floor (although not behind the decks). One scene in particular I found empowering as a young woman in a club: In the downstairs club which was packed with dance-ravishing people, a circle of young men had occupied a good portion of the dance floor, who in turns jumped to the centre and showed off with their (more or less) skilful breakdance moves. It was an energetic, and also slightly aggressive, mode of demonstrating masculine dominance, and the girls (including my friend and myself) increasingly felt stopped in their dance, because we were repeatedly jostled and pushed away. I observed the women in the room starting to look at each other, expressing their discomfort. Then a female dancer came up to me shouting in my ear: 'we'll count down and smash the pit.' The conspiracy was extended throughout the room, via eye contact, and then we started counting down from ten, and by zero collectively danced our way inside the circle, breaking it open, dancing through and with the crowd in a very positive, cheerful manner which left the boys baffled, but no one really complained. The table was turned, and the party went on. It was a moment of female solidarity which I perceived also as reaching across and beyond social markers such as race and class.

My subjective view based on my personal experience as a 21-year-old white woman new to London was – and it had to be – in many ways complexified and problematized by a lot of different accounts I became aware of on the *Anokha* nights in particular, and South Asian music scenes in London more generally, as articulated by British Asian club goers, academics and music producers I met during my research. I was exposed to these accounts only a little later when I started to study postcolonial literature, cultural studies and cultural anthropology in Frankfurt/Main, when my knowledge in South Asian dance music, migration and postcolonial histories, narratives and discourses became more nuanced and founded.

I only then learned more about the so-called Asian Underground scene, which actually has never been one homogenous scene at all, and of which Anokha was counted to be a significant part. I learned about the variety of South Asian musics across different genres that had been part of British Asian communities in the UK for decades. One of the books that were crucial in this for its critical and cutting-edge stance was *Dis-orienting Rhythms: The Politics of the New Asian Dance Music* (edited by Sanjay Sharma, et al., in 1996), a book which continues to be seminal in the field.

When I was embarking on this project in 2007, one of the initial questions was what the particular sonic and cultural legacies of the so-called Asian Underground were, and how this sound has shifted with the general and more specific shifts and transformations in UK dance music and in society at large.

I conducted ethnographic fieldwork in London mainly in 2008, with a few shorter visits in 2006/2007 and 2009/2010. This period turned out to be a special moment in the history of South Asian Dance Music in the UK, which can be described as a moment of heightened popularity and mainstream recognition for musics emerging from South Asian music producers, and, simultaneously, an increasingly racialized discourse of nationalism, (street) crime, terrorism and surveillance that developed in the context of the terrorist attack of 9/11 in 2001 and the London bombings of 7/7 in 2005, which 'bolstered a longstanding Islamophobia in Britain whose prior existence had been evidenced by such events as the Salman Rushdie affair in 1988', as Falu Bakrania's aptly points out in his 2013 book *Bhangra and Asian Underground: South Asian Music and the Politics of Belonging in Britain* (Bakrania 2013: 188). British Asian bands such as Asian Dub Foundation, Fun-Da-Mental and M.I.A. have created powerful sonic, verbal and visual expressions and statements that commented and critiqued these tendencies, as will be elaborated in this study.

Throughout 2008, I conducted participant observation in a number of clubs and concert halls in London featuring South Asian dance music, in the contexts of which I recorded interviews with musicians, music producers and DJs across different musical genres and scenes, including Nihal Arthanayake, at the time radio producer and host of Bombay Bronx club night at Notting Hill Arts Club; Ritu Hirani aka DJ Ritu, broadcaster, DJ and host of Club Kali and other club nights; Nerm Chauhan and Dee Dhanjal aka Nerm and D-Code, radio producers, DJs and founders of artist collective Shiva Soudsystem; Steve Goodman aka Kode9, electronic music artist and scholar, Nathan 'Flutebox' Lee flutist and MC; Ash Chandola, music promoter and co-founder of collective and club night Swaraj and artistic director at *Alchemy* festival at Southbank Centre; Martin Clarke aka Blackdown, label owner and music producer, amongst others.

After talking with musicians, label owners and radio producers, the question that I wanted to investigate was how, in concrete musical productions, sounds of different musical genres and traditions were mixed together, and how these sounds were cut, pasted and manipulated to become an entirely reworked transcultural fabric, a critical and transformative material which was tweaked to challenge the binary constructions of culture that were still so dominant in popular and academic musical discourses at the time and so often neatly packed, labelled and sold as 'World Music'.

My focus is on five case studies – five examples of how transcultural sound practices can be studied as cultural transformation. These five particular examples of musical works and performances by artists and bands Apache Indian, Asian Dub Foundation, M.I.A., Dusk & Blackdown, and Nathan 'Flutebox' Lee formed the five case studies analysed in Part II of this book, in connection to which the interviews worked as a highly valuable resource.

At the end of the second decade of the 2000s, while finishing the manuscript of this book, nationalist and right-wing extremist parties throughout Europe have been gaining power for several years, which has been accompanied by growing hostility to the immigration of refugees, and a growing anti-Islamic rhetoric and Euroscepticism, which is not least reflected in the current social debate about and concrete social consequences of Brexit. This has not at least also influenced the perception of South Asian communities in Britain, with a notable decrease in the visibility of South Asian cultural production, and a tendency of South Asian music production going more underground again. One manifestation of this – or rather, a reflective turn to one of the key moments in the pinnacle of the *Asian Underground* – might be British Asian band *The Asian Dub Foundation*'s release of a reissue of their revolutionary 1998 studio album *Rafi's Revenge*, on coloured vinyl and with an expanded CD/Digital version (London Records, 22 March 2019). The album's release is accompanied by a new documentary in which the founding members of ADF Steve Chandra Savale aka *Chandrasonic* and Aniruddha Das aka *Dr Das*, retrospectively explain the sonic, political and cultural innovation and power of *Rafi's Revenge* and its creation. Instead of a nostalgic review, the band members emphasize why Rafi's revenge is still a relevant album, in which completely new musical ideas were formed in the juxtaposition of jungle (this very specific interplay of fast beats with half-time distorted bass lines) with punk guitars, synths and samples from a range of musical sources. The band has moved on since the release of their debut album, and in my opinion have grown also slightly less politically and musically innovative over time, with noteworthy musical projects being pursued by band member Dr Das (who left ADF in 2005 and returned to the current line-up in 2013), consistently breaking new sonic ground with his 'Dubnoiz' and 'Dhangsha' projects. In any case, Asian Dub Foundation's work remains groundbreaking – and this applies to some of the other artists I am discussing in this study such as M.I.A. and Nathan 'Flutebox' Lee, in that they have consistently faced (in different ways) the challenges of reimagining Asianness in a transnational, globalized, racist, gendered world. And music was one of the grounds on which the struggle for recognition and for change was taking place, in London prominently, in very concrete locations, cultural institutions as well as the academy, and simultaneously around convivialities and socialities that were formed on the dancefloor, in clubs, in concert halls or in radio shows.

Dance music was one of the vehicles to foster a greater presence, audibility and visibility of the South Asian youths in Britain. And the concrete sound practices – the practices which formed the emerging dance music styles in merging different genres, musical traditions and electronic sound production techniques in whole new ways – became the tools with which the sonic, cultural and social materialities could be accessed, reworked and new claims be made. While working in the very concrete material of sound and music, the analytical work of *transcultural* sound practices might incorporate the capacity to create new sonic narratives, to amplify alternative histories and to forge new relationships between music, politics and the wider social world. It's not the sound itself that is political per se, or that holds a 'sonic agency' (LaBelle 2018) that points in exactly the progressive direction you might envision; but the ways in which sounds are treated, sampled and merged, how they are juxtaposed with lyrics, and performed on stage, can become an aesthetic strategy of navigating affective sonic relationships, which include musical, verbal, visual and performative elements of music production, in a way that indeed may become political: Transcultural sound practices, as a concept, can change the way we listen, and shift the paradigms of who is heard, what is heard and how. *Transcultural Sound Practices: British Asian Dance Music as Cultural Transformation*, as the title of this book has it, is exactly about this. It is not about a culturistic reformulation of ethnic identity in a migratory and globalized world. It pushes beyond identity as a fixed entity, and towards processes of cultural transformation as a repertoire of resources, stances and new sonic fictions (cf. Eshun 1998) and how they have emerged from South Asian cultural production in the UK.

Aspects of Chapter 4 appeared as 'Sonic Modernities: Listening to Diasporic Urban Music' in: Schulze H, Papenburg J (Eds.), *Sound As Popular Culture: A Companion*. MIT Press, Massachusetts, 2016. 173-181.

Theorizations of the concept of sound practices, and portions of the musical analysis in Chapter 6 appeared as 'Sound Practices' in: Schulze H, Papenburg J (Eds.), *Sound as Popular Culture: A Companion*. MIT Press, Massachusetts, 2016. 45-51.

Portions of Chapter 3 appeared as 'Sound Cultures' in: Merten K, Krämer L (Eds.), *Postcolonial Studies Meets Media Studies*. Transcript, Bielefeld, 2016. 179-196.

Acknowledgements

This book, which took many years to complete, would not have been achievable without the indescribable support of my family, and the stimulating conversations with colleagues and friends I met along this journey.

In the very beginnings of this project, during my time at Goethe University Frankfurt, I found a greatly supportive and inspiring research environment. Thank you for inspiring and fun conversations, my colleagues of the NELK research colloquium: Ellen Grünkemeier, Claudia Perner, Mahsa Mahamied, Nadia Butt, Doreen Strauhs, Cosima Wittmann, Jan Wilm, Jenny Diederich, Eva Jungbluth, Zhuang Wei, Ivo Shmilev, Malte Schudlich, Troy Blacklaws, Maria Hüren, Subin Nijhawan, Hanna Teichler. Especially, I would like to express my deep gratitude to Frank Schulze-Engler, who encouraged me to embark on a project in which I had to step out of my disciplinary comfort zone of *Anglistik* and crossing over to *Sound Studies*, to develop an interdisciplinary mode of thinking and listening. My research interest in South Asian British musical production brought me to London, where I had the honour and pleasure to meet many musicians, producers and club owners who generously shared their knowledge, expertise and critical views on the sonic and cultural politics of music in the UK. Special thanks go to DJ Ritu, Ash Chandola, Nerm, D-Code, Dr Das, Chandrasonic, Nathan 'Flutebox' Lee, Nihal and others. Thank you so much for stimulating discussions at various stages of the project (also including those who read earlier versions of the manuscript): Lars Eckstein, Helen Kim, Anamik Saha, Sanjay Sharma, Johannes Ismaiel-Wendt, Thomas Burkhalter, Regina Römhild, Kira Kosnick, Bernd Herzogenrath, Stefanie Kiwi Menrath, Maria Hanáček (†), Harpreet Kaur Cholia, Michael Bull, Les Back, Julian Henriques, Steve Goodman, John Hutnyk, Nirmal Puwar, Melissa Van Drie, Stefanie Alisch, Hannah Fitsch. My special and heartfelt gratitude is for Holger Schulze, my mentor, collaborator and friend, who has always believed in my work and who introduced me to many sound studies scholars who have since become collaborators, colleagues and friends.

This book is simply not thinkable without the love, patience, support and inspiration of my family: My mother Regina Schulzke and stepfather Hans-Ludwig Schmidts, my father Hartmut Müller and his wife Dorothea Thums, and my dearest siblings Kerstin Müller-Schulzke, Johannes Schmidts and Felix Schmidts. And Christa Hoock for extending and enriching our family with her love, and for supporting me. My deep gratitude goes to Christian, my love, who has inspired me and encouraged me in all the moments of dancing and fighting with this book. Last but not least, I thank our children Marvin and Enya for simply being who they are and for letting me hear and see the world in a new way every day.

Introduction

In 2007, when Sri Lankan British musician Mathangi Arulpragasam, also known as M.I.A., released her second album *Kala*, she was awarded 'Best Global Sound' of the year by *Rolling Stone* magazine. What 'global sound' is meant to connote remains vague, since the list does not actually reference any verifiable criterion like the music charts, nor is it related directly to a particular artistic product like an album or a music video (although it is most probably connected to the release of her album in the same month). It could equally be read as a renewal of the assertion that M.I.A.'s music is 'the coolest sound for the coming summer' made by *The Independent* after the release of her first album *Arular* in 2005 (Gill 2005). In any case, there does not seem to be any great urge to clarify the blurry character of the label 'Best Global Sound' – the effect it has as a form of respect for some kind of globalist, subcultural capital seems sufficient.

The term 'global sound' calls up a number of controversial perspectives on the workings of contemporary urban dance musics. First of all, it could be read as an overdue recognition that her music indeed no longer fits into the 'world music' section of any record store (which it never really did, of course). When her first album *Arular* came out in 2005, she was still confronted with the question posed by eager and somewhat puzzled journalists asking her under which section she would actually file the album. She nonchalantly responded that they should just stack it up right next to the cashier. In this sense, choosing the label 'global' could be understood as a concession to the limitations of ethnically connoted musical categories.

Moreover, the term 'global' has already started to function as a more up-to-date substitute for 'world' in music discourses, as in global pop, global beats or global ghettotech, alongside rejuvenated 'world' categories such as worldtronica, world fusion or world music 2.0. Which particular term is used varies depending on whether it is used in announcements of club nights and music festivals, radio shows, online music networks or scholarly investigations of globalized popular music culture. Global fusion, for instance, can be seen as a relatively unspecified musical style, fusing some sort of electronic dance beat with fragments of non-European instrumentation which could range from Australian didgeridoos to Indian sitars to Algerian gaspa flutes. If the particularities of these musical mixings are ignored for the sake of an easy to digest 'exotic flavour' (which is the way in which world music or global fusion is often promoted), 'global sound' would simply revive the old binaries of traditional and modern, East and West, technology and tribalism under the promise of universalized dance music.

One of the questions which emanate from my critique of simple cultural binarisms, and with which the present study will engage, is how we can think beyond 'world music' and other limiting musical categories and listen more closely to the transcultural sound practices in dance music that is transnational in scope and involves diverse and inventive sonic techniques. In the case of M.I.A., her music challenges assumptions about the location of her music in an Indian music tradition. The sounds that she uses do not evoke the image of remote cultures in distant countries playing handmade instruments; these sounds come rather from the areas around urban metropolises such as São Paulo, San Juan and Johannesburg: Brazilian *funk carioca*, Puerto Rican *reggaeton* and South African *kwaito* feature prominently in her albums. These styles themselves share a translocal and inherently transient character which cannot easily be confined to notions of fixed ethnic communities. Moreover, these styles are highly technologized, using drum computers, samplers and other electronic devices in order to produce and disseminate their music, and are thus part of a wider transnational electronic dance music culture. This is a clear contradiction of the biased images of musicians in the global South being unaware of up-to-date musical technology.

While M.I.A. mixes and merges funk carioca, reggaeton and kwaito with London dance music, Jamaican dancehall and US hip-hop, additional noise is explicated through her politicised lyrics dealing with topics of war, immigration politics, surveillance and capitalist exploitation. In this way, the musics which influence M.I.A. are not merely reproduced, but thoroughly reappropriated according to her own aesthetic, cultural and political aspirations. This aspect touches upon another important endeavour of my study, namely the investigation and comparison of musicians and bands of the South Asian diaspora in the UK with distinctly different sound practices, transcultural trajectories and critical agendas.

Another aspect that this book is interested in is in how artists in South Asian dance music have challenged and complicated the cultural politics of sonic production, and its effect on globalized music culture. In the case of M.I.A., she very consciously used her sound practices to raise awareness of political issues. Her politically charged lyrics – which speak her resistance against the disregard of the rights of the Tamil minority in Sri Lanka, and which she also widely expressed on social media platforms such as MySpace and Twitter – granted her another honour, namely that of being named one of the most influential people in the world by *Time* magazine in 2009. The drawback of this award, however, was that media coverage was beginning to focus increasingly on her as an individual rather than on her output as a musician. This was in fact the case right from the beginning of her musical career, when the main interest circled around her experiences of the Sri Lankan civil war, her refugee status in the UK and a father who supported the separatist militant organization Liberation Tigers of Tamil Eelam (LTTE). The controversies around her person reached another peak after the release of a music video for the single 'Born Free' off of her latest album *MAYA* (2010), directed by Romain Gavras. The video depicts the rounding up and massacring of red-headed men and boys – an allegory on the arbitrariness of violence and the interchangeability of the roles regarding 'who is to blame'. The media could not get their heads around it and readily concentrated on M.I.A.'s decline as a credible artist for living with Benjamin Bronfman, son of the CEO of the Warner Music group. In the context of my study, it is important to think beyond 'the conventional reception habits of popular music audiences' which literary and postcolonial studies scholar Lars Eckstein pertinently criticizes in his investigation of the controversial press coverage of M.I.A.'s 'Born Free' video, which almost completely blanks out 'the private, political and artistic spheres of *production*' (Eckstein 2010b: 37, my emphasis). Still, in the case of M.I.A., she herself also contributed in highlighting her outspoken pop persona, in the form of her activism against oppression of Sri Lankan Tamils, which also resulted in the US immigration officials denying entry into the United States in the mid-2000s, and being accused by the Sri Lankan media of supporting terrorism by speaking out for Tamil Tigers.

In June 2019, M.I.A. was awarded the MBE for 'services to music', which she accepts for paying tribute to her mother, tying her economic success back to her working-class background:

I'm honoured to have this honour, as it means alot to my Mother. I want to honour what my mum spent many hours of her life doing! She is one of the 2 women in England who hand stitched these medals for the last 30 years. After receiving asylum my mum and cousin took this job in 1986, because it was the only non English speaking manual labour she could find. She spent her life in England hand sewing 1000s of medals for the Queen. No matter how I feel or what I think, my Mother was extremely proud of the job she had. It's a very unique situation for me where I get to honour her most classiest minimum wage job ever. #TAMIL #UKTAMIL #REFUGEE survival story #LIFECYCLES #whomademymedal. (miamatangi, Instagram, 6 June 2019)

Knowing about her critical stance towards British immigration- and international war politics which might have her more likely decline the honour, she uses the publicity surrounding the MBE award to draw attention to the realities of refugees (then and now), by firmly grounding her popularity to her own upbringing as a refugee in London. This is a quite different positioning than that of other musicians who rejected the MBE, including Asian Dub Foundation's co-founding member John Pandit (see Chapter 4) and highly acclaimed producer and composer Nitin Sawhney (OBE 2007), who told the BBC:

I wouldn't like anything with the word 'empire' after my name. One of my heroes, [the Bengali polymath] Rabindranath Tagore, gave back his knighthood to the British after the Amritsar Massacre. I felt very strongly about what had happened in Iraq, and I thought it would be hypocritical to take any award that said 'empire' in the wake of this country invading another country and killing women and children. I don't want to be part of that world. (Hebblethwaite 2018)

While M.I.A.'s music is often acknowledged as playing an important role in getting across her ideas and as a medium for constructing her pop persona, there is little attention being paid to how her music itself deals with the formulas of world music and global pop. The music itself is hardly ever described in any detail. There are exceptions, however, when music journalists indulge in creative celebrations of M.I.A.'s tracks, as can be exemplified by this description of her 2005 track 'Galang', the single to her debut album *Arular*:

'Galang' began with a curious, lurching, roughed-up slappy-clappy beat before a woman's laconic rap wrapped up a massive cultural shift with a simple verse: London calling, speak the slang now, boys say 'wha gwaan?' girls say 'wha-wha?' The song built from there, the beat jamming along like an '80s world music machine gone haywire and spewing out a mathematics of chimes, tweaks and squeaks while the MC at the mic chatted slangy non sequiturs that only occasionally emerged from the gauzy flow ... purple haze, galang-a-lang-a-lang ... razor blades, galang-a-lang-a-lang ... some impenetrable lyrics. A mess. Perfect. (Robinson 2006)

Although such exuberant reviews are highly compelling to the fan (which admittedly applies to the music enthusiast in me, too), this citation emphasizes a gap between a celebratory mode of describing the music's materialities and textualities (which this book will take much more seriously), and a popular discourse that wants to 'place' a musician, geographically and culturally. Moreover, the entanglement between sonic signification and its wider cultural, social and political frameworks is often underexposed. Cultural studies approaches are clearly no exception, as writer, critical theorist and filmmaker Kodwo Eshun remarked in *More Brilliant than the Sun*:

In CultStud, TechnoTheory, and CyberCulture, those painfully archaic regimes, theory always comes to Music's *rescue*. The organization of sound is interpreted historically, politically, socially. Like a headmaster, theory teaches today's music a thing or 2 about life. It subdues music's ambition, reins it in, restores it to its proper place, reconciles it to its naturally belated fate. (Eshun 1998: 004)

M.I.A. is clearly an example of how music does not need to be rescued. Indeed, it is precisely the blurry and 'unmanageable' character of the sound which can become the starting point for investigating sound practices as 'a wider syncopation' as cultural studies scholar John Hutnyk proposes (Hutnyk 2012: 6). To clarify this, I use the musicological term 'syncopation' which describes a variety of rhythms which are unexpected in some way, in that they deviate from the strict succession of a regular 4/4 beat. These include a stress on a normally unstressed beat or a rest where a beat would normally be stressed. It is an engagement with the 'normally unstressed beat', for instance, which is used by musicians to break new sonic ground, to experiment with new sounds or to recombine different sonic sources to challenge and reinvent musical ideas and cultural repertoires. This is where my research interest lies, in investigating how exactly a sonic and cultural analysis of music and its concrete sound practices could work. This book thus proposes an analysis of transcultural sound practices in South Asian dance music to reach beyond the limiting view that music simply reflects culture, and thus to extend the repertoire of how scholars (and others) can speak about music without necessarily being musicologists (or able to 'read the notes'). This would then allow an analysis of concrete musical ideas as they are generated within the music itself.

Regarding the scope of this book, this study focuses on South Asian dance music in the UK, roughly spanning three decades from the late 1980s to the late 2000s, with some more recent examples, of South Asian diasporic music production, and concentrating on five artists and bands in particular who have mainly lived and worked in London or Birmingham. Any attempt to create a comprehensive account of the various musical productions, their musical networks and forms of organization and institutionalization would immensely exceed the scope of the current study and would necessarily fail. Therefore, and this is my desirable aim, my focus is on five specific artists and their music – Apache Indian, Asian Dub Foundation, M.I.A., Dusk & Blackdown (the only non-Asian artists of my case studies), and Nathan 'Flutebox' Lee – in regard to which I will investigate how music becomes a particular site of cultural politics, technologies of sound reproduction and sonic fiction. The reason to choose this historical period in particular is that it enables an engagement with some significant moments – or rather, temporary aggregations – in South Asian cultural production, in which concrete transcultural sound practices, which work on the miniscule level of a musical track, or a live performance on stage, anticipate, or negotiate, shifts in the wider cultural and social politics in the UK.

The specific interests of this study are therefore: how can *sound* be analysed as an expressive form which plays a crucial role in the transformation of culture? And, related to this question: if this *sonic perspective* is taken into account, what ramifications does it have on the ways in which scholars think about culture as a concept?

Part One of this study, entitled 'Towards a Cultural Analysis of Sound Practices', accordingly outlines an encompassing analytical framework for the description and interpretation of sound practices in South Asian dance music. This section is organized around two chapters, highlighting my interdisciplinary approach of situating the discussion at the intersection of cultural studies, postcolonial studies and sound studies.

Chapter 1 sets the scene for renegotiating culture in the age of South Asian Dance Music, beginning with a clarification of the concept of transculturality. It is argued that the aesthetic, cultural and political practices involved in the production, perception and dissemination of diasporic dance music in the UK challenge discourses around culture which depict cultures as homogenous entities that are delineated by geographically locatable places. Music can serve as a particularly pertinent example of the 'dangerous crossroads'[1] of creative musical practices and the politics of cultural representation and ethnic identity

(Lipsitz 1994). The notion of transculturality helps to create an alternative concept of culture and cultural formation which questions received notions of culture that rely on cultures which are territorially or nationally defined. A number of scholars have postulated a decline of the nation as the primary reference for cultural formation, critiquing it as part of the 'ideologies of difference' and British superiority (Dawson 2007: 6). In this sense, transculturality can be regarded as the result of the discontinuities and transnational entanglements that take place against the grain of a linear history or national boundaries and identities. There have been research efforts in various disciplines to look at how culture is renegotiated in literature, the visual arts, performance art or music and how artists work around simple binaries such as traditional and modern, East and West, technology and tribalism.

In order to further delineate the field of enquiry in which my case studies are situated, an overview is given of the genuinely transcultural musical spheres which started emerging in the 1980s and continued into the early 2000s, spanning various synthesized post-bhangra music styles. These innovative musical forms can be conceived of as highly dynamic formations at the intersection of globalized music production and local musical practices and are shaped by and interact with the changing premises of cultural, social, economic, political and ideological power structures. What unites all these styles is their turn to digitalized modes of production, and the ways in which musicians recombine different musical influences through digital sampling and lyrical performance, thereby creating new forms of sound reproduction which challenge the listening conventions of music consumers and critics. It is argued that processes of cultural transformation have to be analysed as a dynamic relationship between the concrete aesthetics and the sonic forms of diasporic Asian dance music in London and the wider context of urban cultural politics and transnational culture.

Chapter 2 brings a discussion of sound into the centre of attention by elaborating on the analytical concept of transcultural sound practices. This section critically reassesses studies on sound from a perspective of postcolonial and transcultural studies with a focus on the hierarchies that were established between the different senses, and how this is related to (neo-)colonial logics of cultural representation. The chapter then deals with how sonic particularities, as well as the specific social or cultural functions of sound in a certain time at a certain place, have changed over time. The sound of a church bell in early modern England could serve here as an example as relevant as that of the muzak in a shopping mall or the heavy bass that reverbs from a London underground club. In this respect, a link can be drawn between ubiquitous everyday soundscapes and musical sound. Listening to musical sound is not confined to the musical score, or the musical recording, but extends it – it is cultural praxis: of listening, of feeling, of orientation, of the creation of an individual experience and of collectivities. From a cultural analysis perspective, the exploration of sound is relatively new; since the seventeenth and eighteenth centuries thought was highly dominated by a visual perspective of the world, on human beings, on cultural artefacts and on thinking itself. Only recently has a growing body of work been devoted to sound in the humanities, science and technology studies, anthropology, architecture (to name just a few prominent ones) in relation to various areas of cultural and artistic production, such as literature, architecture, audio-visual media, functional sounds, music and sound art (Pinch and Bisterveld 2012, Sterne 2012, Bull and Back 2015).

This chapter discusses some of the established and some more recent research in sound studies and auditory culture with a focus on everyday sounds, music and transcultural formations. Starting with a detailed and critical account of R. Murray Schafer's pioneering book *Soundscapes: The Tuning of the World* (1977), this section brings up the studies of three scholars in particular in order to exemplify the temporal, spatial and material qualities of sound and how they can be made useful for the elaboration of a cultural analysis of music. These studies include: Steven Feld's anthropological enquiry into the relationship between the music and speech patterns of the Kaluli people, Michael Bull's study of the renegotiation of the urban space in the iPod culture and Julian Henriques' study of the affective dimensions of reggae sound systems.

Focusing on the concrete techniques and technologies of sound, the concept of transcultural sound practices is established as a new perspective from the field of cultural analysis that aims to both explore concrete musical techniques, and to investigate sound as part of a wider framework of cultural technologies and practices. It is argued that sound practices such as sampling should be regarded as a *cultural* technology which is not restricted to the actual technological devices, namely the sampler, or the sequencer. This section thus defines technology in a broader sense and asks how it can in turn become useful for a critical study of music that disrupts the binary opposition between technology and tribalism (in the sense of a traditional culture that apparently does not engage in any way with sonic technologies) that is often maintained in discourses on diasporic music culture. While the concept of sound practices is broadly defined here, in the subsequent sections of Chapter 3 it will be more specifically developed as the major methodological approach for the analysis of the musical tracks that were chosen as case studies.

A special emphasis is on the implications of digital sampling as a specific sound practice, and looks at the particularities of production techniques as they are largely found in urban dance music styles such as hip-hop, drum'n'bass or dubstep. The concept of sound practices is further specified, and exemplified by the technique of digital sampling. The main aim of this section is therefore to ask how specific sound practices can be analysed in order to find out how music from different sources is recontextualized. Moreover, this section argues that it is important to conceive of dance music pieces as *tracks* rather than as *songs* in order to underline their multilayered and open structure.

Finally, the chapter aims to introduce an interdisciplinary methodology for a cultural analysis of music. It provides the terminology and key tools which will be used in the analysis of the subsequent case studies. Rather than claiming to be a fully detailed and developed method, this sonic tool kit will be further refined and elaborated in the analysis of the actual musical tracks. Therefore, the chapter discusses how the concept of transcultural sound practices can be defined so as to denote a particular sonic constellation and specific practice in a musical track. Part of the basic terminology with which I aim to investigate specific sound practices is the term *key sound*. The original term *keynote sound* was coined by R. Murray Schafer and Barry Truax as part of their 'World Soundscape Project' and is adapted here in the context of musical analysis. The use of the term 'key sound' also marks a shift away from the original meaning of keynote sound that refers to 'the anchor or fundamental tone' (Schafer 1994: 9), that is, for instance, a characteristic sound of a specific place. Rather than understanding key sound merely as the characteristic sound of a musical piece that refers to a certain musical style, key sound will be elaborated and refined in order to describe the complex sonic constellations in a musical track.

Part Two of this book, 'Listening to South Asian Dance Music', is dedicated to a detailed analysis of specific artists and tracks: Apache Indian, Asian Dub Foundation, M.I.A., Dusk + Blackdown and Nathan 'Flutebox' Lee. As already mentioned above, the chosen examples do not exhaustively represent South Asian–influenced dance music by any means. Rather, they are highly selective and taken as exemplary case studies for a transcultural analysis of sound practices.

Chapter 3 investigates how the reggae musician Steven Kapur aka Apache Indian mixes Jamaican dancehall reggae with Punjabi-derived bhangra on his

1992 album *No Reservations*. Apache Indian is regarded as a musical innovator, defying pop music conventions as well as 'world music' categories. Kapur grew up in Birmingham, where his musical socialization was highly influenced by Jamaican reggae and dancehall. This section will discuss how Apache Indian reinvents UK bhangra by refusing (and re-fusing) its traditionalist connotations and reclaiming its dance music qualities in the context of British dance music culture. A particular focus is placed on the track 'Arranged Marriage', which is significant with regard to both the concrete sampling techniques and lyrical performance; a merging of African-Caribbean and Punjabi styles, as well as the lyrical content in which questions of post-migrant[2] realities and imaginaries are negotiated on the level of ethnicity, gender, and class.

Chapter 4 deals with how the musical and political projects of the multi-ethnic band Asian Dub Foundation demystify Asianness. Originating in a youth community project in East London, Asian Dub Foundation's music is intricately linked with a critical stance regarding narrations of second- and third-generation South Asians in Britain and their anti-racist activism. However, as will be demonstrated with regard to their 2000 album *Community Music*, their music is more than just a tool for transmitting their political views and claims, but they create new musical ideas across musical genres and established production techniques on deep material and structural level that establishes new ways of listening.

Chapter 5 analyses transcultural sound practices in the work of musician, producer and visual artist M.I.A., a Sri Lankan Tamil who was born in to the UK, grew up in Sri Lanka and returned as a refugee to the UK with her mother and sister at the age of ten. The focus is on her first album, *Arular* (2005) and investigates her unique sound practices of sampling and lyrical performance with special attention to the linkages of music, politics and gender which are established in the music. In order to communicate her provocative and conflicting sonic fictions, M.I.A.'s music extends the transnational musical repertoire of London dance music once more by drawing from the sounds and styles of the global South.

Chapter 6 turns to an investigation of aspects of performance, technology and the body by examining Nathan 'Flutebox' Lee's unique fluteboxing technique of playing the flute and beatboxing at the same time. A live performance as well as the recorded sound on his 2010 *Flutebox* EP is at the core of the analysis. Nathan Lee is the child of a white British father and an Indian mother with ancestors from the Indian diaspora of West Africa. The composer and performer innovates London's dance music scene with his unique performance technique and receives acknowledgement for this as Emerging Artist in Residence (EAR) at London's Southbank Centre in 2009.

Chapter 7 analyses the aesthetics and politics of place as they are sonically, verbally and visually produced on Dusk + Blackdown's album *Margins Music* (2008). Coming from the context of post-2000 London dance music, and grime and dubstep in particular, composers and producers Martin Clark and Dan Frampton aim to create an alternative soundtrack of London which captures the multilayered fabric of the transcultural soundscapes on the margins of London society. They draw from various musical styles such as Hindi film music, bhangra or Chinese drums, which they interweave into the steady, yet syncopated, rhythmic patterns of grime and dubstep. Taking into account their positionality as white British artists, this section claims that there is friction between the intricacy of their practices of sonic reproduction and the way in which the album's visual and textual accompaniment is presented. While creating compelling musical ideas, the visual presentation of these ideas fails to live up to the complexities of the sound reproduction practices, and instead reproduces old cultural binaries of margin and centre, East and West, sound and light.

Part Three consists of the two final chapters. Chapter 8 concludes by drawing together the main analytical outcomes and proposes a refined methodology for an analysis of South Asian dance music and transcultural urban dance musics more generally.

Chapter 9 revisits some of the aspects of this book which engaged with sonic thinking and analysis which was not confined to music but highlights aspects of sound as cultural transformation in everyday life, the (sonic) arts and the urban space and points towards some more recent examples to further establish transcultural sound practices in and beyond music.

My hope is that this study will pass on some of my own fascination with and affection for this multifaceted music, forms of musical expression which are often underexposed in academic texts, particularly within cultural studies. The following discussion will attempt to carve out the interdisciplinary framework which may assist in an improved understanding of how listening to transcultural sound practices transforms the way we think about culture.

Part One

Towards a Cultural Analysis of Sound Practices

1

Renegotiating Culture in the Age of British Asian Dance Music

This study investigates the juxtaposition of South Asian sounds and urban dance music in the UK as a diverse cultural practice in which the local effects of globalized communication, transnational migration and musical production are negotiated, and examines how these local practices of music production and perception affect and transform discourses of cultural formation.[1] In order to create new ways of thinking about cultural formation in this fast-changing, highly dynamic world, this chapter seeks to critically revise received concepts of culture which are based on territorialized identities, and questions nationality and ethnicity as a primary frame of reference for cultural identification. The chapter argues that the specific musical practices which generate transcultural urban musical styles such as UK bhangra or British Asian electronic music also constantly reconfigure the conditions of cultural and discursive formation, and that, consequently, the focus of analysis should be on the concrete practices of production, perception, and dissemination of these musics.[2] In order to specify my conception of transcultural South Asian dance music, one important trajectory is the understanding of the significant relation of music and diasporic culture. This was pertinently expressed by Virinder S. Kalra, Raminder Kaur and John Hutnyk in *Diaspora and Hybridity* in their statement:

> The intermingling, interpenetration and blending of cultural traditions, in what Dick Hebdige (1987) called, borrowing from black musical culture, the 'cut'n'mix' of contemporary culture, enables the production of hybrid, syncretic and creolized forms [...] Yet, unlike those anthropological approaches which have marked this process as a re-creation of tradition or a reproduction of social forms in a new place, Stuart Hall maintains that these innovations of culture are not and never can be simple re-creations because they are the product of new material conditions. (Kalra et al. 2005: 37)

The authors refer to Paul Gilroy's *Black Atlantic* for an exemplification of this significant interrelation of music and diasporic cultural production:

> Music is the vehicle that 'brings Africa, America, Europe and the Caribbean seamlessly together. It was produced in Britain by the children of Caribbean and African settlers from the raw materials supplied by Black Chicago but filtered through Kingstonian sensibility' (Gilroy 1991: 5). This kind of patterning can be repeated in many other contexts as well as with other forms of cultural production. What is specific about Gilroy's stance on musical expression is the relationship forged between expressions of resistance and expressive forms. In a similar manner the routes marked by the musicians in the Bands Asian Dub Foundation and Fun^da^mental produce a different diasporic space, one that takes in South Asia, the Middle East, England and North Africa but shares a common tradition of resistance through cultural praxis with those musicians described by Gilroy. This is a music that finds its material rooted in the inner-city areas of London and Birmingham, yet nevertheless draws its inspiration from a multi-locational, multi-musical set of sources and, of course, is consumed globally. (Kalra et al. 2005: 38)

Considering the presence of South Asian cultural productions in contemporary UK, one finds equally significant productions of literature, theatre or visual arts which are all part of the transcultural fabric of the UK.[3] Moreover, as will be shown, this fabric renders old dichotomies of tradition and modernity, East and West, heritage and innovation questionable.

One of the main ramifications of cultural globalization is the decreasing importance of the nation-state as primary reference for cultural formation (Appadurai 1996, Beck 1998, 2009). Cultural theories that relied on a singular grand narrative of European modernity conceived of nations as fixed and homogeneous entities with their own unique, firmly attached cultures. However, more recent perspectives developed in cultural, literary and postcolonial studies (Bhaba 1994, Schulze-Engler 2004, 2006, 2009), as well as sociology and anthropology (Clifford 1988, 1992, 1997, Gupta and Ferguson 1992, Featherstone 1995, Urry 2000), have started to investigate the complexity of the relationship of the nation and the global frameworks of cultural formation and have shifted the focus onto 'multiple modernities' and 'entangled histories' (Chakrabarty 2000, Welz 2004, 2009). In the former Eurocentric model, a notion of Western culture was established which included the nation states of the northern hemisphere (particularly Europe and the United States) and was defined in opposition to all other cultures, which more or less included the nations of the southern hemisphere. However, the complex political, economic and cultural constellations of colonialism, imperialism and postcolonial migration clearly transcend the limits of fixed nation states. Against the backdrop of the transnational trade of goods (and enslaved people) during the colonial era, the various politically and/or economically motivated migration processes which took place during the decolonization process, as well as the contemporary forms of mobility and exchange, created multiple 'transnational connections' (Gilroy 1993, Hannerz 1996, Ong 1999) and fostered ideas about a new social, cultural and political world order (Giddens 1999, Castells 2000, Hardt and Negri 2000, Mignolo 2000).

There has therefore been a growing awareness that people, consumer goods and ideas are not fixed to one place, nation or community, but that they are in a 'flow', and that cultural formations are fundamentally influenced by these dynamic and multidirectional movements. Thus, the spatial parameters have changed. Popular music can serve as a particularly pertinent example of the 'poetics and politics of place', as George Lipsitz compellingly argues in his book *Dangerous Crossroads: Popular Music, Postmodernism and the Poetics of Place*:

> Popular music has a peculiar relationship to the poetics and politics of place. Recorded music travels from place to place, transcending physical and temporal barriers. It alters our understanding of the local and the immediate, making it possible for us to experience close contact with cultures from far away. Yet precisely because music travels, it also augments our appreciation of place. Commercial popular music demonstrates and dramatizes contrasts between places by calling attention to how people from different places create culture in different ways. A poetics of place permeates popular music, shaping significantly its contexts of production, dissemination, and reception. (Lipsitz 1994: 3-4)

Lipsitz suggests that the production, uses and circulation of popular music play a significant role in the negotiation of place – and thus of power relations and constructions of cultural identity. Music transcends national boundaries and follows various transnational trajectories:

> Like other forms of contemporary mass communication, popular music simultaneously undermines and reinforces our sense of place. Music that originally emerged from concrete historical experiences in places with clearly identifiable geographic boundaries now circulates as an interchangeable commodity marketed to consumers all over the globe. Recordings by indigenous Australians entertain audiences in North America. Jamaican music secures spectacular sales in Germany and Japan. Rap music from inner-city ghettos in the U.S.A. attracts the allegiance of teenagers from Amsterdam to Auckland.

Juke boxes and elaborate 'sound systems' in Colombia employ dance music from West Africa as the constitutive element of a dynamic local subculture, while Congolese entertainers draw upon Cuban traditions for the core vocabulary of their popular music. (Lipsitz 1994: 4)

Lipsitz makes a valuable point here in emphasizing the multiple musical linkages that propose a more multilayered conception of culture. In this respect, transculturality means that people are not constricted by either the one or the other culture. However, this quotation still exhibits a fixation on the contemporariness of musical exchange which could imply that globalization is a new phenomenon which presupposes a past in which culture was still ordered along 'clearly identifiable geographic boundaries' (Lipsitz 1994: 4). I would argue that there is no *before* and *after* globalization, but that it is rather the discourses about globalization, global communication and diasporic cultural formation which have only recently been explored more thoroughly. Furthermore, the means of communication and global exchange have surely changed considerably with the development of digital media technologies, and it is on these new forms of circulation and use that analyses have started to focus. The aspect which is core to the sort of analysis upon which this study concentrates is that the specific *musical* connections are worth investigating with regard to the specific spatial, temporary and transcultural entanglements. In contrast to a number of critics who have been apprehensive of the growing influence of Americanization on popular music and thus homogenization of global popular culture, Lipsitz and others have argued that rather than leading to a homogenized space inhabited by a global culture, global developments have significant impacts on local places and significantly reconstitute local music culture. It is therefore argued here that transculturality is the result of the discontinuities and cultural entanglements that happen against the grain of a linear history and across national boundaries and identities.

In order to relate these thoughts to the context of post-war Britain, Britain's attachment to the concept of the nation has to be critically examined, as it still has an impact on how questions of ethnicity and cultural identity are discussed in both political and pop-cultural debates. As Benedict Anderson already claimed in his well-known 1983 book, nations are *Imagined Communities*, and nationalities can be conceived as cultural artefacts which are based on 'multiple significations' that change according to specific historical, social and cultural conditions (Anderson 1991: 4). Ashley Dawson problematizes the way in which the nation has continuously been defined as an exclusivist concept, in the context of the UK. In *Mongrel Nation*, he claims that Britain's adhesion to the framework of the nation has often been analysed as a reaction to the ubiquity of globalization processes and an ensuing insecurity and loss of control; Britain's reluctance to become part of the EU could also be attributed to this. Dawson remarks, however, that the zeal for a distinctively 'British' culture was grounded in Britain's experience of losing its standing as an imperialist power:

> Long after Britain lost its colonies it retained its insular sense of cultural superiority. Indeed, the more potency they lost on the global stage after the eclipse of imperialism, the harder some Britons clung to the illusionary status symbol that covered their bodies – their white skin – and the immutable cultural difference that it seemed to signify. (Dawson 2007: 6)

Dawson argues that '[t]hese ideologies of difference and innate superiority' helped to create 'enduringly exclusionary discourses of national identity' that have formed, and continue to form an integral part of British political and cultural life (Dawson 2007: 6–7).

One example for how this was accomplished is the way in which, in the mid- to late 1990s, Tony Blair's New Labour party aimed at constructing a new image for modern Britain. In fact, the outcome was an exclusivist cultural politics. The tendency of commodifying the 'other' is reflected in practices such as the designation of chicken tikka masala as 'a true British national dish' (Cook 2001).[4] These ventures should also be regarded as deliberate strategies in New Labour's project to aggregate the threatening 'other' into a manageable 'we' while maintaining an alluringly exotic twist.[5] At the same time, there has been a tendency to deny, or neglect, the impact of South Asian diasporic cultural production on British popular culture and discourses.[6] Referring to a more recent example, Dawson analyses the British government's responses to the July 2007 bombings, which in his view 'germinated from the deeply racialised manner in which British identity has been framed for the last half-century' and concludes:

> [T]he policies pursued by the Labour government are driven by a *cultural racism* that hinges on the defence of putatively homogeneous national values against an alien threat. This is [...] an institutional and ideological racism that is grounded in exclusionary discourses of national identity disseminated across the political spectrum and deeply inscribed in British culture. (Dawson 2007: 176, original emphasis)

Consequently, the racialized discourses of national identity continue to have an impact especially on postcolonial post-migrant communities, i.e. the successive generations of Caribbean, African and Asian migrants living in Britain.

Particularly with regard to complex migration processes, people develop multiple linkages across the confines of nation states. Following Nina Glick-Schiller's notion of transmigrants, migration practices can no longer be seen as one-way processes in which people leave their culture of heritage behind and subsequently enter the culture of the host country. She argues that '[c]ontemporary immigrants cannot be characterised as "uprooted"' as they 'maintain multiple linkages to their homeland' (Glick-Schiller 1995: 48). The notion of transmigrants that is established by Glick-Schiller proves particularly useful to differentiate the various motivations (economic, political, etc.), practices (transnational kinship relations and social networks) and effects (financial support of the family in the homeland) of migration in the contemporary world (Glick-Schiller 1995: 48).

Investigating the particularities of diasporic cultural production, Dawson criticizes the effects of Britain's essentialist cultural politics and illustrates how, as expressed in both literature and music, '[d]iasporic communities in Britain denaturalised the confining boundaries of the nation-state' and therefore profoundly challenged Britain's 'insular sense of cultural superiority':

> [B]y enacting fresh ways of being British, members of the postcolonial diaspora helped to reconfigure social categories such as race, gender, and sexuality that cemented conventional definitions of national identity. Although many white Britons found the novel cultural practices of postcolonial migrants profoundly threatening, the newness introduced to Britain by members of the Asian and African diaspora also offered important routes of escape for many from stultifying local traditions. (Dawson 2007: 7)[7]

Dawson argues that diasporic cultural practices do not only have considerable ramifications for the lives of individuals, but that these practices reconfigure the cultural, social and ideological condition of British society as a whole. He thus explores the critical interventions of bands such as Fun-Da-Mental and Asian Dub Foundation into public discourses of post-9/11 and post-7/7 racism and Islamophobia:

> The anti-imperialist cultural politics of engaged artists such as Fun-Da-Mental and Asian Dub Foundation point toward a radically different and truly postimperial Britain [...] The stinging criticism such groups offer of Britain's

imperial legacy makes them part of the chorus of voices that have sought over the last five decades to decolonize Britain and, in so doing, to make of it a truly mongrel nation. (Dawson 2007: 188)

While Dawson relevantly points out how diasporic writers, scholars, artists and musicians have profoundly transformed and continue to transform the British cultural and social landscape, in the above quote, the limitation of his overall concept of 'mongrel nation' becomes apparent: it reproduces a kind of methodological nationalism. Although Dawson adequately observes how the notion of the nation is insufficient in capturing the creative and conflicting dynamics of contemporary cultural production, the category itself, albeit contested, remains intact as the fundamental reference point in Dawson's methodology.

A work which is particularly compelling in its attempt to transgress the conceptual confines of nationality is Ali, Kalra and Sayyid's collected volume *A Postcolonial People: South Asians in Britain* in which they implement the term 'BrAsian' to deconstruct the dichotomy of Britishness versus Asianness. Sayyid claims in the introduction that there was a continuous effort in the past to maintain a 'colonial framing of ethnically marked populations,' which was, according to the author, 'most vividly demonstrated by the chequered trajectory of the various labels deployed to identify people from South Asia who settled in Britain in the wake of the (formal) decolonisation of British India: Black, British Asian, Asian British etc.' (Sayyid 2006: 4). In opposition to this stance, the editors set out to employ a different, more productive, term to write a book about South Asians who settled in Britain, and one which might also not tie them to the 'postcolonial condition':

[T]here is an obvious problem as postcolonial marks something beyond colonialism but not something intrinsic in itself, in other words, the 'post' in the postcolonial reminds us that we have not arrived at something that can have its own name. (Sayyid 2006: 5)

Therefore, the term BrAsian is suggested in order to speak about people in Britain with a South Asian heritage so as to express 'the need for a category that points one in a direction away from established accounts of national identities and ethnicised minorities' (Sayyid 2006: 5). On the one hand, BrAsian is used to differentiate 'British' Asians from people associated with Asia outside of the British context (where Asian often refers to people of East Asian or South East Asian heritage). On the other hand, BrAsian implies a deconstruction of

Britishness, a term Sayyid deems particularly problematic due to its inextricable bond with the era of the British Empire. Sayyid argues that 'such a transformation of Britishness cannot be accomplished without the dis-articulation of coloniality in its constitution' (Sayyid 2006: 6).

Particularly significant in the context of the present study will be how an exclusivist notion of ethnicity has to be critically revised with regard to South Asian-influenced dance music. In one of the contributions to *A Postcolonial People*, Sanjay Sharma applies the term BrAsian to South Asian music from the UK. He argues that writing about BrAsian popular music 'is like charting a map without legitimate borders and boundaries', a picture which he sees further complicated by the nowadays 'customary [...] claim that all modern music is syncretic or hybrid' (Sharma 2006: 317). To come to terms with the highly diverse range of BrAsian popular music, the central characteristic marker seems to be its detachment from a cultural or ethnic 'origin':

> What is common to this music is not simply the ethnic marker of 'Asian', rather its concomitant articulation of 'roots' (identity, belonging, place) and 'routes' (cultural flows, movements, translations). The global musical adventures of Fun-Da-Mental, Talvin Singh and Nitin Sawhney and their collaborations with other international artists make it difficult to fix the origin of their sounds, especially as it is produced in places such as Mumbai, New York and Johannesburg, as well as in London. Nevertheless, it is argued that their music is uniquely 'made in Britain', even if it is clearly not wholly of it. (Sharma 2006: 326)

It can be concluded from Sharma's analysis that rather than being able to identify a 'BrAsian' musical/cultural identity, these musics are influenced by various musical traditions and created on multiple sites of production that point to a heterogeneous field of possible musical identifications and cultural appropriations. Moreover, although the British context seems to play a role, 'BrAsian' musicians seem to see themselves as just as much part of a global music scene as a local one. While the authors of *A Postcolonial People* productively reframed the essentialist paradigm of Asian cultural production in Britain, the term BrAsian itself might not have the capacity to become a new concept in its own right, evidence of which being the fact that the authors themselves have not continued to employ it in subsequent publications.

Concerning the 'global musical adventures' Sharma speaks of with regard to diasporic music, Aiwha Ong's *Flexible Citizenship* makes a significant contribution by putting forward a more fluid conception of cultural formation. Focusing on cultural as well as economic processes of globalization, she establishes the 'trans' concept to depict movements which refer to defined as well as undefined spaces:

> *Trans* denotes both moving through space or across lines, as well as changing the nature of something. Besides suggesting new relations between nation-states and capital, transnationality also alludes to the *trans*versal, the *trans*actional, the *trans*lational, and the *trans*gressive aspects of contemporary behaviour and imagination that are incited, enabled, and regulated by the changing logics of states and capitalism. (Ong 1999: 4, original emphasis)

Therefore, transferring Ong's conceptualization to transcultural music production, these productions can be seen as transversive in terms of their crossing of geographic divides, transactional in communicating and exchanging ideas across music styles and music scenes, translational in terms of lyrical and sonic forms of musical appropriation, or transgressive in reconfiguring cultural identities and spatialities, as well as musical and listening conventions. Graham Huggan, who develops the notion of transculturality with regard to postcolonial literature, proposes thinking of this paradigmatic shift from inter to trans in terms of a 'transcultural turn' (Huggan 2006: 56).

In investigating global trajectories along with local practices, Ong emphasizes their inextricable entanglement:

> [A] model that analytically defines the global as political economic and the local as cultural does not quite capture the *horizontal* and *relational* nature of the contemporary economic, social, and cultural processes that stream across spaces. Nor does it express the *embeddedness* in differently configured regimes of power. For this reason, I prefer to use the term *transnationality*. (Ong 1999: 4, original emphasis)

This conceptualization of transnationality is eminently useful (and can be transposed on transculturality) as it emphasizes the mutual interconnection of global and local coordinates of diasporic cultural production. To elaborate on this concept I would like to draw on George Lipsitz, who in his study *Dangerous Crossroads* surveys the transnational entanglements of music, and emphasizes the 'peculiar relationship [of music] to the poetics and politics of place':

> Recorded music travels from place to place, transcending physical and temporal barriers. It alters our understanding of the local and immediate, making it

possible for us to experience close contact with cultures from far away. Yet precisely because music travels, it also augments our appreciation of place [...] A poetics of place permeates popular music, shaping significantly its contexts of production, distribution, and reception [...] Intentionally, and unintentionally, musicians use lyrics, musical forms, and specific styles of performance that evoke attachment to or alienation from particular places. (Lipsitz 1994: 3-4)

Therefore, the global dynamics of musical production have significant local ramifications and *vice versa*, and, following Lipsitz, these dynamics are most tangible at the 'dangerous crossroads' between people, sounds and places which create crossroads of conflict and creativity. Arjun Appadurai makes an important point with regard to a critical account of the concept of the nation, as shown in the following citation: 'The imagination is now central to all forms of agency, is itself a social fact, and is the key component of the new global order.' What can be imagined here are more complex forms of cultural, ethnic and technological collectivities which Appadurai respectively calls *ideoscapes, ethnoscapes or technoscapes* (Appadurai 1996: 31).

Transculturality can serve here as a pertinent concept to describe dynamic and multifaceted diasporic cultural practices. With respect to the analysis of South Asian dance music, the dynamics of the multifaceted correlations between diasporic cultural productions can no longer be captured within the category of the nation. In order to address cultural, social, economic and political institutions, the concept of nation and the implemented notion of national identity needs to be deconstructed and replaced. Rather than conceiving of culture as a homogeneous enclosed entity, Wolfgang Welsch poignantly claims that 'multiple cultural connexions are decisive in terms of our cultural formation' (Welsch 1999: 3). Thus, drawing from Lipsitz that '[t]oday, shared cultural space no longer depends on shared geographical space' (Lipsitz 1994: 6), culture can no longer be regarded as bound to one place, but as generated in a dynamic interplay of various connectivities that refer to different places at the same time. On the level of cultural practices, as will be shown in my analysis with regard to South Asian dance music, the notion of transcultural sound practices seems particularly productive.

In the course of this section, I was able to specify the question posed in the beginning regarding how a transcultural approach on musical sound can be productive in the reconceptualization of received frameworks of culture and ethnicity. While taking into account the various ways in which scholars engage with culture as a highly contested field of research, it emerged that, with regard to South Asian dance music, the question should not be what kind of cultural identity is reflected in the music, but how specific musics create culture and generate discussion of the cultural politics that are involved in this process. Therefore, the following subchapter investigates in more detail the cultural politics of music in relation to musical styles such as UK bhangra, South Asian inflected electronic dance music, grime, dubstep and the various new musics from the global South – demonstrating how these diverse styles resonate in the urban dance music cultures in the UK.

The cultural politics of South Asian dance music in the UK

There has been an increasing interest with regard to transcultural South Asian dance music in recent years, as the contributions from various interdisciplinary perspectives show, ranging from studies on musical borrowing and appropriation (Born and Hesmondalgh 2000) to renegotiations of national identity (Zuberi 2001) and investigations on the alterity of Asian sounds (Sharma 2004). What all these contributions share is that they do not aim at a 'conclusive report on the current state of play of the children of the diaspora' (Sharma et al. 1996: 2). Rather than confining the complex cultural practices of post-migrant generations to exoticizing and ethnicizing identity categories, these approaches call for a critical debate about the possibilities of taking South Asian dance music seriously as an object of academic research; and seek to resist the stereotyped conventions of a cultural politics which is based on hegemonic power structures (Sharma et al. 1996: 2). Dichotomies such as high culture versus popular culture, Western culture versus non-Western culture, British chart music versus ethnic world music are often based on essentialist ascriptions which have more to do with power relations than with aesthetic or cultural differences. In relation to the transnational flows of goods, ideas and people, as well as globalized music production, binarisms such as those mentioned above are increasingly questionable because they often rely on notions of homogeneous, territorially defined cultural spheres. In actuality, these musics reveal complex and highly dynamic temporal and spatial interrelations which transgress either purely British or purely Indian musical traditions.

In discourses about popular music, 'British Asian' music has often been dealt with in terms of its expression of an identity, often in the highly ambivalent manner of either emphasizing the problems of multicultural identity formation or celebrating a mystified, exotic Other. These musics, like many other 'fusion' musics, were mostly dealt with under the 'world music' label, a term which became highly popular in the 1980s within pop-cultural and academic discourses. World music has largely been communicated as part of a marketing strategy to sell 'non-Western' music to a white mainstream audience.[8] Record stores piled everything from East African drums to folk music from Fiji, from Bollywood music to Senegalese hip hop under the single rubric of world music. Erroneously, these musics were mostly referred to as part of one national culture, although the respective musical styles were to a great extent already highly influenced by different cultural and musical traditions:

> Therefore, within the genre of World Music, particular musics and artists are divided by their national origin. The diversity of these very different musical forms, often belonging to specific localities that either have little to do with the hegemonic national culture or cross the boundaries of nation-states, is nevertheless subsumed into these units of national culture. In World Music marketing practices, a pervasive strategy has been to promote specific artists as representations of authentic ethnic musical cultures. (A. Sharma 1996: 23)

Regardless of this fact, and in order to increase the marketability of world music, the music industry has tried to emphasize the music's 'otherness' to enhance its appeal of 'authenticity' and 'realness'. Consequently, musicians with a South Asian cultural background were asked to musically represent a marginal community, an expectation Mercer has accurately termed 'the burden of representation' (Mercer 1994: 235).

Significantly, as Ashwani Sharma argues in *Dis-Orienting Rhythms*, it is no coincidence that a concept such as world music was not established at a time when more 'technologized' musical styles such as hip hop emerged 'which had posed a challenge to the racist structures of the music industry and wider Western public culture' (A. Sharma 1996: 23–24). According to this view, the creation of the world music genre can be seen as an attempt to work against explicitly political, anti-hegemonic musical innovations and to aim instead at creating a 'sane world of all cultures' celebrated at world music festivals such as Womad. Sharma further argues that '[t]his differentiation between "black music" and World Music is also an attempt to firmly bifurcate the syncretic metropolitan cultures from the authentic Third World' (A. Sharma 1996: 23). This dichotomization of black music and world music becomes increasingly questionable given the multidirectional crossings of musical influences and practices that musical styles such as bhangra or various other popular and dance musical styles constantly undergo. Another concept which is often used in this context is *fusion*. The term 'fusion' has become a buzzword in discourses on globalized popular culture. In cuisine, music or design, fusion is constructed as the fundamental characteristic of contemporary, cosmopolitan 'world' culture. Much like other pop cultural terms, fusion has become a fashionable tag, mostly serving marketing interests rather than being concerned with a specific creative process, a musical quality or a transcultural social encounter. Fusion can stand for everything that sounds 'cool' and is influenced by many things, or by any exotic flavour of the week. With regard to transcultural musical styles, the term fusion has often been used very broadly to describe the various ways in which sounds, instruments and musical traditions are mixed together to form a new musical style. Besides the slightly more concrete term *fusion jazz*, referring to a distinct style which evolved in the 1960s and fuses jazz with funk and rock music, there is no common understanding of what a piece of fusion music actually sounds like. Exactly this vagueness has seemed to make the term particularly easily applicable to discourses of world music or New Asian Kool, within which the notion of musical fusion is transposed to equally blurry notions of hybrid culture. The fundamental problem with regard to the term 'fusion' is the presumption that two formerly distinct sounds, styles or traditions are mixed and merge completely to create one new musical expression. This is misleading, however, since music per se implies different musical influences and cultural connotations. There is, therefore, no clear line that could be drawn between one pure musical style, or tradition, and another. Furthermore, with regard to the sound practices that are explored in this study, the different sounds, rhythms and textures that become part of the same piece of music do not fuse together completely. On the contrary, the differences that they display and the tensions that they produce are integral to the musical performance on stage or a recorded performance in a musical track. There is a danger, therefore, to lose track of the particularities of how different sounds intermingle and to reach one of the discursive dead ends of empty pop music catchwords. This study therefore engages in a musical analysis which disrupts the ways in which ethnicity has been written into music, and investigates how transcultural sound practices generate new ways of thinking about culture.

    A common denominator of new musical developments across the globe has been their attachment to urban space. The specific role of music in the construction of urban space is investigated in Sheila Whiteley's edited volume *Music, Space and Place*, which seeks to explore how urban space becomes a contested space in which culture is negotiated through the practices of musical creation and consumption. This study is especially concerned with how cities become central for the creative and conflicting potential of the diverse diasporic communities which inhabit that space, and how music is conceived as a tool both to connect and to disconnect urban subjects. In her introduction, Sheila Whiteley claims that music has the power to 'bond displaced peoples, effectively bridging the geographic distance between them and providing a shared sense of collective identity articulated by a symbolic sense of community' (Whiteley 2004: 4). She argues that the spaces which these communities construct for themselves are not primarily structured along the lines of a particular, nationally defined identity, but could rather be conceived as what Appadurai has termed 'ethnoscapes':

> According to Appadurai, such are the global flows of people and 'culture' that contemporary urban spaces are most effectively conceptualized as ethnoscapes, that is 'landscape[s] of persons who constitute the shifting world in which we live: tourists, immigrants, refugees, exiles, guestworkers and other moving groups and persons.' (Whiteley 2004: 3, quoting Appadurai 1996)

Although the critique of the nation as a framework for the diverse cultural and musical practices is valid, it is highly questionable whether the notion of the ethnic is actually a very pertinent construct in that context. Instead of re-establishing ethnic boundaries which divide the different groups that inhabit a city, the multilayered musical practices of African-Caribbean and South Asian people in London permanently challenge concepts of ethnicity. Drawing on Gilroy's notion of a 'common fund of urban experiences' that people of the African diaspora share, Whitely notes that in this context music can be conceived as a 'creative resource in the context of urban [...] spaces' (Whiteley 2004: 7). In Lee Watkins' contribution to the volume, which deals with hip-hop in Cape Town, he emphasizes the specificity of urban space in relation to global hip-hop culture in stating that:

> Around the globe, hip hop inhabits spaces on the periphery of urban centres. The common thread running through these scattered localities is that hip-hoppers use the music, break-dancing, spray-painting, and the effects of technology as a source of strength in their struggle for recognition. (Watkins 2004: 124)

Watkins is interested here in the subversive potential of hip-hop culture and focuses primarily on the significance of hip-hop music in the context of gang politics. However, although there are many examples to show that hip-hop has been a strong reference point for localized struggle, Watkins does not relate these local subcultures to the mainstream status of hip-hop in the United States and Europe. For instance, with regard to the influence of hip-hop in the context of the UK, the boundaries between subculture and mainstream are becoming blurred, and the relation between urban dance music and their subversive potential has to be explored in detail with regard to concrete examples. A more complex picture is drawn in Ashley Dawson's *Mongrel Nation*. He claims that urban space becomes a contested space on a variety of levels. Afro-Caribbean derived musics are seen as situated at the periphery of urban centres, and can serve as a tool which connects the ghettoized spaces of London, Kingston and Johannesburg. At the same time, the music serves as a vehicle which can be used to move into the centre, through the growing economic success of these musical styles, and thus can also become an opportunity for change for marginalized communities. With regard to South Asian musics, which are a particular focus of this study, it is interesting to explore how notions of the margin and the centre are constructed with regard to music. In this sense, the creative and conflicting fabric of urban space seems to create a kind of continuum of discontinuities which is worth exploring.

In the following, an overview of the history of South Asian dance music will be given along three important strands: Bhangra, Asian Underground and South Asian dance music in post-2000 UK. Although there is a chronological trajectory, the described musical developments cannot be regarded as part of a linear and coherent history, but the detailed discussion of musical styles and the pop-cultural discourses surrounding them is crucial to understanding the context in which the case studies of Part II of this study are situated. However, the artists – Apache Indian, Asian Dub Foundation, M.I.A., Dusk & Blackdown, and Nathan 'Flutebox' Lee – and their music cannot be neatly situated within clear-cut genre categories, or as belonging to a specific music scene. And this is also why I chose these artists, not others, as examples. Without being contained by one genre or style, they have in different ways, broken new ground, while being influenced by and actively reshaping traditional, established or cutting-edge musical styles and techniques. As will be demonstrated, Apache Indian, who produced his most acclaimed albums in the early 1990s, uses bhangra music and turns it, though his dancehall beats and lyrics, into a new style he calls *Bhangramuffin*. Asian Dub Foundation, who formed in 1993, use samplers and turntables as part of their dub and punk music and thus create new sounds that might be also associated with other artists who were put under the umbrella term Asian Underground, without ever representing this scene (which never really was one at all, as will be demonstrated). M.I.A., who released her debut album *Arular* in 2005, is already situated in post-2000 urban dance music, being rooted in UK club culture and using sounds derived from globalized music productions in the Global South. Nathan 'Flutebox' Lee can also be situated in the late 2000s with his flute playing that is firmly situated in his practice as a jungle MC of the early 1990s and thus reinvents the instrument in adding bass to it. Dusk & Blackdown with their 2008 album *Margins Music* have been part of the grime and dubstep scene for many years as DJs and producers, and perceive South Asian sounds as one facet of the sonic fabric of London's club music culture. This example also intends to highlight the complicated relationship of 'white' artists using South Asian musical references. The relevance of these artists for my discussion of transcultural sound practices, as will be demonstrated in Part II of this study, lies in the ways in which their music and sound practices challenge and complicate essentialist notions of culture, not matter-of-factly, but through the reworking of sonic, verbal, corporeal repertoires, techniques, stances and discourses.

Bhangra

Bhangra music is a highly danceable music style which prominently features the sound of the dhol drum, a double-barrelled drum that is played with a stick and with the hands. The basic bhangra beat pattern is recognizable across all bhangra tracks and builds its rhythmic spine. Bhangra music usually features other accompanying instruments and, very importantly, Hindi vocals that are sounded out in a melodic and catchy fashion. The following part of this chapter deals with the diverse mutations of bhangra in the UK and investigates its relation to the growing visibility of British Asian cultural production from the late 1970s onwards.

There are a number of ways in which the story of South Asian popular music in the UK, and bhangra in particular, has been told. Most of the academic accounts dealing with Bhangra in the UK begin this story with the music's origin in the Punjab region, and continue with how this musical style was transformed from a 'traditional' Indian folk dance into an eclectic mix of British and Indian instrumentation and pop-musical patterns. However, as has been highlighted by Rajinder Dudrah, bhangra music, as it travelled to Britain in the post-war period of the second half of the twentieth century, is not one homogeneous musical style. Rather, it developed from different musical styles which existed in the Punjabi region prior to the 1947 partition of the Indian subcontinent, and was transformed after the partition into several distinct musical styles in both the Pakistani and the Indian part of the Punjab (Dudrah 2007). Furthermore, and this is the focus of my study, UK bhangra styles have undergone similarly wide-ranging musical developments across and beyond migrant and post-migrant communities and music scenes. Another way of telling the bhangra story has been via the popular reference to the Beatles, and especially the musical encounters between George Harrison and Ravi Shankar. However, music critics have tended to present this story mainly as an *inter*cultural dialogue between India and Europe. Musically, their meeting was regarded as a 'fusion' of the Indian classical music tradition (and exotic appeal) represented by the sitar and Western pop music. This contrasting relationship between the traditional Indianness, represented by the sitar, and modern Britishness, represented by the songs of the Beatles, has helped to maintain a Eurocentric view of Indian and South Asian music culture in Britain.[9]

In contrast, Sanjay Sharma has proposed a much more productive way of telling the story of Bhangra in the UK. His analysis accounts for the multifaceted cultural and socio-political entanglements of the South Asian musical presence in the UK. In his review of the 'Soho Road to the Punjab', an exhibition that took place in London and Birmingham in 2007, he commented upon the diverse perspectives of 'fifty years of Bhangra music, culture and style'. Sharma emphasizes how Bhangra has become an integral part of the British cultural sphere and claims that there is 'something culturally disruptive' about this music in its resistance to assimilate into British culture (Sharma 2007). Sharma precisely detected three moments (or periods) of the presence of Bhangra in Britain, which roughly cover the three decades of the 1970s, 1980s and 1990s. These periods can be characterized by *invisibility, marginalisation* and *ambivalent recognition* respectively. Significantly, Sharma warns not to see these moments as part of a linear development. He argues that the story of bhangra has been part of 'divergent global geographies and places' that have constituted South Asian cultural formation in the UK (Sharma 2007).

Concerning the first moment, the moment of *invisibility*, he concludes that 'South Asians were not part of the national culture, it's like we didn't exist' (Sharma 2007). Here he refers to the fact that although Indian communities all over Britain were engaging in music throughout the 1970s, and the first British Asian bhangra bands were formed at that time, bhangra music remained confined to a space in the popular music sphere that ran parallel to the mainstream musical consciousness and the British charts. Instead, 'Bhangra offered an alternative space of community formation, and an alternative subterranean "popular-public" sphere' (Sharma 2007). Bhangra bands had performed widely at family celebrations, but from the late 1970s onwards, a growing Bhangra scene developed, with thousands of people attending Bhangra festivals which took place outside of the city borders of London and Birmingham. Simultaneously, bhangra daytimers were established and became an integral part of the local music scene across South Asian communities. However, there was hardly any popular recognition of the participation of South Asians in the social and cultural life of the UK, and music was no exception. The popular discourse tended to focus on the issue of immigration policies and problems of either successful or failed integration of South Asian communities into the host society, and the media coverage focused on young women who fled their restrictive family structures. Thus, music provides a good example in this respect because it throws light on the gap that existed between the variety and creativeness of South Asian musical production, and the visibility of these musics in the wider public sphere.

As far as the popular music press was concerned, there was hardly any interest in the music itself, the distinct sounds or the new musical styles that evolved from bhangra and other musical influences. Therefore, although there were already a few British Asian broadcasting stations in existence in the 1970s playing bhangra and Hindi film music from the recent Bollywood movies, South Asian sounds were far from popular amongst the non-Indian population.[10] As will be elaborated below, bhangra became interesting for the music industry only once it became marketable in ways that spoke to the average (white middle class) music consumer. Otherness became fashionable. Exotic sounds became cool. The problem here was that the discussion of music was mostly confined to questions of cultural identity, which often resulted in an essentializing of British Asian music culture. These debates were frequently guided by a multicultural ethos which tried to give more attention to 'minority communities', but sometimes failed to reach beyond a form of positive racism.

The second moment that Sharma identifies is that of *marginalization*. Here Sharma raises the issue that 'South Asians now appear to be entering into national culture, but considered still as ethnic others - on the periphery' (Sharma 2007). He is here referring to the growing visibility of bhangra music (and British Asian cultural production in general) in the UK. In the early to the mid-1980s, the presence of bhangra became obvious through a growing audience at bhangra festivals which took place on the outskirts of London and Birmingham. The various new 'home-grown' UK varieties of the musical style changed the face of bhangra fundamentally. Bands such as Alaap (founded in 1977) and Heera (founded 1981) appeared on the scene and mixed bhangra with Western instrumentation and synthesizers, incorporating 'disco influence such as synthesizer-sound and electro beats into Bhangra's dhol and thumbi beat' (Gajaweera 2005: 11). The British Asian station Sunrise Radio was founded in 1988 and started as a pirate radio station. However, there was hardly any recognition by the wider public of these new cultural productions. Bhangra occupied an alternative musical and social sphere, with hardly any connection to the popular music industry of the 1970s and 1980s. It was mostly produced in small studios, recorded on music cassettes and distributed through corner shops in Southall and some East London boroughs. Significantly, while being only marginally recognized within the UK, bhangra bands such as Alaap gained popularity in the South Asian diaspora in India and elsewhere and thus had, from the beginning, a decidedly transnational dimension.

The third moment, which, according to Sharma, was 'structured by a multicultural logic', is that of *ambivalent recognition* (Sharma 2007). Ambivalent recognition implies that, despite the growing popularity of bhangra and Bollywood music in the UK, South Asian musicians were still faced with marginalizing cultural politics. Sharma attributes this moment primarily to the 1990s, and it is only in this decade that scholarly attention was paid to the relevance of this music in the context of transcultural formations in the UK (see Back 1996, Bauman 1996, Bennett 2000). The British Asian music scene also changed significantly in the 1990s, an account of which is given in this clearly partial, but still poignant, statement by DJ and musician Nerm Chauhan:

> When I was growing up, [bhangra and Bollywood music] wasn't particularly cool, it didn't resonate with me. And when I heard more underground applications of Asian Sounds, that's what caught my ear, that's when I thought, wow, brown people can actually be cool, as opposed to being a picked-on minority. That was a major turning point. (Chauhan 2008, personal interview)[11]

As far as the marketability of UK bhangra and related styles is concerned, terms such as 'Asian Kool' became the hip substitute for the British Asian version of 'world music', as Sanjay Sharma observes in his article on 'The Sounds of Alterity':

The new-found hypervisibility and popularity of 'hybrid' Asian fashion, film and music, summed up by the specious label 'Asian Kool' (created by the style media) signifies a splitting of Asian cultural representation in terms of a 'postmodern hybrid' against a traditional, ossified culture. (Sharma 2004: 411)

Garnished with a slightly more edgy attire, 'hybrid' Asian culture is still presented in the same exoticizing, marginalizing rhetoric, and controlled by the same market-driven logics. In this way, the complexity of the specific musical, cultural and political elements which made up British Asian cultural production in the 1990s was continuously simplified in order to be instrumentalized for British mainstream pop culture, as Sharma states:

> The complex processes and politics of mixing, fusion, syncretism of contemporary youth culture have been seized by the master concept of hybridity, something that seems to get cultural commentators and theorists alike all worked up. The zeal of journalists from fashion style bibles such as i-D and The Face for all things hybrid has been faithful in celebrating a new-found British multicultural cool in which the rise of a vibrant syncretic Asian youth culture plays a pivotal role. (Sharma 2004: 410)

To simply celebrate an alleged subversiveness of diasporic subjects, however, would enhance the marginalized status in relation to British mainstream culture. That the musical developments which grew out of bhangra clearly enhance frameworks which try to establish simple binaries between Asianness and Britishness, or subculture and mainstream, becomes particularly clear when looking at more recent developments in the British Asian musical spheres. As DJ and radio producer Ritu Hirani aka DJ Ritu sums up:

> You just got lots of different sectors. You've got British Asian artists making R'n'B, and it's pure R'n'B, and they're having some mainstream success with that, people like Jay Sean for example. Then you still got your Asian Underground guys, State of Bengal, and Nitin Sawhney, they're still doing exactly what they were doing fifteen years ago. And then you've got a kind of Asian rock scene that started to emerge. And then, there is still a very strong bhangra scene here, lots and lots of young guys and young women making very traditional bhangra tracks [...] In the Indo-Jazz scene there is a guy called Arun Gosh, a clarinet player, then there's Nathan 'Flutebox' Lee [...] On the r'n'b/bhangra side you have Richi Rich, H-Dhami and vocalist Mona Singh.[12] (Hirani 2008, personal interview)[13]

This highly selective account of established and emergent songwriters, musicians and producers provides good insight into the diversity and heterogeneity of South Asian music in the UK. This musical variety thus defies any one-dimensional thinking which would conceive of British Asian music as either purely traditional in terms of musical influences, or purely following the latest musical trends.

Bhangra can hardly be conceived of as a homogeneous musical scene. Rather, elements of bhangra music in the UK have featured in a number of different musical styles and across diverse music scenes. Why is it pertinent here to speak of musical scenes at all in this context? From a broad perspective, there is a twofold trajectory of bhangra in the UK, one of which could be said to claim bhangra, or desi, for that matter, to be the focal point of identification, and one which is much more diversified and conceives of bhangra sounds only as one of many influences in the musical mix. However, both trajectories are closely linked, albeit in different ways, to the UK popular music realm. To define the first trajectory more precisely, bhangra refers here to the young tradition of UK bhangra. Here, the lyrics tended to be continuously sung in Punjabi, and the lyrical content did not differ significantly from that of the traditional bhangra folk songs. They were 'centered around themes of drinking, dancing, chasing girls and nationalistic pride', as Ritu Hirani puts it in her entry on UK bhangra in the *Rough Guide to World Music* (Hirani 2000: 92, quoted in Gajaweera 2005: 12). Significantly, there seems to be a strong link between bhangra music and 'desi' identity, as sociologist and ethnographer Helen Kim argues in her 2014 book *Making Diaspora in a Global City*:

> The notions of 'desi' too is a site in which differences of race, class, gender and sexuality bring to bear different versions and meanings of identity that validate or invalidate 'desi' as a significant marker of their identity. (Kim 2014: 3)

Kim's study is very precise in working out how notions of desiness are negotiated as locally and socially specific expressions of these identities-in-process:

> I argue that [South Asians'] construction[s] of themselves as Londoners challenge and de-center straightforward notions of belonging and identity such that identities aren't formed out of an unquestioned assumption of a one-dimensional British identity. Instead, through the messiness and ambivalence that is so much a part of London's urbanness, they help to produce more complex and deliberate links to people, networks and communities beyond the rooted frameworks of territory, place, neighborhood and nation. (ibid.: 2–3)

Therefore, regarding one of the central questions posed in this study of how difference is generated in music, it becomes clear that difference is not confined to the dichotomy of South Asian versus British Culture, but difference is generated on a much smaller scale, between different music scenes, and, even more importantly, through different sound practices.

Asian Underground

Asian Underground refers to musical activities which took place in London mainly in the second half of the 1990s, focusing attention on British Asian musicians, producers, label owners and radio presenters. The independent music labels *Nation* and *Outcaste* were established by young musicians and featured bands like Fun-da-mental, Hustlers HC, Sister India and Asian Dub Foundation. During the same time-period, Talvin Singh, tabla player and electronic dance music producer, established a club night called *Anokha* which featured 'beats, breaks and tablas, bits of rap, Indian female vocal samples, swirling basslines, very "electronic" and danceable', as London-based DJ Ritu defined the distinctive sound of the Asian Underground in a compilation's booklet (Hirani 2003). Moreover, Ash Chandola established *Swaraj*, a club night and platform which featured musicians from the UK and India, promoting new musical encounters between the two countries. The ambiguity of the term Asian Underground becomes apparent, therefore, when one tries to define it as either a particular musical style or a homogeneous musical scene. It should be emphasized here that Asian Underground does not refer to a particular musical style, although a common denominator might be urban dance music. Generally, the styles which were subsumed under Asian Underground were geared more strictly towards club-oriented electronic music styles such as jungle and drum'n'bass, but also included other urban music styles such as rap, punk and dancehall. Interestingly, Sharma et al. described New Asian Dance Music as including the various bhangra-related styles, also in an attempt to remove the 'traditional' tag from it. If bhangra played a role in the context of urban dance music, it was rather in the form of bhangra samples which were added to the mix of established dance music styles such as reggae dancehall (see for example reggae artist Apache Indian) or drum'n'bass (see for example Shiva Soundsystem, a group of producers and DJs). Significantly, as Gajaweera has noted, '[t]he [Asian underground] scene was different than [...] the Bhangra scene as it allowed accessibility to non-Asian audiences unable to cope with Bhangra's heavy Punjabi-ness' (Gajaweera 2005: 12). While the adaptability of Asian sounds to electronic dance music can be seen as a move towards an opening up of London's club scene in terms of different cultural influences, some scholars criticized the tendency that it was mostly a white audience that attended club nights such as *Anokha* and regard it as emerging new forms of exoticism (Hutnyk 2000). Anamik Saha highlights the danger of celebrating the transgressive potential of the 'Asian Underground':

> This [unique and innovative sound] invariably grabbed the attention of postcolonial and cultural studies theorists who saw in the scene the quintessential expression of hybridity, destabilizing nationalist discourses that construct British Asian youth as absolutely Other to their white British counterparts. However, problems with this reading arise when we consider production of Asian music against the context of global capitalism, where we see how its uniquely syncretic qualities perversely become a source of fetishization, captivating an Orientalist gaze that exoticizes South Asian cultures. (Saha 2011: 437)

Saha draws attention to 'the effects of industrial cultural production upon the British Asian text – especially at the marketing and distribution stages – in order to truly grasp the political effectiveness of particular cultural strategies' (Saha 2011: 438).

Asian Underground has been used as an umbrella term for diverse and vibrant musical activities which included bands and musicians of various musical styles. As Ritu Hirani and others have claimed, however, the term was often used in a restrictive way, as if it were represented solely by a handful of artists, namely those who had gained the most popular acclaim, such as Talvin Singh, Bally Sagoo and Nitin Sawhney. Hirani emphasized in an interview I conducted with her in 2006, that these artists were only responsible for a small part of the diverse musical releases, parties and other events which were happening in the 1990s but might not have attracted as much attention from the British music industry (Hirani 2006, personal interview).[14] This restrictive definition of Asian Underground also resulted in the refusal of some British Asian musicians and producers to being subsumed under this label. Therefore, it seemed paramount to create an alternative space in the wider public sphere to disseminate the various activities, ideas and viewpoints that had accumulated in British Asian (sub-)culture. One endeavour in this regard was the *2nd Generation Magazine*. The editors combined concert and album reviews with urban street fashion and critical commentary on the state of Asian culture in the UK, and thus worked against the grain of the popular/mainstream discourse about British Asians which dominated British media. The articles in this magazine demonstrated that the activities of British Asians in London and beyond could hardly be constricted to one homogeneous scene. However, the fact that *2nd Generation* primarily focused on British Asians as their target audience became increasingly limiting. While the magazine did work as a relevant and timely statement on a creative and critical Asian presence in the UK, the activities of the contributors and the music and activities they wrote about and were part of continuously transgressed the confines of ethnic communities, or '2nd generation migrants'. Nevertheless, this does not minimize the relevance of magazines such as *2nd Generation*, labels such as *Nation Records*, or club nights such as *Swaraj*, since negative and/or exoticizing representations of South Asians in Britain have remained an issue that needs to be resisted. However, the Asianness of these cultural productions was always only one point of reference in the broader urban music culture to which British Asians belonged.

Therefore, it would be limiting to conclude that everything that happened under the label of Asian Underground was simply part of a marketable brand for all things Asian. As will be shown in the case studies with regard to Apache Indian and Asian Dub Foundation who were highly productive in the 1990s, these musics could not be contained by fashionable or exoticizing labels. On the contrary, the newly generated impulses created new spaces for creativity, and resistance.

South Asian dance music in post-2000 UK

The thesis that this chapter will present is that the concrete musical narratives that are created have the capacity to move beyond the cultural territorialism of Britishness against which 'other' cultures are perceived. This is particularly relevant with regard to the lack of recognition of this perspective in the media coverage of urban dance music. Zuberi writes:

> While [contemporary dance music] has been highly mobile, much of the commentary on this music in journalism and websites centres on 'placing it', situating it, marking its boundaries, and making critical claims about its authenticity, success or failure based on its belonging to a place or places. Popular music discourse, inside and outside academia, manifests a territorializing imperative and desire for enclosure that is integral to the boundary-making of music cultures, but may also be linked to wider anxieties about aliens and borders. (Zuberi 2001: 180)

There is a clear connection between the territorialization of diasporic music and the marking of it as premodern in terms of its cultural heritage that re-establishes and reinforces binary oppositions between the modern and the traditional, or the West and the East. In his book *tracks 'n' treks* (2011), musicologist Johannes Ismaiel-Wendt elaborates an analytical framework, which he terms TRX studies, that synchronizes a subjective mode of close listening, a reflection of postcolonial theories of spatial deterritorialization, and notions of transcultural transformation. With what he calls 'postcolonial ear training,' Ismaiel-Wendt challenges the established causal relations between sound (Lautbild) and idea (Vorstellungsinhalt) in order to open up new perspectives on diasporic music as 'performative spaces' (Ismaiel-Wendt 2011: 25), in which sampling, layering, instrumentation and production techniques charge our perception with imagined geographies that are saturated with folkloristic associations, or train our ears to discern and critique exoticizing sonic strategies to arrive at a mode of listening that acknowledges the transatlantic and transcultural links between these musics (ibid.: 53). It is in regard to this sonic space, which is also an imagined space, that South Asian dance music should be situated and analysed.

These musics must therefore be regarded against the background of racialized discourses of nationality, (street) crime, terrorism and security, which still dominate much of the popular discourses in Britain. In fact, British mainstream media deliberately and forcibly use national and ethnic identity 'to stimulate controversy for higher ratings' (Zuberi 2001: 184).

In post-2000 UK, the British Asian music scenes grew increasingly diverse and it became even more difficult to pin it down to the Asian factor. Moreover, a number of South Asian music producers moved increasingly to the centre of the mainstream music industry, while simultaneously new varieties of South Asian sounds and their creators firmly established themselves within underground club culture. In my interview with Nerm, a producer, DJ and radio presenter, he states:

> It all tailed off I think around about 2002 when Punjabi MC was number one in the charts, Bombay Dreams was released as the Bollywood musical by Don Black and A.R. Rahman, and that's when things changed. I think even Swaraj tried getting more commercial. I was firmly in the underground, and Shiva Soundsystem kind of grew out of Swaraj, a loose connection of DJs and musicians which then became an organisation, a music label and organising club nights and so on. (Nerm 2008, personal interview)

Shiva Soundsystem also hosted a number of parties in a warehouse in Dalston/ Hackney, which, in Nerm's words, 'put the [Asian] Underground back on the club map I think, but more in an underground way which was never overtly Asian':

> We'd never talk about the Asian sound, it would just be there. And I think that's quite critical, when a movement goes beyond making a point, it becomes part of Britain, it becomes part of club culture. Because if you create things for a minority that's fantastic, but as soon as you ring-fence it, it becomes a ghetto, and you never get any further. So the idea now is, as an artist, your roots and your culture would always come through, but there is no need to sort of wave a flag and say 'Yeah, we're Asian', 'cause anyone with a pair of eyes can see that, anyone with ears can hear a certain element coming in. But it's not what defines us. What defines us now is British underground culture. (Nerm 2008, personal interview)

British underground culture in post-2000 Britain is a thriving, diverse and fast-changing urban club culture which produces a large number of artists from a wide range of musical (sub)styles that have mainly been emerging from London and Bristol. While the dance music culture of the early 1990s generated music styles such as dancehall, dub, rave and acid house, a burgeoning pirate radio scene and the establishment of independent record labels have inspired new musical developments, from hardcore, jungle, drum'n'bass, UK garage, 2-step, grime and dubstep. What these styles have in common is the influence of Afro-Caribbean diasporic popular music (and especially styles such as free-jazz, reggae and dub), and specifically its focus on the beats and the sub-bass which make it particularly danceable and thus predestined for the club context.

These styles have been constructively discussed by scholars such as Kodwo Eshun (1998) and Steve Goodman (2010) under the concept of Afrofuturism. The term Afrofuturism was originally coined by Mark Dery (1994) in the context of Black science fiction. In Eshun's *More Brilliant than the Sun*, he finds new ways of describing Black musical styles through fictionalizing his listening experiences that are very inventive and creative, using his 'sonic fictions' (a term that he elaborates) to break with the ethnicized myths that surround popular and academic music discourses. Eshun claims that this myth, which is actually based on a neocolonial rhetoric of black and white, female and male, traditional and modern, creates a dichotomy between white guitar music and black soul music. In contrast, the concept of Afrofuturism defies essentialist dichotomies. In my interview with Goodman at Clandestino Festival in 2009, he explained the concept in the following way:

It is an attempt to identify traits or characteristics in the new music that is around today and create an alternative history of those musics in relation to Afrofuturism [...] Firstly, Afrofuturism recognises the fact that whether the music is black or white, the most important influence has come from black musical culture. And secondly, that influence of black musical culture has interacted with new technologies of production and recording, synthesis and manipulation. So it's this combination of a certain orientation of technology and – irrelevant of the people who are actually making the music – the most important influence on the music being from black popular music. (Goodman 2009, personal interview)[15]

Instead of putting sociology before music, Eshun and Goodman seek to argue against and challenge the common rhetoric of the music industry and music journalists as well as academics, who try to make sense of music from a sociological point of view, trying to put themselves in the alleged position of knowing more than the producer, or the listener of a musical track, knowing better how to interpret and valorize music. Therefore, and this is very close to the approach pursued in this study, Eshun demonstrates a 'close hearing' of the music, taking sound first before superimposing some kind of ideological framework: '*More Brilliant* goes farther in. It lingers lovingly inside a single remix, explores the psychoacoustic fictional spaces of interludes and intros, goes to extremes to extrude the illogic other studies flee' (Eshun 1998: 004).

In the context of this chapter, the notion of Afrofuturism is constructive in emphasizing 'roots and routes' of these musics and underscores the multiple linkages that were mentioned earlier in this chapter which defy the confinement of music or culture to frameworks of nationality or ethnic origin. The new technologies of production and recording that were mentioned by Goodman in the quote above have also simplified transnational exchange of music. More people can now afford computers due to decreasing prices of hardware and music software, and along with the new developments in digital media technology this has also led to an increase of home-recorded music (rather than having to pay a lot of money for professional recording studios) and a simplification of exchanging sound files through the internet. Musicians as well as music consumers exchange ideas and share music through social networks and in chat rooms; they remix music and create new styles. As Jace Clayton states, 'the line between producer and consumer blurs, and most songs end up being given away for free' (Clayton 2009). DJs, curators and authors of blogs promote new musical styles and thus influence the birth of new genres (Burkhalter 2010). These new musics set trends in the club scenes in global cities such as London, New York, New Delhi or Brazil, and new terms have been created in order to characterize this new musical development, among which is a term which attempts to redefine world music in adding a suffix which stands for the music's embeddedness in digital media culture: world music 2.0 (Clayton 2009, Burkhalter 2010).

Although the musical styles which are subsumed under this label differ tremendously concerning their sonic characteristics (and this immediately indicates the old problem of the generalizing tendency of such terms), there are scholars who regard the term as reflective of the inventive and critical capacities of these emergent musical styles. Thomas Burkhalter suggests that one conceive of world music 2.0. artists as being associated with avant-garde artists such as those active in musique concrète and similar movements in the twentieth century which aimed to break with the dominant musical canon, to redefine the role of music in society and use it as a form of protest (Burkhalter 2010). Not unlike the artists of musique concrète, world music 2.0 artists incorporate noises from their local environment and manipulate technological tools, thereby reappropriating them as part of their experimental sound practices.[16]

Another term which has been used to describe the various urban dance music styles that emerged from the global South and were mixed and merged with British dance music is *global ghettotech*, coined by Wayne Marshall on his blog in order to emphasize its inherent link to Western and non-Western electronic music that started to come out of the social and economic peripheries of urban spaces. I prefer global ghettotech as opposed to world music 2.0, because it is more effective at highlighting the contradictory and controversial relationships that it teases out and enacts. A more detailed discussion of this term and a concrete application of it in the context of musical analysis are demonstrated in Chapter 5 which presents an analysis of M.I.A.'s music. What is discussed here more generally is the broader perspective on the globalized and transnational entanglements of urban dance musics across the globe and their influence on South Asian dance music in the UK in particular (and specifically London).

The digital and transnational forms of musical exchange have continuously shaped and transformed urban dance music in the UK. With regard to the diverse British Asian music culture, this is no exception.[17] As Zuberi states concerning Afro-diasporic and electronic music cultures, 'these recordings also incorporate musical codes from multiple genres and even more dispersed sources, and have themselves been repeatedly modified, remixed, edited and sampled in other genres' (Zuberi 2001: 180). The dispersed sources that Zuberi mentions here are not further specified, but in the context of this study and looking at dance music of post-2000 UK, the musical developments have been shaped, besides the aforementioned Afro-Caribbean musical continuum, by a range of other musical styles especially from the global South. This can be observed also in regard to urban dance music artists in the UK, of which songwriter and producer M.I.A. is one example. Her style, in particular, features musical styles from Brazil and Puerto Rico such as reggaeton and funk carioca. Reggaeton has been described as a form of global ghettotech for its reluctance to be pinned down to a specific origin. As Juan Flores states in the foreword to the edited volume *Reggaeton*:

> Reggaeton may well go down in that history as the first transnational music, in the full sense of the term. Not only that it becomes transnational by its massive and far-flung spread in the world, a process that has become more rapid and intensive with every new generation of technology and global shrinkage [...] Reggaeton kicks that remarkable process up still another notch by being an eminently popular form of music without any single specifiable place of origin, with no *cuna* (cradle) in the sense of a 'hood' or even national setting from which it sprang. The contention over whether it's Panamanian, Jamaican, Puerto Rican, or Nuyorcian will most likely seethe on, since it seems to be a style brewed in a multilocal, transnational cauldron from the beginning. All of these parental claims are valid, yet none of them are, because the "location" of origin in this elusive, perhaps unprecedented case is at the very crossroads of many diasporic, migratory, and circulating communities of taste and generational solidarity. (Flores 2009: x)

What becomes clear from the above statement is that this music can by no means be received, interpreted or understood in the framework of a linear music history, but has to be regarded, from its emergence, in its transnational connectivity and transcultural fabric. There is no longer a 'point of origin' which can be identified, and no 'tradition' which can be ascribed as its original cultural heritage. The discontinuities and multiple sites of musical production, performance and dissemination are not the result of a former continuity of time and space, but rather constitute the very precondition of these productions. The productive aspect offered by this perspective is that it makes new cultural trajectories and dynamic interrelations audible, visible and tangible; trajectories and interrelations which are normally hidden behind the effort to understand music as a reflection of a culture that has to be traced back to some one origin.

Another case in point is funk carioca, which is influenced by a number of musical styles and influenced urban dance music in the UK in a similar way. The specific mixture of 1970s funk, 1980s US rap and Afro-Brazilian beats is characteristic for *Miami bass*, from which funk carioca took a lot of inspiration. Miami bass, as well as funk carioca, is characterized by rough and minimalistic beats and rap-style lyrics which are often saturated with violent and sexually explicit lyrics. The US group N.W.A. (an acronym for: Niggaz With Attitude), composed of the rappers Dr Dre, Eazy-E and Ice Cube, are often referenced as pioneers of Miami bass, something which is now often referred to, in a highly generalizing manner, as *gangsta rap*. However, it is important to differentiate the different attitudes that were representative of the early phase of hip-hop from the United States. Significantly, Public Enemy, who also emerged in the late 1980s, pioneered a rough and aggressive rap style and sound in combination with a socially and politically conscious message transported through their witty and thoughtful lyrics. In contrast to Public Enemy, N.W.A. 'celebrated the violence and hedonism of the criminal life, capturing it all in blunt, harsh language' as noted on their official website. However, both bands significantly influenced the sound of hip-hop throughout the following decades and beyond the national borders of the United States. N.W.A.'s rapper Easy-E signature voice can be highlighted here in particular, as it influenced the subsequent generations of rappers, as described on the band's website:

> With his high-pitched whine, Eazy-E's urban nightmares now seemed like comic book fantasies, but that fulfilled the fantasies of the teenage, White suburbanites that had become their core audience, and the group became more popular than ever [...] Although the group was no longer active [from 1992], their influence – from their funky, bass-driven beats to their exaggerated lyrics – was evident throughout the '90s. (NWA 2010)

As far as funk carioca is concerned, the sound and attitude of Miami bass was reappropriated in the local context of Rio de Janeiro. DJs from Rio were highly interested in the latest musical trends from the United States, and Miami seemed to be the closest city which offered the opportunity to get hold of a wide range of US records. This is why the Miami-specific sound features prominently in Funk

Carioca. However, funk carioca can be called a music style in its own right: The lyrics are sung in Portuguese, and the minimalistic and syncopated beat patterns feature Afro-Brazilian percussive elements:

> Besides Miami Bass-style beats, funk carioca also uses some traditional Afro-Brazilian rhythms. A West Coast Electro Bass track entitled 808 Volt (Beatapella Mix) by DJ Battery Brain was widely sampled, and became the common background for various funk carioca songs, recycled time and again with the inclusion of more percussive elements as the "tamborzão" beat style became popular. (Adam 2008)

Taking into consideration the different musical influences, the transnational dimension of funk carioca becomes evident. As Adam notes on his blog about funk carioca, a distinctly Brazilian version of Miami bass was created already in the late 1980s when '[l]ocal music producers began mimicking these [Miami] importers'. He also notes that '[t]he influence of Miami is also reflected in the prominence of freestyle-style synth melodies' (Adam 2008). While in the 1980s DJs and producers had to rely on the suppliers from Miami, in the 1990s, they increasingly used the internet and digital technology to obtain, (re)produce and disseminate music:

> The emergence of readily available digital music technologies in the early 90s changed the face of the Funk Carioca movement in Rio de Janeiro, Brazil. Funk Carioca can be traced to many different musical genres ranging from Brazilian samba to European techno. Although Brazilian Funk started using mixed vinyl tracks that mimicked the scratch, loop and break techniques made famous by Bronx artists like Afrika Bambaataa and Miami Bass legends 2livecrew, the movement is currently almost exclusively digital. Beat machines and automated loop technology have revolutionized the genre. (Adam 2008)

From the beginning, issues of copyright were raised. This development also resulted in a shift from being a local subculture to being globally recognized.

In the context of this study, it is particularly important to take into account the various practitioners and the multifaceted forms of organization of British Asian music culture. As was demonstrated with regard to the early developments of bhangra in London and Birmingham in particular, from the beginning musical developments have been dependent on alternative channels of production and distribution. Regarding the musical developments of later stages, across musical scenes of bhangra, Bollywood and the Asian underground, the creation of independent record labels, club nights and radio shows has been imperative and integral to the new musical formations. Most of the people I talked to in my expert interviews or informal meetings are practitioners who incorporate several functions, being musicians, label owners, club night hosts and radio promoters all at the same time.

Drawing together the transnationality of musical exchange and the diversity of musical practices on a local level, it is paradoxical to think that South Asian urban dance music from the UK could somehow be contained by the geographic borders of the UK, taking into account the long history of exchange between Britain and India and the Subcontinent (and, of course, the other territories of former British colonial rule). What has been called 'British' culture in modern times had already been morphed and changed by cultural influences from many parts of the world. Therefore, the idea that along with the post-war South Asian migration to Britain, there was suddenly a presence of 'foreign' cultural habits, artefacts, and languages invading the pureness of British culture has to be seen in relation to the intention of constructing a national identity for Britain, which needed 'ethnic difference' to create an 'other' in order to reinforce the construction of a British national identity. The only way in which the advocates of a British national culture were willing to deal with the Indian and South Asian presence was by looking at their culture in terms of a 'heritage' culture. This perspective was applied not only to the works that could be called 'classical', but with contemporary culture, music and literature. 'South Asian culture' was constructed as being a reflection of the past. They ignored the fact that the South Asian diasporic communities in Britain were producing work which was being created *here* and *now*. It was happening in the contemporary context of London, or Leeds, or Birmingham, and not in former times in India. This construction of a temporary and spatial difference was a means to keep South Asian culture at a distance, to justify the idea that South Asians did not belong to Britain, and to justify their failure to recognize the influence, presence and significance of South Asian cultural expression in contemporary Britain, a factor which was not just adding to British culture, but transforming it. Thus, the dichotomies which have been established between tradition and modernity, or the East and the West, are highly artificial. Cultural practices which are only perceived along the lines of these geographically or time-based constructions become enclosed, rigid, irrelevant. This chapter gave an overview of some of the musical, temporary and spatial trajectories along which transcultural sound practices are generated.

With regard to this study, there are three interconnected questions which I want to emphasize and which emerge from the theoretical and music-cultural elaborations of this chapter: what kind of critical and inventive thinking is required to bring the various developments and mutations of South Asian sounds in urban dance music to the domain of cultural studies? What sonic particularities are emerging which demand and incorporate new ways of thinking *through* sound rather than *about* music? How can a capacity be developed for listening differently and more thoroughly to the sound practices of these musics?

2

The Concept of Transcultural Sound Practices

There is a widely quoted phrase from French philosopher Jaques Attali's *Noise: The Political Economy of Music* in which Attali claims that 'Western knowledge' has been dominated by the visual paradigm as its primary framework for making sense of the world, and that '[it] has failed to understand that the world is not for the beholding. It is for hearing. It is not legible, but audible' (Attali 2006: 3). Particularly relevant in the context of my study on transcultural sound practices is Attali's claim that in order to grasp emergent social, cultural and political formations – contemporary and historical – a shift is needed towards a greater awareness of the sonic dimension of these formations which are often *anticipated* in the sounds of music. With regard to the endeavour of this chapter to develop a concept of sound as a specific cultural *practice*, the questions which lie at the heart of this endeavour are: How can *sound* be analysed as an expressive form which plays a crucial role in the transformation of *culture*? And, related to this question, is another one: What are the ramifications for the ways in which scholars think about *culture as a concept*, if this *sonic perspective* is taken into account? One of the preconceptions which lie at the heart of such an endeavour is that sound is not a natural given, nor is it universal. There are a number of instances which show how sonic particularities, as well as the specific social or cultural functions of sound in a particular time and space, have re-constituted the world in which we live, how we perceive it and make sense of it. The sound of church bells in an early modern French village could serve here as an example as fruitful as that of the muzak in a New York shopping mall or the heavy bass that reverbs from a London underground club (Corbin 1998, Goodman 2010, LaBelle 2010). This study aims at utilizing the notion of transcultural sound practices, a concept which will be established in the course of this chapter to focus on the particularities of contemporary urban dance music, and particularly the diasporic musics which combine South Asian sounds with urban dance music styles. The act of listening to these musics cannot be confined to the musical score, or to the musical 'work', but extends beyond that – it is cultural praxis: in the form of listening, feeling and orientation; as a creator of individual experiences and of collectivities. Music is understood here not as a mere *result* of social and cultural constellations, but is conceived as a space in which meanings are actively shaped, and received cultural, social and gendered inscriptions are constantly contested and renegotiated.

Nevertheless, the exploration of sound is relatively new, since modern Western thought was highly dominated by a visual perspective of the world, of human beings, cultural artefacts and thinking itself. Recent discussions dealing with the 'hierarchy of the senses' which prioritizes the visual over the senses of listening, touch, taste and smell have emphasized how such a hierarchy has influenced epistemologies of culture and cultural formations (Jenks 1995, Bull and Back 2003, Cox 2006, Schulze 2008). However, as will be shown, the hierarchy of the senses is not a stable construct, but serves here as a point of departure to investigate how certain conceptualizations of the human senses are related to hierarchies of meaning creation, and how these conceptualizations have continuously – until today – influenced conceptions of culture. Thus, this chapter highlights some of the instances which demonstrate the intricate relation between visuality and knowledge production, and then proceeds to investigate alternative approaches which emphasize the historical, cultural and musical dimensions of sound as a way of thinking culture.

One of the aspects which show that visual culture is more widely reflected upon is the fact that everyday speech is intricately interwoven with visual associations: having a certain perspective on something, something being obvious, something being looked at or reflected upon are visual depictions of reasoning, validating, and sense-making (Bull and Back 2004). Comparing the allusion of vision in everyday speech to that of the auditory, there is a notable disparity in the frequency and accuracy of the use of aural and visual expressions. Additionally, although sound is as ubiquitous to everyday life as vision, sonic experiences seem to be less tangible than visual experiences, the former alluding to the subjective, emotional and the inner. This imbalance of visual and auditory associations in language is not part of a naturally given order, but based on powerful constellations which can be conceived as deeply rooted in history reaching back to Aristotle, as Eric Leigh Schmidt notes in 'Hearing Loss':

> For both knowledge and delight, the sense of sight was, according to Aristotle, 'above all others'; it was the most developed sense, the clearest and most discerning, the one most able to bring 'to light many differences between things'. Hearing was a close second, superior for its conduciveness to learning. Taste and touch, associated with animality, had the 'least honour'. Smell fell as a mediator in the middle. (Schmidt 2004: 43)

The dichotomous relationship which is established here between the bright sense of sight, which alludes to knowledge and clarity, and the soft sense of hearing, which is related to the realm of knowledge only in its function as a facilitator, is further intensified by the emphasis on the senses of taste and touch as completely dissociated from any ability of abstraction and sense-making. Smell functions in this framework as a socially conditioned olfactory sensor able to differentiate the 'scentlessness' of reason from the 'foulness' of base bodily desires. It can thus be argued that this hierarchical paradigm of knowledge production is based on a body–mind split, which places the sense of sight completely outside of the body. The epistemological effect of the objectification of visuality is that it becomes linked to the objectification of knowledge. Although the significance of aurality has not been completely absent from the classical and modern literatures, as Schmidt emphasizes with regard to Aristotle,[1] as a normative concept the supremacy of the visual has continuously been inscribed and re-narrated in the Western literary canon:

> Whether in Francis Bacon's aphorism, 'I admit nothing but on the faith of the eyes', or in Thomas Reid's, 'Of all the faculties called the five senses, sight is with no doubt the noblest', [historian Martin] Jay lifts up vision as 'the dominant sense in the modern world' [...] Sight, 'the most comprehensive of all our senses', as John Locke concluded in his Essay Concerning Human Understanding, reigns with unquestioned supremacy over the Enlightenment enterprise. (Schmidt 2004: 44)

Particularly in the context of conceptions of culture it is relevant to look at how notions of the visual have given shape to the idea of Western culture, especially with regard to the embeddedness of such a concept in experiences of colonialism, and contemporary (postcolonial) racism. As Nicholas Mirzoeff argues in *The Visual Culture Reader*, '[t]he futile quest to visualise racial difference was a key part of Western visual culture throughout the modern period and its effects are only too apparent in contemporary everyday life' (Mirzoeff 1998: 281). In referring to Timothy Mitchell's contribution to the same volume, which deals with the orientalist implications of the world exhibitions in Europe in the nineteenth century, Mirzoeff emphasizes that:

> [O]bjectiveness was a matter not just of visual arrangement around a curious spectator, but of representation. What reduced the world to a system of objects was the way their careful organization enabled them to evoke some larger meaning, such as History or Empire or Progress. (Mirzoeff 1998: 282–283, in reference to Mitchell 1992)

Therefore, colonial authority was to a great extent maintained and reinforced through forms of visual representation in which objects, as well as peoples and cultures became objectified and thus 'manageable'. In this way, the binary of 'self' and 'other' was stabilized through visual projection. With regard to contemporary accounts of racialized knowledge production which rely on the visual paradigm, McLuhan's construction of a mythology of modern Western visuality is a significant example. In creating a discursive polarity between 'Western' and 'primitive' cultures, McLuhan opposes a visually adept, technologically progressive Western world with an 'ear culture' of uncivilized, non-literate peoples in which aurality has a spiritual connotation:

> With an unreflective colonialist lens, McLuhan made Africa his imaginary for constructing through black-and-white contrast a sense of which [sic] modern Europeans and North Americans were at their epistemic core. 'The African' lived in 'the magical world of the ear', while modern Western 'typographic man' lived in 'the neutral visual world' of the eye. The one was a world of vision, objectification and progress; the other a world of sound, magic and timelessness. The animated intensity of the auditory was something that the lettered had been forced to set aside but that oral peoples all experienced – tribal worlds, which were characterized by an 'overwhelming tyranny of the ear over the eye'. (Schmidt 2004: 46–47)

While visuality in this example represents Western culture as proprietor of typography and thus of rationalized knowledge and progress, aurality evokes romanticized images of distant cultures, and an implicit desire to escape from the technology-oriented Western world.[2] What becomes obvious here is how the visual paradigm has become constitutive of racialized narratives. The dichotomous relation which is created between visual and aural worlds make tangible how the hierarchy of the senses becomes an arena for the negotiation of specific cultural politics. The opposition of sight and sound functions here as a way to justify and re-establish essentialist and ethnicizing frameworks of culture. Although deliberations such as these made by McLuhan in 1962 seem unequivocally essentialist and exoticist today, the underlying binarisms (of tradition and modernity, East and West, etc.) continue to exist, for instance in world music discourses, as has already been discussed in Chapter 2.

This short and selective account of the relation between the visual and concepts of culture exemplifies how visually generated hierarchies of cultural difference have been, and still are, inscribed into the dominant discourses of culture and modernity. However, a simple reversal of the visual and the aural perspectives would not suffice to disrupt the underlying powerful structures on which such essentialist concepts of culture are based. While this chapter will concentrate on the relation of sound and cultural formation, it is also pertinent to note that the academic field of visual culture has changed considerably within at least the last three to four decades, and that practices of visual perception have also changed. The expanding realm of visual culture in architecture, art, design, advertising, photography or film has challenged the old hegemony of the visual as mediator of objective truths. In *The Visual Culture Reader*, Nicholas Mirzoeff suggests creating new forms of engagement with, and new narratives of, visual culture:

> Such a history of visual culture would highlight those moments where the visual is contested, debated and transformed as a constantly challenging place of social interaction and definition in terms of class, gender, sexual and racialized identities. (Mirzoeff 1998: 4)

Disrupting the visual paradigm involves critically attending to the ways in which visual forms of representation constantly influence human beings on all levels of social interaction across cultural boundaries. This notable shift towards a critical analysis of visual culture is closely linked to a number of scholars' endeavours that are related to cultural studies approaches from the late 1960s onwards: above all in relation to the CCCS (Centre for Contemporary Cultural Studies) in Birmingham, which posed innovative questions concerning the politics of cultural representation and the transgressive potential of cultural and artistic practices. It is part of the endeavour of my study to work towards a critical analysis of musical sound.

The shift of the notion of visual culture from objectified representation to an everyday cultural practice is highly relevant when it comes to the study of sound and the diverse developments of what has been called auditory culture (Bull and Back 2004, Sanio 2010). Mirzoeff has highlighted that visual experience can no longer be defined in textual terms (Mirzoeff 1998: 6–7). In a similar way, acoustic experience can no longer be grasped visually or textually. For example, Jim Drobnick suggests that sound and music have particular dynamics which cannot be grasped visually; the study of sound and music, he claims, requires a *sonic turn*, which conceives of sound and music as specific forms of cultural articulation, taking into account its distinctive qualities (Drobnick 2004: 9–15). Sound holds, he says, 'not only a temporal, dissipative dimension, but also an inherent performative and a social orientation' (Drobnick 2004: 10). However, Drobnick is well aware of the relativity of such terminological shifts and adds that:

> To postulate a sonic turn, however, is more than just a matter of adroitly exchanging one trope, one sense modality, for another [...] Yet, however apparent sound's unique qualities may be, it is important to guard against essentializing sound as an autonomous realm. Many of the texts and artworks [...] integrally link sound to the other senses, visual culture, technology, and various kinds of artefacts, and when the relation is not explicit, it often exists on an implicit level. (Drobnick 2004: 10)

Therefore, rather than speaking about another paradigm shift which is captivated in an either/or dualism, it is more relevant to emphasize the particularities of sound and listening as a cultural, discursive and performative practice alongside, and in interaction with, the other senses. As Holger Schulze has noted, an inclusive approach to the study of the human senses is more adequate in describing cultural productions. Such a study would aim to move:

> away from a supposed opposition between visual and acoustic communication – and towards a project with a broader goal: the understanding of the whole world of artefacts, in their diversity of sensory perceptions, as being designed. (Schulze 2008: 15, my translation)[3]

Understood in this way, sound should be conceived of as a *cultural practice* that implies an engagement with how sound is perceived, produced and performed in everyday life as a form of identification and socialization. Moreover, the particularities of specific sonic practices can be studied in relation to visual and linguistic practices, rather than as separate from the other senses. Conceiving of sound practices as a cultural practice means, then, thinking about how sound is related to and intervenes in discourses of race, class and gender and how specific sound practices generate and transform these discourses (and thus become *discursive* practices in their own right). Another important dimension of sound practices that is related to the aforementioned is the understanding of sound practices as performative practices, which implies investigating sound as a specifically creative and constitutive act that happens in the 'here and now' of sonic production and reproduction. With regard to the received visualist framework outlined above, it is relevant to recognize how '[t]he reduction of knowledge to the visual has placed serious limitations on our ability to grasp the meanings attached to much social behaviour, be it contemporary, historical or comparative,' as Bull and Back accurately pointed out in *The Auditory Culture Reader* (Bull and Back 2004: 2). Thus, the strong focus on visual culture has created a blind spot when it comes to the study of music. With regard to the study of diasporic urban dance music, which is the focus of my study, and taking into account music's complex means and multiple sites of production, it is necessary to develop a new conceptual and methodological repertoire to describe these forms. This study puts its main focus on sound, but it studies sonic practices also as assemblages of sonic, visual and verbal practices.

Everyday sounds, music and transcultural formation

While visual culture can be regarded as an established field of study in the humanities and social sciences, a cultural analysis of sound is still an emergent field, loosely spanning different academic disciplines and artistic realms.[4] While sound studies as an interdisciplinary research field gained recognition only in the 1990s, there were endeavours in the study of sound previous to this period. R. Murray Schafer's pioneering book *Soundscapes: The Tuning of the World* can serve as a case in point here to illustrate how an approach to auditory knowledge acquisition moves beyond the old visuality-knowledge bias. Schafer claims that human beings possess a 'sonological competence', a competence which 'unites impression with cognition and makes it possible to formulate and express sonic perceptions' (Schafer 1994: 274). Thus, sonological competence does not simply refer to the physical ability to receive sound, but, more precisely, to the ability to differentiate sounds, and to make sense of the world through sound. In establishing the term 'soundscape' as a combination of sound and landscape, he describes soundscapes in order to show how people orient themselves in their environment in reference to specific sounds. Referring to the sounds of a busy market place in the middle of a town, birdsong in a rural landscape or the church bells in a small village, Schafer claims that the sounds of a particular place hold characteristic and recognizable connotations for the people who live in that place. Thus, as Alain Corbin points out in his essay on church bells in early modern French villages, characteristic soundscapes can evoke a sense of belonging to a particular place:

> The emotional impact of a bell helped to create a territorial identity for individuals living in range of its sound. When they heard it ringing, villagers, townsfolk, and those 'in the trade' in the centres of ancient towns experienced a sense of being rooted in space. (Corbin 2004: 117)

The question how people create different territorialized identities in different parts of the world is part of the endeavour Schafer, Truax and a few other scholars pursued in *The World Soundscape Project*. This project, which was pursued mainly during the late 1970s and the 1980s, introduced sonic ecology, a field that aimed at improving the soundscape of inhabitants' environments. One example of this form of ecology is the use of urban architectural design to control noise pollution. Schafer claims that in order to improve a soundscape, it has to be understood in terms of the geographical and habitual particularities of a certain place and culture. Thus, he formulates his aim to:

> study the rich symbolism sounds have for man and [to study] human behaviour patterns in different sonic environments in order to use these insights in planning future environments for man. Cross-cultural evidence from around the world must be carefully assembled and interpreted. (Schafer 1994: 5)

Although the work of the soundscape project is unprecedented and indeed outstanding with regard to the richness of collected audio footage and the creation of a terminology to describe soundscapes, the underlying preconceptions of culture which are formulated in *The Tuning of the World* need to be critically revised, since they tend to rely on received paradigms of cultural difference and ethnic essentialisms. His comparative analysis of 'cross-cultural' sonic characteristics is based on the assumption that cultures are geographically rooted in a certain place. The theoretical problem of this supposition does not lie in the fact that people experience sound in different ways, but in the assumption that these differences are perceived as being naturally given and ordered along the boundaries of distinct and homogeneous cultural entities.[5] Another aspect which bears the risk of essentializing territorialized identities is the act of attaching fixed meanings to a certain area in the first place.

Therefore, rather than drawing clear-cut conclusions about territorially fixed cultural identities from acoustic markers, the challenge of the present study lies in the investigation of sound *practices*: rather than simply collecting sounds and defining their inherently given meaning, this study understands the production, perception and performance of sound as part of complex *transcultural* practices which transgress geographical confines and continuously reconfigure place.

There is, however, no intention to dismiss Schafer's enquiry of sound and listening conventions, however. His analysis of the relationship of everyday sounds and music will be discussed in some detail below, and special attention will be given to the quest for a terminology to describe the sonic particularities of rural, urban or musical soundscapes. Schafer aimed at devising a history of everyday sounds, reaching from the birdsong to the sounds of the 'electric revolution' (see Schafer 1994: 88–99).[6] Investigating the historical perspective of sound and listening, Schafer draws mainly on literary sources, in which he finds myths and stories which describe acoustic experiences and their sociocultural contexts. These depictions, however, cannot be read as objective accounts of past sonic events, but as an engagement in an historical anthropology of sound (Picker 2003, Erlmann 2004, 2010, Smith 2004, Howes 2005, Schulze 2008). Moreover, Schafer developed a terminology to describe everyday sounds by combining terms from musicology, geography and psychology.

Three terms which are relevant in this context are *keynote sound*, *sound signal* and *soundmark*. To exemplify sound signals, Schafer mentions the bells of a church, small bells, jingles or whistles, as well as the voice of street criers announcing the closure of the shops or the beginning of the night's rest (Schafer 1994: 53–67). These signals did not only embody an informative value; for the people who heard and recognized these signals, they functioned as an orientation which guided them through the day, it structured their day, and the repetitiveness of their occurrence also evoked an emotional connection to these sounds.

Another term which Schafer uses is *keynote sound*, a term deriving from musicology and denoting the key of a musical piece. In the context of everyday sounds of a town or village, keynote sounds denote the specific background noises with which people recognize and identify. These sounds do not have a direct signalling function but build a characteristic sonic background. Schafer exemplifies keynote sounds by referring to the sound of metal wheels of a horse carriage on the cobbled street of an early modern village (Schafer 1994: 60–63), but keynote sounds could equally be referring to the sound of car engines or the rattling of an overground train in a contemporary urban environment. Sound signals and keynote sounds can become *soundmarks*.

Soundmarks describe sounds which become a common marker with which people identify. To come back to the example of the street crier, if the street crier stands at the same corner proclaiming the same message each day, this recurring sound event becomes a collective reference point which might make the people familiarize themselves with it and which in turn would connect them to a certain time and space. Transferred to the contemporary context, and taking into account a comparative perspective, the noise of the approaching underground train and the specific noise of the opening and closing doors can evoke the familiar feeling of being at home in the city in which one lives. As far as the historical dimension of soundmarks is concerned, church bells can be conceived as a characteristic soundmark of the early modern village, as churches, together with market places, constituted the central node of the village.

Two other pertinent terms he introduces are *figure* and *ground*. Schafer tries to detect different layers of sound that are found in natural or urban soundscapes. In using the terms 'figure' and 'ground', he differentiates sounds which are in the foreground from sounds which are perceived as background sound. As will be shown, these terms will prove pertinent with regard to this study when they are translated into the context of music, and musical analysis. Particularly with regard to urban dance music, or popular music in general, the terminological repertoire provided by classical musicology, which often relies on the musical score as its creative and analytical base, does not suffice here to describe the complex and highly dynamic sound practices involved in the creation of music that is mostly produced on the computer. The notion of sonic layers, as well as the investigation of the materiality and spatiality of sounds, thus resonates much better with the musics that are analysed here and become integral to the concept of transcultural sound practices developed in this study.[7] A more detailed account of the use of this terminology for the research of sound in urban dance music will be given in Chapter 2.

A major aspect in the context of this study is the conceptualization of sound practice as a cultural practice, and, related to that, sound as constitutive of a particular space and time in order to concretize the particularities of auditory culture. This implies, again, that sound does not simply *belong* to a geographically locatable place, but that sound as a creative force generates notions of place which point beyond that place – moreover, it is always an imagined place which is not confined to its geographical/cultural properties. To demonstrate this, three examples will be given which emphasize the temporal, spatial and material qualities of sound.

Steven Feld conducted a study that focused on an anthropological enquiry of how people respond to the soundmarks of a certain place, and how these soundmarks are appropriated to the musical practices of the people who live in that place. In his article 'Rainforest Acoustemology', Feld describes how the Kaluli people[8] have developed their music and speech patterns in relation to their everyday soundscape.[9] Rather than analysing his observations through the colonial gaze, Feld's aim is 'to study how human experiential patterns and practices construct the habits, systems of belief, knowledge and action we call "culture" ' (Feld 2004: 223). The sounds of the trees and the wind are soundmarks which become part of the specific sonic narratives that do not simply reflect, but design the language, music and social life of the Kaluli. What is relevant about such an investigation is how the study of sound practices can be transferred to different temporal and spatial constellations. In his article 'Tuning into London c.1600', Bruce R. Smith asks, '[w]hat sort of relationship could be traced between ambient sounds and the music and speech patterns of the Londoniensis people of WC1?' (Smith 2004: 128). This question could be enlarged to look into how this relationship has changed in contemporary urban London in consideration of its mediatized and technologized sonic coordinates.

Another relevant approach is Michael Bull's *Sound Moves* (2007), in which he investigates how a specific 'technology of the self'[10] is generated through the use of the iPod. He relates this listening practice to the increasing polycentric and polyphonic structure of modern urban space. In comparison to the geographical location of the village church, which is situated in the centre of the village and expands its sonic radius from the centre outwards and thus draws the attention of the people towards this centre, contemporary urban environments tend to have a polycentric structure which could be arranged around a shopping centre, a set of office buildings, an important local train station, not to mention numerous other, much more subtle, multidirectional and overlapping sonic coordinates, created by cars, trams or shopping streets. Thus, even though the churches are situated in the same place as they were 300–400 years ago, the centres of the cities have shifted, and ambient noises around the centres have become much more polyphonic. Technological developments, as well as the modification of practices of socialization and consumption, are closely related to the changing development of the specific soundscapes which are part of the continuous transformation of cities. Michael Bull has noted that '[s]ound and movement are closely related in the navigation of urban experience' (Bull 2007: 299).[11] He studied the relation of sonic experience and urban space in relation to what he calls iPod culture, and particularly highlights the 'privatisation of experience through sound' through the use of the iPod:

> It is a hyper-post-Fordist culture in which subjects construct what they imagine to be their own individualised schedules of daily life – their own daily soundtrack of media messages, their own soundscape as they move through shopping centres, their own work-out soundtrack as they modulate the movement of their bodies in the gym. With its enveloping acoustics iPod users move through space in their auditory bubble, on the street, in their automobiles, on public transport. In tune with their body, their world becomes one with their 'soundtracked' movements; moving to the rhythm of their music rather than to the rhythm of the street. In tune with their thoughts – their chosen music enables them to focus on their feelings, desires and auditory memories. (Bull 2007: 3)

Bull is creating here the notion of the urbanite as an 'isolated, yet mediated, urban subject,' which only randomly takes part in the collective buzz of the urban soundscape (Bull 2007: 4). He argues that the city consists almost entirely of 'non-spaces' (Bull 2007: 5),[12] to which the iPod users attach meaning while walking along listening to their music and thus creating their privatized soundscape. Seen in this way, meaning is not generated here with reference to the auditory and emotional qualities of the space itself, but only as a space mediated through the experience designed by the music a person listens to on his or her iPod. Although Bull detects a tendency towards the privatization of people's individual urban experience, he also emphasizes the innate fear of social isolation. He argues that the use of the iPod also functions as an interface between the individual and the urban social world: 'This contradictory desire for privacy and fear of social isolation is resolved through the use of mobile sound media' (Bull 2007: 5). Bull argues that the music people listen to on their iPods does affect the way the city is ordered:

> iPod culture reorders the social spaces of the city, giving greater prominence to media-generated forms of privacy whilst distancing users from the 'proximity' of others. iPod users live within a mediated and perpetual sound matrix, each user inhabiting a different auditory world. (Bull 2007: 7)

The users of the iPod manage 'to liberate themselves from the perceived oppressive rhythms of the city' (Bull 2007: 7) and regain control through the creation of their own private auditory spaces – a dynamic which Bull situates between the affective realms of ' "warm", representing the proximate, the inclusive' and '"chilly", [representing] the distant and exclusive' (Bull 2007: 9).

Bull explored the individualized auditory spaces which are created by iPod users, and conducted interviews with iPod users in New York and London in an attempt to determine how they create their own version of the city, and of themselves, by creating their personalized 'soundtracks' (Bull 2007: 3). In this way, complex connectivities between people and urban spaces are created that intersect with other auditory, (in)visible and geographic markers of the city. The significance of Bull's investigation for the research of my study is that it shows how sound, and listening in particular, become creative agents in the (re-) configuration of urban space. How this relationship is then transferred to the realm of musical creation will be investigated in Chapter 4 with regard to Dusk + Blackdown's album *Margins Music*, in showing how the sonic coordinates of margin and centre, East and West, tradition and modernity are negotiated.

As far as the material and affective dimension of transcultural sound practices is concerned, Julian Henriques' investigation of the reggae sound system is notable in demonstrating how the sonic can be analysed in the context of the contemporary urban space as a complex site of social interaction. He establishes the concept of sonic dominance by investigating the materiality of the sound of the bass which is the most striking sound heard and felt when standing in front of a sound system's speakers:

> The first thing that strikes you in a Reggae sound system session is the sound itself. The sheer physical force, volume, weight and mass of it. Sonic dominance is hard, extreme and excessive. At the same time the sound is also soft and embracing and it makes for an enveloping, immersive and intense experience. The sound pervades, or even invades the body, like smell. Sonic dominance is both a near over-load of sound and a super-saturation of sound. Your [sic] lost inside it, submerged under it. This volume of sound crashes down on you like an ocean wave, you feel the pressure of the weight of the air like diving deep underwater. There's no escape, no cut off, no choice but to be there. (Henriques 2004: 451–452)

Henriques' notion of sonic dominance does not primarily imply the dominance as power *over* somebody or something, but rather emphasizes the sonic as 'a life force' which connects people and is able to create 'something that even defies communication – joy' (Henriques 2004: 453). In a sound system, the boundaries between the inside and the outside become fluid. First, the sound system itself is mobile and thus 'inseparable from movement not only through time, but also through space' (Henriques 2004: 454). Second, there is no clear separation between the artists and the audience, since '[u]sually the speaker stacks are used in a triangular configuration to point inwards into the "Dancehall crowd" or audience, rather than directed outwards onto an audience' (Henriques 2004: 454). And third, '[s]ound systems are microcosms of the social, cultural and economic sonic relationships in which they partake' (Henriques 2004: 454). These sonic relationships become part of a process of socialization and negotiation between the people who happen to be sharing this time and space that the sound system offers.

Moreover, and this alludes to the comparative perspective, there is, through musical sound, a link from this specific microcosm of a London street to West Kingston, where a lot of the tunes are produced up until today, and where the sound system culture started to develop in the 1950s. The relevance of Henriques' study for my investigation of transcultural urban dance music lies in the contextualization of transcultural sound practices in terms of urban dance music's Afro-diasporic *routes*.[13] The significance of the affective dimension of these musics is summed up in Steve Goodman's *Sonic Warfare*, which will be quoted here in some length:

> What makes these Afro-diasporic music cultures key here, aside from their content as music, is that they generate bass ecologies within underdeveloped zones of megalopian systems. As such, they have cultivated, with Jamaican sound system culture as the prototype or abstract machine, a diagram of affective mobilization with bass materialist foundation. Taking the staples of popular electronic music, from hip-hop to house and techno, and mutating them to their local desires, spraying them with local voices, these musics also, hand in hand with their pirate economics, propose models for affective collectivity without any necessary political agenda [...]. They always possess a power of transversal application into other aesthetic, sociocultural, and economic fields. Perhaps the contagiousness of such cultures and their analog and digital sonic transmissions make them an audio portal, offering them innovative techniques for synthesizing modes of collective assemblage, production, and distribution through the construction of temporary and mobile vibrational ecologies. (Goodman 2010: 175)

What becomes clear from the examples given is that urban space is more than a mere auditory landscape that can be read like a cultural map. Rather, the sonic fabric of urban space is constantly transformed according to the ways in which people move through it, the ways in which they manipulate it, or use it to interact with other people, and other sonic and musical textures and vibrations. But how do these urbanity-saturated sounds resonate in South Asian urban dance music? How can the specific sound practices that are central to the development of transcultural urban dance music be described?

Coming back to Jaques Attali's notion of the anticipation of social change in music, the relationship between music and sound in everyday life will be elaborated in some detail in the following section. Schafer investigates the relation between music, social life and everyday soundscapes and claims that '[m]usic forms the best permanent record of past sounds, so it will be useful as a guide to studying shifts in aural habits and perceptions' (Schafer 1994: 103). The assumption that music and everyday life have always been intertwined and have influenced each other is not new. Nevertheless, a thorough investigation of the interplay between social change and artistic and musical expression is still an inexhaustible enterprise. Studies of music and urban space can benefit from Schafer's exploration of how the imitation of nature played a significant part in musical composition and the arts in the eighteenth century, a time when urbanization successively enhanced the unnatural; and music and the arts became sites to underscore and to 'stage' this difference:

> The conscientious imitation of landscape in music corresponds historically to the development of landscape painting, which seems to have been first cultivated by the Flemish painters of the Renaissance and developed into the principle genre of painting in the nineteenth century. Such developments are explicable only as a result of the displacement of the art gallery farther and farther from the natural landscape in the hearts of growing cities. Imitations of nature were then created to be exhibited in unnatural settings. Here they functioned as so many windows, releasing the spectator different scenes [...] By means of this metaphorical fenestration we break out of the confinements of the city to the free paysage beyond. (Schafer 1994: 104)

In this example, music not only comments on recent developments in society, but it becomes an arena where new meanings are created, where change itself becomes the artistic subject. This artistic potential evokes creative and conflicting dynamics. And composers themselves register this ambivalent potential. Schafer states that Handel, who lived in the city, was one of the first composers to be influenced by the bustle of urban activity and is said to have derived inspiration from the singing and noises in the streets (Schafer 1994: 104). But there were other composers, and scholars, who felt distracted by the noises of the street, and turned against street criers and loud music in particular, having the effect that noises of a certain loudness and quality were forbidden (Schafer 1994: 65–67). Instead, the music of the high classes took place remote from the hustle and bustle of the busy street, in concert halls or private salons, and thus closed itself off from the disorganized noise of the city. However, the noises of the city, as well as the specific ideological mindsets of the people, also became audible in the contemporary classical compositions. Schafer emphasizes how the belief in technological and social progress at the time of the industrial revolution influenced musical compositions. Quoting Lewis Mumford:

> Here, then, in the constitution of the orchestra, was the ideal pattern of the new society. It was achieved in art before it was approached in technics [...] Tempo, rhythm, tone, harmony, melody, polyphony, counterpoint, even dissonance and atonality, were all utilized freely to create a new ideal world, where the tragic destiny, the dim longings, the heroic destinies of men could be entertained once more. Cramped by its new pragmatic routines, driven from the marketplace, and the factory, the human spirit rose to a new routine in the concert hall. It's greatest structures were built of sound and vanished in the act of being produced. (Mumford 1934, quoted in Schafer 1994: 108)

The orchestra of the nineteenth century articulates, in idealized form, the celebration of the Industrial Revolution. The orchestration was extended by wind instruments, drums and other bass-intense sounds, and the harmonium was substituted by the grand piano (Schafer 1994: 108–109). Thus, the loudness was enhanced and fundamentally altered the sonic conventions of modernity.

The way in which creative musical practices challenge listening conventions and can serve to intervene into hegemonic social structures has been widely discussed in relation to the groundbreaking work by John Cage. While some nineteenth-century composers wanted to create 'ideal soundscapes of imagination', musicians such as John Cage in the mid-twentieth century intended to bend the boundary between music and social life. Schafer states that '[w]hen John Cage opened the door of the concert hall to let the traffic noise mix with his own, he was paying an unacknowledged debt to Russolo' (ibid.: 111).[14] The ordered structure of the concert hall seemed to have the function not only to reflect, but to enhance, the dominant order of the privileged classes, and reflected back into the musical compositions themselves. Schafer emphasizes that '[t]his blurring of the edges between music and environmental sounds may eventually prove to be the most striking feature of all twentieth-century music' (ibid.: 111).

In the context of twentieth-century musical avant-gardes, innovative sound practices have been realized with the tape recorder, which significantly altered the notion of music as an ideal reflection of society and instead investigated the destruction of the 'real'. The sound itself became increasingly central to musical creation:

> With this device sounds can at last be suspended, dissected, intimately investigated. More than that, they can be synthesized and it is in this that the full potentiality of the tape recorder is revealed as an instrument uniting impression, imagination and expression. The tape recorder can synthesize sounds impossible for the voice. (ibid.: 154)

This created the basis for the inventors of the musique concrète, who set out to explore the creative possibilities of the cassette recorder and thus generated new musical practices of composition:

> In the practices of musique concrète it became possible to insert any sound from the environment into a composition with tape, while in electronic music the hard-edge sound of tone generator may be indistinguishable from the police siren or the electric egg-beater. (ibid.: 111)

Brandon LaBelle provides a pertinent differentiation between John Cage's work and the artists who were engaged in musique concrète:

> As mentioned, what we hear in the work of Cage, and reflected in works such as 4'33", as well as Cartridge Music (1960), which calls for the amplification of small objects, is an emphasis on the very source of sound itself, as objects, electronic circuits, and real bodies [...] The work establishes a sensitivity to sound, and listening in general, by showing us the direct place from which it springs [...] Thus, we are asked to understand the liberation of sound in relation to material conditions: the material of objects, the material of sounds, the material of our own bodies and the space in which we are positioned. These become conditions that refer to themselves rather than signifiers of some *other* reality; for Cage, liberation only occurs by insisting on sound, and by extension, direct perception, beyond representation or mediation, as found within the location of the real [...] Against such thinking, musique concrète locates sound's liberation through ideal configurations, harnessing sound's intrinsic ambiguity or malleability so as to create distinct auditory experiences abstracted from an original source, beyond or in spite of material reference. [...] Thus, to a certain degree, experimental music's initial steps oscillate from concentration on a social architecture in which sound figures to a concern with the body of sound as an object in its own right. (LaBelle 2007: 24–25)

This differentiation can be analysed in terms of two forms of sonic re-embodiment. In the case of John Cage, the music is freed from the abstract realm and led back to the physicality and materiality of the space and the body to the here and now of sonic perception. With regard to the musique concrète, the re-embodiment works through a detachment of sound from a detectable source and explores sound as sound. This sound as sound then develops a very unique materiality which is somehow generated outside of the body, but can be perceived only through embodied sonic perception. While the former gives some clues about how we experience musical sound in a certain space in relation to our own body, and the bodies of those who share that space (e.g. Henriques' reggae sound system), the latter would refer more to a specific musical technique, such as sampling, for instance, where an aesthetic practice predates its re-attachment to the discursively formulated semantic organization of meanings.

Therefore, there is a link that can be drawn between analogue practices of collage and practices of digital sampling and remix, as media and sound studies scholar Rolf Großmann (2011) summarizes in his article on musical reproduction. While facets of musical reproduction already developed in the 1960 and 1970s with analogue techniques such as tape recorders, dubplates and manipulated four-channel mixing boards, sampling and digital audio only developed from the 1980s onwards – 'continuing the analogue tradition with digital means' (Großmann 2011: 125, my translation). What is radically different from the analogue era is 'the availability of audio-compatible hardware and software and the interconnectedness through the world wide web' that came along with digital communication technology (Großmann 2011 125). What can be concluded from this is that the idea of remixing and collage is not confined to digital processes of reproduction. But the actual practices of sampling, remixing and collage took on new forms through the digitalized ways of production, perception and dissemination. Significantly, an increasing number of people are now able to get involved with these practices and share their sonic ideas with people all over the world, something which shapes and transforms contemporary music culture in significant ways.

Sound practices: Techniques and technologies

Popular music is often defined through its categorization into pop music styles such as hip-hop, rap, reggae, dub. All these styles are often treated as fixed categories equipped with certain characteristic features: the rhythmic patterns in hip-hop, the use of guitars in rock music, the use of distinct sorts of distortion in punk and heavy metal, or the use of certain music equipment such as the 12×12 guitar box, samplers, percussion instruments or the cowbell. Although there might indeed be certain sonic characteristics that are shared by musical styles, the music should not be restricted by these characteristics since that might result in a limiting view on music which ignores the complex transformations of musical styles across musical genres, locations and modes of production. The descriptions which are often given of music, especially in the music press, frequently intend to emphasize a certain 'style' which is often not aimed at being precise about the concrete features of a song. Instead, these descriptions want to evoke a feeling, and a lifestyle that involves something about a certain musical scene, including clothing, habits, certain spaces in which the music is performed; it intends to sell the music, advertise it. In addition, more importantly, there is a political implication in the description of music, which becomes highly dominant when looking at music from different cultural backgrounds. Terms such as 'fat beats', 'sexy sounds' and 'hot rhythms' often evoke ethnicized and racialized images, as has already been elaborated in some detail in Chapter 2 in looking at how these popular descriptions of music have been perceived with regard to certain forms of negotiation of cultural identity, and ethnic identity. These descriptions contain aesthetic judgements, which aim at creating fixed ethnicized and sexualized markers for certain musical styles or genres. The present study seeks to understand musical styles not as 'containers' equipped with clearly defined sound characteristics. Bhangra, Indi-Pop and Asian Underground are instead understood as concepts which on the one hand are generated by concrete musical practices, but on the other hand are linked to diverse social, cultural, economic and musicological aspects of music.

Over the last twenty years at least, a growing body of scholarship from a range of disciplines has explored the influence of pop-cultural expressions of the South Asian diaspora on British culture. When it comes to the investigation of specifically urban musical developments in the UK, Ashwani Sharma, John Hutnyk and Sanjay Sharma's book *Dis-orienting Rhythms: The Politics of the New Asian Dance Music* was clearly an innovative contribution when it was released in 1996, in that it raised some overdue questions about the contemporary South Asian dance music and the politics of identity, and paid special attention to the commodification of exotica with regard to these musics.[15] Drawing mostly from cultural studies and anthropology, the authors of *Dis-Orienting Rhythms* share a 'commitment to critical Marxist critique and radical political agendas' as Jazeel notes in his article on 'British-Asian Soundscapes' (Jazeel 2005: 234). Although this book is still highly relevant in highlighting the capability of these musics to counteract the 'exuberant celebrations of a depthless British multiculture', Jazeel critically remarks in his article that 'this body of scholarship has characteristically declined from any serious examinations of the musicality of any of the music with which it engages' (Jazeel 2005: 235). He argues:

> Musical analysis seems to not go beyond explorations of the lyrical expression in Bhangra music and in ADF tracks. These are analyses of music and politics, where the 'and' marks a gap, a deferral from the political event to its mediated, musical representation. (Jazeel 2005: 235)

Therefore, the main attention is given to the explicit articulation of political messages, and the lyrics become the adequate medium to deliver this message.

In contrast to this, Jazeel's approach 'signposts a fully integrated analytical approach that evokes both the multiple ways music is always fully inside a society that is dynamic, and the multiple stakeholders (composers, performers, listeners, dancers, etc.) involved simultaneously in the doing of musical activity and the doing of society' (Jazeel 2005: 235). Especially when transcultural musical styles are concerned, music is analysed in terms of the cultural background, or the social conditions under which the music was created, performed or distributed. And, of course, there are highly relevant aspects to consider about the contextual level of music production. But these discourses often ignore the discourses that the music itself provides (see Eshun 1998).

The aim of this study is to analyse the specific sound practices of South Asian-influenced urban dance music from the UK. The main analytical focus with regard to the sonic material, namely the musical tracks, is the investigation of how digital sampling is used as a creative sound practice in which sounds are decontextualized from their 'original' source, and recontextualized to form a new piece of sound. In general, sampling technology plays a pivotal role for the development of urban dance music. However, this subchapter refrains from conceptualizing technology in a deterministic way, but understands sampling as a cultural technology which is not restricted to the technological device of the sampler, or the sequencer.

To clarify, in *Capturing Sound*, Mark Katz states that 'the technology of sound recording, writ large, has profoundly transformed modern musical life' and proposes thinking about the specific ways recording influences musical practices by introducing what he calls the 'phonograph effect' (Katz 2004: 3). He describes phonograph effects as the 'manifestations of sound recording's influence' as intricately related to the specific practices of its users:

[I]t is not simply the technology but the relationship between the technology and its users that determines the impact of recording. It is important to add, too, that the influence I describe does not flow in one direction only, from technology to user [...] users themselves transform recording to meet their needs, desires, and goals, and in doing so continually influence the technology that influences them. (Katz 2004: 4)

One of Katz's central claims is that creative musical practices (including both composition and production) were constantly appropriated to the developments of recording technology, and that recording technology at the same time changed according to the ways in which the technology was used. One instance Katz highlights to exemplify the phonograph effect is when the phonograph was first invented and made it possible to record musical performances:

When Igor Stravinski composed his Serenade for Piano in 1925, he wrote the work so that each of the four movements would fit the roughly three-minute limit of a ten-inch, 78-rpm record side [...] Stravinski was not alone. Many composers of classical and especially popular music followed a similar compositional approach. (Today's tree-minute pop song is a remnant of this practice.) (Katz 2004: 3)

While this example applies the phonograph effect to the structural level of musical composition, Katz highlights other significant effects of sound recording technology on the perception, production and dissemination of recorded sound. Significant examples are how violinists in the early twentieth century 'intensif[ied] and expand[ed] their use of vibrato' in response to recording technology, or how the phonograph became a 'compositional tool' in the context of avant-garde music in the 1920s and 1930s. In the context of the music which is analysed in my study, Katz's investigation of turntablism and digital sampling is pertinent in showing how audio and recording technology not only changed musical creation, but how people used these technologies in new ways, thereby reinventing them.[16] Therefore, the ways in which recording technology has been rebuilt and redefined by the ways in which music is composed, produced and performed by musicians, producers and DJs – and, likewise, how it is perceived, translated and judged by the listener – cannot be underestimated and is a precondition of the concept of transcultural sound practices which is developed here.

What makes this broad definition of technology useful for a critical study of South Asian dance music is that it disrupts the dichotomy between technology and tradition. In debates about popular music, musical technology is often narrated as belonging to the modern world, and 'handmade' instrumental music as belonging to a traditional world of folk music styles. In contrast to that, conceiving of all forms of music as part of technology in the broad sense means understanding classical and folk music techniques as technology in the same way as sampling techniques.[17] Jayachandran Palazhy, artistic director of *Attakkalari Centre for Movement Arts* in Bengaluru (formerly Bangalore), makes some relevant remarks in relation to his understanding of technology. In his own work as a performer, choreographer and producer, he combines classical Indian dance moves, contemporary dance and digitally generated sounds and visuals, which are then staged in various site-specific performances. In a roundtable discussion at the Southbank Centre London as part of the *Alchemy Festival 2011*, he was asked how he negotiates the polarities of tradition and modernity, heritage and technology. Palazhy claimed not to be contained by these static categories and suggested a wide and incorporating conception of technology by stating that from his viewpoint, religious rituals, social dances or site-specific performances can all be conceived as technologies of movement, of the body, of sound, light or colour. This notion of technology thus transgresses the divide between a tradition which is somehow caught in the past, and a technology which directs us towards the future and aims at an understanding of embodied knowledge which is rooted in the present:

> For me it is more about a continuum. Particularly for people like me working with the body. For me, images, technologies, relating to the space and other people, is all part of an inherited knowledge that is a created knowledge responding to the contemporary reality. (Palazhy 2011, my transcription)

In considering technology as a continuum, Palazhy suggests that one could think of any form of movement as being saturated by body technologies. Interestingly, he does not claim that people who 'belong' to a certain culture somehow naturally inherit these technologies. Although people have an 'inherited knowledge', it is always a knowledge that has to be re-acquired. Although he is primarily concerned with performance art, his notion of technology can be transferred to specific sound practices as well. Following Paul Théberge's concept of technology established in *Any Sound You Can Imagine*, technology is not confined to the technological device alone, but always incorporates a material and social aspect:

> The focus, then, is not so much on technology per se as on 'technique', understood in its broadest possible sense. I refer to the notion of technique not

simply in the limited sense commonly employed in music (e.g., performance or compositional technique) but in its full sense as the organisation of means – material and social – employed for musical ends. (Théberge 1997: 160)

To support this view, he also suggests using the concept according to Frederickson's idea of 'social technology', and, returning to Frederickson, he claims that '[s]ocial technologies are distinct from, though they may be related to, specific "machine technologies" ' (Théberge 1997: 160, quoting Frederickson 1989: 194–197).[18] In the context of music, Théberge thus adequately differentiates 'musical technology' (to refer to 'musical instruments, recording devices, and so on') from the notion of 'technology of music' in reference to Michel Foucault's expression of the notion of a 'technology' of sex:[19]

> I examine certain 'technologies of music'; that is, technologies in the form of discourses, institutions, and practices – aesthetic, scientific, pedagogical, legal, or economic – that 'produce' representations of music that have concrete ideological or material effects on music making. (Théberge 1997: 160)

To relate the notion of technology which has been developed here to sampling, sampling can be conceived of as a tool to create dissonance, discontinuity and dislocation, and thus challenges notions of temporality, spatiality and community that insist on linearity and progress (Weheliye 2005: 8). As Alexander Weheliye notes in *Phonographies*:

> Sound technologies not only shape and reshape the temporality of modernity, they also significantly recast its spatiality. The city as the sine qua non of modern spatiality illustrates the varied ways in which these machines and their usage re/configure this sphere, adding an aural dimension to the generally visual considerations of modern geographical constellations. (Weheliye 2005: 144)

Consequently, he insists that 'sound technologies are a vital element of the musical text rather than supplementary to its unfolding' (Weheliye 2005: 2), which has significant ramifications for the analysis of sound practices. Therefore, the notion that sound practices are conceived of as specific forms of cultural activity functions as a precondition for a more detailed analysis of distinctive sounds and forms of musical reappropriation.

Besides the broad understanding of technology which is suggested here, there are two other points which distance the analysis of sound practices from conventional (pop) musicology. First, in relation to the critique of musical styles as analytical categories elaborated in Chapter 2, relying on the rigid divisions between guitar music and electronic music is unproductive for the revealing of the significance of the specific sonic 'modes' of its production.[20] Théberge suggests looking at some of the concrete characteristics constitutive for the formation of new musical forms:

> What is important to determine, however, is precisely the manner in which selected characteristics – physical, acoustic, stylistic, or aesthetic – which constitute the total 'accumulated sensibilities' of a piano, a guitar, an orchestra, or even a computer, interact with a variety of musical and extra-musical factors to create innovations in musical form [...] In this sense, musical instruments are not 'completed' at the stage of design and manufacture, but, rather, they are 'made-over' by musicians in the process of making music. (Théberge 1997: 160)

Théberge draws from Robert Walser's analysis to show how specific modes of sound production such as 'specific uses of distortion and sustain' and 'power chords' have been used, thereby re-inventing the guitar and creating new musical forms (Théberge 1997: 159, in reference to Walser 1993: 42–51).

Along the same lines, it will be demonstrated in Chapter 4 how Nathan 'Flutebox' Lee redefines the flute with his new mode of percussive beat-boxing and thus transgresses the confines of fixed musical categories, and moreover, of expectations of 'traditional' Indian music. Furthermore, the concept of the musical 'work' needs to be critically revised. Most of today's popular music is produced on the computer. While, with regard to most guitar music, real instruments are recorded in real time, dance music styles such as hip-hop, jungle or drum'n'bass have moved the whole process of composition to the sequencer. Plug-in instruments are digitally stored and endlessly manipulable, which implies that the sound becomes more important than the song. This sound practice is more about sonic layers than about symphony. This perspective could be considered limited because the way in which music is perceived as music has not changed altogether, and song structure is thus still an important feature that makes a piece of music 'work'. However, with regard to urban dance music, this structure tends to be much more open, and bendable. Therefore, *song* will here be substituted by the term *track*, and the focus will be more on ways to describe sound and sonic constellations, than on musical histories of songs and genre.[21] In this respect, it is important to highlight Stan Hawkins' (2002) account of the contextualization of popular (and especially urban dance) music. As Peter Wicke sums up, Hawkins aims at '[combining] analysis with hermeneutics to explore both the sonic structures and the cultural relations within which [musical pieces] are located and meaning is unfolded' (Wicke 2003: 14, my translation). What is especially interesting concerning the sound concept of Hawkins is that it is tightly related to the musical piece as an 'open audio space':

> No amount of transcription or conventional musical analysis can ever render the pop score fixed. As I was writing this book, I imagined a score without manuscript paper, without staves, without bar-lines, without time signatures, an open audio space to occupy in whatever way one deems most appropriate. [...] Ultimately then, the pop score is an abstract and experiential one. It is based not only on the dynamics of the pop recording but also on the individual listening patterns, emotions, aesthetics and cognitive responses we have to sound. In this sense, the score symbolises the recorded soundtrack of our memories, experiences, and musical reflections – everything that makes music fun and meaningful. (Hawkins 2002: 13, quoted in Wicke 2003: 112)

This notion corresponds with my idea of the track, and particularly resonates with the sound practice of sampling, which can be seen as a 'generative procedure':

> The concept, proposed by Hawkins, of an open and multidimensional sound space which would be understood more as a set of generative procedures than as a fixed structural context, is tremendously productive and goes far beyond the question of the possibilities and limits of notation practices. (Wicke 2003: 112, my translation)[22]

Rather than depicting a musical piece as being determined by a notational score, or as representative of a certain musical style, the analysis of sound practices can be conceived as an investigation of musical, sonic, cultural and social fabrics that are interwoven and influence each other. Rather than representing a fixed meaning, the sound practices generate meaning through multiple processes of production, performance and mediation. This is particularly relevant with regard to the investigation of the transcultural implications of South Asian–influenced dance music.

Another aspect which needs to be taken into account is the dominance of analyses of the lyrical content of popular music within cultural studies. In his article 'The World Is Sound? Geography, Musicology and British-Asian Soundscapes', cultural geographer Tariq Jazeel critiques approaches which focus on the lyrical content without recognizing their embeddedness in music and suggests that it is necessary to be more attentive to the musical performance than the lyrics. He argues that although cultural studies has done a great deal to critically investigate the cultural politics of South Asian dance music, 'this body of scholarship has characteristically declined from any serious examinations of the *musicality* of any of the music with which it engages' (Jazeel 2005: 235, original emphasis). If the musical pieces are examined in any detail, the focus lies mostly on the lyrical content:

> Musical analysis seems to not go beyond explorations of the lyrical expression in Bhangra music and in ADF tracks. These are analyses of music and politics, where the 'and' marks a gap, a deferral from the political event to its mediated, musical representation. (Jazeel 2005: 235)

Thus, the main focus is placed on the articulation of politicized messages, and the lyrics are depicted as the appropriate medium for the dissemination of these messages. In contrast, Jazeel suggests a different approach on musical analysis which aims at:

> [signposting] a fully integrated analytical approach that evokes both the multiple ways music is always fully inside a society that is dynamic, and the multiple stakeholders (composers, performers, listeners, dancers, etc.) involved simultaneously in the doing of musical activity and the doing of society. (Jazeel 2005: 235)

Jazeel thus proposes that rather than seeing music (or lyrics, for that matter) as an expression of a particular political, social or cultural condition (or critique of that condition), musical activity is seen as *constitutive* of society – a social and cultural practice. Following that perspective, and aiming to include in the analysis, besides the lyrical content, the musical techniques, the specific sounds, and the lyrical performance, this chapter seeks to analyse the dynamics that are involved in the multilevelled configurations of musical tracks. Therefore, the goal is to relate some of the significant questions which cultural studies have posed about identity constructions, alterity and the cultural politics of music, and to read those questions along the lines of concrete sound practices in order to develop an understanding of the dynamic relationship between musical and cultural formation.

Elaborating on the particularities of music as a means to transgress the confines of rigid concepts of culture, musicologists Georgina Born and David Hesmondalgh's book *Western Music and Its Others* is particularly relevant in critically confronting earlier approaches to popular musical forms which conceived of music either as an articulation of cultural and social relations *per se*, or as 'music for music's sake'. In more recent accounts, the authors see a paradigm shift in popular music studies and ethnomusicology, 'away from a cultural imperialism approach to global cultural flows and toward theories of postcoloniality and globalisation' (Born and Hesmondalgh 2000: 25). While cultural studies perspectives on music have been mostly interested in the social and cultural *context* of musical production, the cultural analysis of musical sound that is pursued here takes the sound of music seriously and sets out to *listen* attentively to the sonically generated cultural negotiations. But rather than projecting postcolonial analysis upon musical pieces, the authors claim a new methodological and ontological approach by attending to the 'complexity of musical signification', as Born explains:

> Music exists and generates meaning in a number of different, simultaneous forms: as musical sound, and this as mediated by notations, by technological and visual forms, by the practices and sociality of performance, by social institutions and socioeconomic arrangements, by language in different guises (lyrics and dramatic narratives, theoretical, and critical exegeses, and other discourses) and, relatedly, by conceptual and knowledge systems. (Born 2000: 37)

To preliminarily define my concept of sound practice, the underlying goal is a cultural analysis of music which will bring the concrete sound practices into the centre of analysis. I refrain here from a musicological approach, but rather emphasize sound practice as a cultural practice. From this perspective, sound practices are conceived of as a discursive field upon which culture is renegotiated. This is the broad understanding of sound practice that I am pursuing. The more narrow perspective which is also implied by my concept of sound practice is the conception of sound practices as the concrete techniques of musical production, for example sampling, using certain melodies and manipulating them, using effects such as reverb, and so on.

The interesting point in my analytical endeavour is how these different sound practices evoke different and dissonant conceptions of 'Indianness' or 'Britishness'. There has been a tendency to either confine Indian music to a notion of Indian culture as a homogeneous entity, or to celebrate its 'hybridity' while losing track, in both cases, of how the specific practices generate certain ideas about culture, or cultural identification and spatiality. A question which needs to be addressed is who actually judges a piece of music to be 'still' Indian, or 'already' British, or global, or hybrid? And what is the underlying conceptualization of culture? The specificity of transcultural sound practices which are found in the music analysed here will hopefully bring out the multilayered cultural conceptions which are generated in the music.

As will be shown with regard to sampling, key sounds take on something new while remaining distinctive. Key sounds become key in generating difference when one key sound is perceived against another one. My analysis aims to show how the diverse key sounds interact and transform the musical semantics, intensities and fictions.

Sampling as sound practice

This section seeks to develop the notion of digital sampling as a sound practice. With regard to the musical pieces that will be analysed in the following chapters, I am particularly interested in sampling as a creative tool of musical creation and critical intervention. In *Capturing Sound*, Katz defines sampling as 'a type of computer synthesis in which sound is rendered into data, data that in turn comprise instructions for reconstructing that sound' (Katz 2004: 138). From a single snare drum sound to a whole passage of a recorded musical piece, the creative possibilities of what can be sampled are limitless, especially given the dissemination of new technological tools such as sequencers, digital samplers and recording equipment that have made this practice relatively easily accessible. The actual creative enterprise starts when the synthesized sample is manipulated and reconstructed to form a new piece of sound. This can be pursued in a number of ways, some of which are listed by Katz: 'Tempo and pitch can be increased or decreased, [...] sounds can be reversed, cut, looped, and layered; reverberation can be added; certain frequencies within a sound can be boosted or deemphasized' (Katz 2004: 139).

In the context of this study, the goal is to show how sampling is used to create distinct new sounds, how sounds are re-contextualized, and how this distinct form of musical appropriation generates new meanings.

What is particularly valuable in Mark Katz's case studies, in which he deals with the sampling practices of Public Enemy's 'Fight the Power' or Paul Lansky's 'Notjustmoreidlechatter', is the way in which he combines the concrete analysis of digital sampling with wider discourses of cultural production and consumption, stressing the social and political agencies and effects of sampling practices. In this respect, the analysis which follows in the subsequent chapters focuses on the question of what sampling *does* to sonic material.

I argue that it is not sufficient to conceive of a sample-based track merely in terms of the textual, semiotic structure of a sequence of sampled sounds.

Rather than being merely a semiotic strategy, what qualifies digital sampling as a sound practice is precisely the performative and material qualities of sonic recontextualization. It is a form of sonic transformation which disrupts the linearity of the musical (con)text.

In the same book, Mark Katz analyses the sampling practice in the song 'Praise You' from electronic dance music producer Norman Cook, in which everyday sounds are used as the raw material for an electronic dance music track (Katz 2004: 146). This is relevant in the context of my study, because Dusk & Blackdown, one of my case studies, also uses street noises in his grime track 'Darker than East' (see Chapter 4). In his example, Katz explores the beginning sequence of the recording, where the samples of a piano, background sounds of a bar and the voice of a female singer are recontextualized in such a way that it evokes the mental image of a piano player who accompanies the singing of a woman in a busy bar environment. He realizes, however, that the female voice is a capella taken from Camille Yarbrough's soul/funk song 'Take Yo' Praise', and the piano playing and the background noise have been added in the studio. Katz thereby shows how '[t]hrough the technology of digital sampling, Cook has at once decontextualised and recontextualised Yarbrough's voice, giving it new sounds, functions, and meanings' (Katz 2004: 145). The soundscape that is created 'offers a sense of occasion, of liveness, and of place', as Mark Katz accurately describes the soundscape of the beginning sequence of 'Praise You'.

The sound collage is not an objective reflection of a certain place at a certain point in time. It is an interpretation, and an artistic reproduction of a sonic experience. What is similar in the use of everyday sounds in both musical productions is the way in which the sounds are detached from their original source, and in which space is reinscribed into them through the sound practice of sampling.

Listening to it in this way, the audio footage is the sonic material in a creative musical process. It does not represent a certain place, but an idea about a place, one that only exists in the context of the track. In his conclusion, Katz opposes the recurring view that sampling is an act of technological quotation; he states instead that 'sampling is most fundamentally an art of *transformation*. A sample changes the moment it is relocated. Any sound, placed into a new musical context, will take on some of the character of its new sonic environment' and conceives of sampled sounds as 'raw materials, waiting to be mined and refined' (Katz 2004: 156). The aspect of liveness and the creation of place will be taken up in the analysis of Nathan 'Flutebox' Lee's studio recordings, in which exactly the effect 'of occasion, of liveness, and of place' that Katz highlighted (see quote above) is created by using a room microphone and recording some of the verbal and musical communication that happened before the actual song was recorded; in this example, it is a form of staged liveness that could be regarded as a technology not unlike the one Norman Cook uses, although here it is an aesthetic decision taken in the postproduction of a live recording (see Chapter 7).

With regard to the overall question of the present study of how difference is generated through music, the sound practice of digital sampling and thus the fragmentation of the musical 'work' has significant consequences for the received representativeness of culture. When it comes to the politics of representation, the consequences of digital sampling have to be critically negotiated, also with regard to questions of copyright.[23] This becomes particularly relevant when 'non-Western' sounds are sampled by 'Western' musicians, an issue which is also discussed with regard to Dusk & Blackdown's use and handling of South Asian vocal samples. David Hesmondalgh has adequately outlined the implied controversy:

> What are the implications for our understanding of the ethics of cultural appropriation when the sound of a Pacific island women's choir becomes the hook of a club hit in Europe, without reward, recompense, or credit for that choir? And when that hook is then lifted into a Coke commercial? To what extent does the act of recontextualization, the placing of the sample next to other sounds, mean that authorship (and the resultant financial rewards) should be attributed to those sampling, rather than those sampled? How, in other words, are issues of cultural 'borrowing' and appropriation reconfigured in the era of digital sampling technologies? (Hesmondalgh 2000: 280)

To elaborate this, I would like to draw on Katz again concerning his notion of the transformative nature of sampling. Investigating Public Enemy's 'Fight the Power', an early hip-hop track which consists in its entirety of more than one hundred samples from different hip-hop and funk tracks. With regard to this track, and the appropriation of Trouble Funk's 1982 song 'Pump Me Up', he develops the thought that sampling is also transformative 'in that it blurs the traditional distinction between ideas and expressions':

> [D]oes the passage sampled in Public Enemy's 'Fight the Power' remain Trouble Funk's expression when it no longer bears any resemblance to its unaltered state? Isn't Public Enemy's use of that sound an expression distinct from Trouble

Funk's? And if so, does that make the Trouble Funk song the raw material of an idea (or even a wholly different idea) for Public Enemy? (Katz 2004: 157)

Thus, to judge a sampled sound primarily in terms of its 'original authorship' would also disregard the creative potential of the various forms of reappropriation. However, copyright practices are highly important to ensure that they don't become imperialist strategies of cultural and economic exploitation.

What is particularly relevant with regard to South Asian-influenced dance music is that a sample-based track cannot be conceived as an accumulation of authentic, or original bits of culture. Instead, sampling is a pertinent example of the deconstruction of cultural authenticity, because, as a concept, it constantly involves pastiche, and a critique of originality. As Alastair Pennycook notes in reference to Schusterman:

> Rap music's appropriation of sound and music bites and questioning of authorship and creation, its eclectic mixing of styles and use of new technology challenge 'modernist notions of aesthetic autonomy and artistic purity' and emphasize 'the localised and temporal rather than the putatively universal and eternal'. (Pennycook 2007: 11–12, quoting Shusterman 2000: 61)

Sampling functions as an agent of dissonance, discontinuity and dislocation. While 'dissonance' is a term deriving from classical musicology, in the context of electronic music, and sampling in particular, dissonance can be detected with regard to rhythm, broken beats, gaps, dropping the bass – all of which will be explored in detail in the analysis chapters. Jaques Attali is particularly interested in the tensions between music and noise, and conceives of noise as a creative form of distraction, one which bears the potential for transformation (Attali 2006: 3). Sampling generates distractions and thus enables transformative moments. With regard to discontinuity, there is a constant interplay between sonic continuities and sonic discontinuities. Discontinuities are generated, for instance, through the decontextualization of sound bits from other sources which distract received narratives. On the other hand, electronic dance musics such as techno, drum'n'bass or dubstep, in particular, are produced in such a way that the listener actively creates rhythmic continuities, when, for instance, a pulsing bass line suddenly stops and a spheric sound comes in. While the bass line is dropped, the listener imagines a steady rhythm until the bass comes in again. Much of dubstep, for instance, relies on sub-bass sounds, which are sometimes barely heard, but felt, or 'unreliable' syncopated beats which are greatly slowed down.

Thus, in the process of digital sampling and sound manipulation, difference is generated. How this is accomplished cannot be generalized, but one way to study this generation of difference is to analyse the ways in which the different sonic layers interact with each other and reference other sounds, within or outside of the realm of what is actually heard. Schafer's terms 'figure' and 'ground' can be accordingly used as a tool to describe the different locations of sound within a track. Difference is generated, for instance, when a figure suddenly becomes ground, when a sound signal (as a posture, gesture, sign) is introduced to the track. The sonic constellations change, and so do the possible meanings.

The goal of a concrete analysis of sound practices such as sampling is to focus on aspects such as the function of repetition, the effects of sonic recontextualization, and the ways in which vocal styles and musical strategies encode and transgress concepts of place, race, class and gender. A recurring question which is explored in the case studies in Part II of this book is how musical sound creates, negotiates and transforms culturally inscribed and embodied meanings. In the context of the concrete material with which the analytical part of this study is concerned, this question will be further specified as follows: How does a particular sample effect the overall sonic composition? How are sounds used to structure a track? How do different layers of sound interact and form a completely new sonic constellation? How does a sound counteract with the dominant sonic or rhythmic mode of the track? How is sonic material recontextualized to gain new meanings? How do sound samples imitate, mimic or alter other sounds, or other music styles? How do urban sounds seep into a musical track? How do sounds in a track evoke urbanness? How do certain bass frequencies bend the boundaries of the audible? What is the effect when sound is felt rather than heard? How do certain sounds evoke togetherness and others loneliness? How are conceptions of culture renegotiated through sound practices such as sampling, or the use of urban street sounds in a grime track?

To summarize, there are some broader shifts which can be detected regarding the new attention to visual and auditory practices in the humanities in general, as well as cultural and pop music studies in particular. In fact, sound studies, or aural culture as a growing interdisciplinary field which covers historical, social, technological, aesthetic and cultural approaches to sound has developed only very recently, and subsequent to the study of visual culture. As a common ground for the study of visual and auditory culture, cultural studies has played a decisive role in the establishment of an openness towards the constructedness of identities and the investigation of power structures within societies and across national borders. Therefore, the particularities of sounds and their specific practices play a role here, in addition to listening conventions.

The emphasis of my study is not so much on the significance of sound as a *musical* expression as confined to certain musical scenes or musical styles. As a concept, the aim is to show how sound, in its materiality, sociality and performativity has become a tangible object of study and a vital area for the study of cultural formations both in relation to musical and non-musical sound. While the main part of my study deals with the analysis of music, in this theoretical chapter the focus is on a wide concept of sound as way of thinking culture. The main argument here is that sound practices are ways of social and cultural negotiation which are not confined to territorially or nationally defined cultures.

Analysing South Asian dance music

In this part of the chapter, the theoretical preconditions developed in this chapter will be used to create a preliminary method and toolkit with which the concrete musical examples will be analysed. The concept of transcultural sound practices will still have to be concretized in the course of the actual analysis of musical tracks. Significantly, transcultural sound practices are conceptualized here with regard to two different levels: a broad methodological one which defines from which theoretical angle the objects are to be analysed, and a specific one, which refers to a concrete method of how musical pieces can be analysed.

With regard to the broad level, the cultural studies orientation of the concept of sound practices is emphasized. The concept of sound practices established in my study shares many aspects that have been brought up by cultural studies scholars who have dealt with music and other cultural productions. Therefore, the notion of cultural practice that I draw on conceives of culture as something that is fluid rather than stable, and that is constantly reshaped through cultural activity. The *practice* in cultural practice, then, refers to a concrete activity, such as making music, writing or performing dance moves, through which culture is generated, contested and reshaped. With regard to music, musical activity is seen as constitutive of culture, rather than as a mere reflection, or reproduction of stable features that form 'a culture'. Moreover, these practices are not merely habitual or instinctive. Cultural activity is understood in my study as a process of negotiation and transformation that constantly reshapes the cultural codes that surround and permeate these activities.

In this respect, the concept of sound practices is useful in order to investigate how people perceive, create, perform and share sounds, and how this activity is constitutive of cultural formation. Given the special focus on South Asian diasporic and transcultural music, this study investigates the production, perception and performance of sound as a complex transcultural practice which transgresses geographical confines and continuously reconfigures notions of place, ethnicity and gender.

The second level that is fundamental for my conceptualization of the concept of sound practices is a more specific, and method-based, one. This conceptualization is particularly useful as part of my analytical toolkit, as it provides a concrete tool for the analysis of musical tracks. With regard to the mixing and merging of South Asian sounds in electronic dance music in the UK dealt with in the case studies, the main analytical focus is the investigation of how sound practices such as sampling, lyrical performance or playing techniques are used in order to decontextualize sounds from their 'original' source, and recontextualize them to form a new piece of sound in the context of the new track.

In this respect, it is important to note that in the concrete analysis of musical tracks, sound practices are conceived of as particular sonic relations within a musical track in which musical styles and cultural connotations are appropriated and renegotiated. Zooming in on a particular sonic relation in a musical track means moving beyond an analysis of a musical track as a complete and more or less coherent musical work. This is to say that my focus of analysis is on the significance of situative sonic constellations (between different sounds, lyrics, musical references, techniques) and shifts in the sonic aesthetics or narrative of the track.

The conceptualization of sound practice as an analytical tool requires an emphasis on the orientation on sound production practice as a primary frame of reference for thinking about sound practices as concrete sonic relations in an electronic dance music track. In order to clarify how this frame of reference is constituted, it is relevant to bear in mind some of the basic features of electronic dance music production, as summed up by Mark Butler in his book *Unlocking the Groove* (2006):

> Some of the most distinctive characteristics of electronic dance music is the way in which it is produced – namely, through the use of electronic technologies such as synthesizers, drum machines, sequencers, and samplers. Although

increasingly common in popular music in general in recent years, these technologies have always formed the backbone of musical creation in EDM, in which a traditional instrument or a live vocal is the exception rather than the rule. (Butler 2006: 33)

The centrality of production techniques is of importance here because it emphasizes the way in which the processes of production and musical composition are interlinked and should therefore not be separated with regard to the close analysis of a musical track. This alludes to one of the important differences from 'traditional' popular music production in general, and rock music productions in particular, where a song was written and then taken to the recording studio in order to be produced. In electronic music production, from its very beginning roughly in the mid-1970s, digital sound reproduction and manipulation techniques, together with all kinds of performance techniques such as sampling, scratching and filtering have become an integral part of the compositional process. Therefore, Butler's claim that 'these technologies have always formed the backbone of musical creation' in electronic dance music is significant. However, my analysis diverts from simply analysing music production techniques in terms of studio environments and recording devices. In my analysis, sound production practice refers to an interplay of sonic, performative and transcultural aspects of music production.

When the concrete sound practices in South Asian dance music productions are analysed in Part II of this study, this is also taking into account some of the basic structuring elements of working with and producing electronic dance music. This can be very simply illustrated through the way in which electronic dance music tracks are displayed on the surface of a digital music sequencers when working with audio software such as Logic Pro or Cubase: The different audio tracks (e.g. bass drum, snare, bass guitar, synthesizer) that make the musical track are most often organized in vertical order, and the timeline runs horizontally from the left to the right. Thus, each audio track features a different sonic layer of the track, which can be an audio recording of a guitar, or a MIDI track. The significant thing about MIDI (Musical Instrument Digital Interface) is that a rhythmic or melodic pattern can be constructed in a track, and then various different sounds can be chosen from the computer's sonic library (or sampled from elsewhere) and linked to the existing pattern. For instance, a bass drum beat structure can be constructed and then interchangeably feature a bass drum sound from a drum kit or the sound of bongos or tablas. What is significant in electronic dance music production, is that the rhythm patterns and the bass form the basic sonic grid, or skeleton of the musical track to which all the other layers of sound are added, which can in turn be faded in and out of the track: another rhythmic pattern, a melody, a sample, etc. Another important structuring element are the effects (reverb, distortion, etc.) and filters (manipulating the frequencies of single tracks and the frequency spectrum of the sum of all tracks). These basic characteristics of electronic dance music production can be understood as the fundamental logic through which musical ideas are processed. Therefore, the notion of sound practices that I suggest as an analytical tool is also, on a very technical level, based on this logic, but not confined to it.

Therefore, the question that is posed in a cultural analysis of sound practices is not primarily where the sound comes from and what it *essentially* means, but how it plays a role in creating a particular sonic narrative, a particular *sonic fiction*. The particularity of sound practices as *sonic* fictions is that they do not work in uniquely a linear way, as in a novel, or any piece of writing (although music is a sonic organization of time) – sound practices also create fictions through specific forms of *layering* of sounds, rhythms and melodic figures, and sub-bass vibration which organizes sounds and their dynamics in a three-dimensional space. Sound practices, then, mark key moments within a track, in which a specific idea is created, a shift of auditory focus implied or a new sonic relationship established through a specific interaction of a sound and a rhythmic pattern, a sound and a specific effect, or between different layers of sounds.

This is where the term *key sound* comes in. The original term *keynote sound*, which was coined by R. Murray Schafer and Barry Truax as part of their 'World Soundscape Project', is adapted here to the context of sound practices. Key sounds play a particular and decisive role in a sound practice.

Key sounds can be: a melodic figure, a sampled sound, a hookline, a rhythmic pattern, an effect or filter, a vocal figure, a vocal performance. From this characterization of key sound, it becomes clear that key sounds are not confined to the physical traits of a sound (its frequency, loudness and duration), nor does it depict the sound of the mix as a whole (as in production technology), nor does it refer to the sonic characteristics of a particular instrument or its interpretation (as musicologists are interested in with regard to 'musical practice'). What a key sound *is* actually differs from one particular sound practice to another and can only be determined concerning a specific sound practice, a concrete sonic relation within the track in which a key sound generates a shift in the aesthetics or narrative of a musical track.

A key sound does not represent a musical style, or an 'ethnic' sound. For instance, if a Bollywood sound is identified in the analysis as key sound, this means that it has a specific function in a specific sound practice, that is, specific sonic constellation. To continue with the Bollywood example: if a sample of a Bollywood tune is manipulated with filters and looped to accompany a syncopated drum'n'bass beat pattern in the context of a new musical track, the Bollywood sample becomes a key sound in being transformed into a hookline in a drum'n'bass track. The Bollywood sample becomes 'key' in a new sonic constellation, and thus in creating a new sonic aesthetic or narrative. In this way, the Bollywood sample is not regarded in a simple manner as representing an exoticized notion of Indianness. Its function as a key sound in a drum'n'bass track also challenges and transforms the 'ethnic' connotation that Bollywood tunes might conventionally evoke. Therefore, a key sound indicates a shift of sonic qualities, intensities or meanings and in this way becomes a key structuring element in the track. Key sounds have the capacity to intervene into and complicate musical signification in which sounds simply stand for, or represent 'cultures'. Key sounds indicate shifts between ethnic connotations such as 'Indian' or 'British'; they blur and complicate essentialist cause-and effect-relationships between music and culture or cultural identity. Using key sounds as an analytical tool is doing that extra work – where the sonic begins to properly signify the broader contexts of transnational music culture.

Part Two

Listening to British Asian Dance Music

3

Re-Fusing and Reclaiming UK Bhangra: Apache Indian, *No Reservations* (1992)

How can artists and thinkers work around the limiting and prescribed notions of contrasting concepts such as traditional and modern, East and West, technology and authenticity, urban and tribal? This chapter will focus on these questions through an analysis of the sound practices of Birmingham-based, British Asian reggae musician Steven Kapur, more popularly known by his artist name Apache Indian, who mixes dancehall reggae with bhangra beats and Punjabi lyrics. As I will argue, while Apache Indian's sound practices challenge simple binarisms such as those mentioned above in his innovative style of mixing bhangra and dancehall musical traditions, there are also a number of instances in which his use of Indian female vocals and his lyrics also build on and reinforce ethnicized and gendered stereotypes. This becomes very poignant in the particularities of his lyrical performance, and the analysis will thus also have a special focus on how the performativity of the utterance of Apache Indian's lyrics in combination with the beats and melodies of the music becomes constitutive for meaning production that enhances the meaning of the lyrical content alone.

To contextualize his music, in the early 1990s, Apache Indian was celebrated by the British music press as the inventor of an altogether new musical substyle named 'bhangramuffin', combining the terms 'bhangra' and 'raggamuffin'. Dancehall reggae is sometimes referred to as ragga, short for raggamuffin, highlighting its rough and edgy sound, while being based on the characteristic *off-beat* reggae rhythm. The particular musical mix that is referred to in bhangramuffin is significant in the context of Apache Indian's upbringing. Kapur was born in Jalandhar which is located in the northwest of Punjab's capital Chandigarh and migrated to Handsworth, a suburb of Birmingham. Here he grew up in a mostly South Asian and Caribbean neighbourhood, which significantly affected his musical socialization. In *Sounds English*, Nabeel Zuberi quotes from an interview with Apache Indian for *i-D* magazine:

It's a very multicultural, very close community, strongly Asian and black. Very strong reggae vibes seem [to] come from Handsworth. I went to the same school as Steel Pulse and a lot of bands and sound systems come from there [...] I had black friends, white friends, Asian friends, and got to appreciate and understand other people [...] When I had dreadlocks, everyone assumed that I was black, not Asian. (Zuberi 2001: 201)[1]

Apache Indian's affinity with Afro-Caribbean reggae culture is also reflected in his artist name, which can be read as a sign of respect to the Jamaican reggae artist Supercat who was dubbed 'Wild Apache' due to his Afro-Caribbean heritage (Zuberi 2001: 201). Moreover, while a number of tracks on the album feature bhangra rhythms and include Punjabi lyrics, the intersections with dancehall reggae already become obvious when looking at the guest artists featured on the album, namely Maxi Priest and Frankie Paul, two highly acclaimed dancehall vocalists from Jamaica. This affinity with reggae culture is fervently expressed in his lyrics and sound practices, as will be discussed in detail in this chapter.

Although 'bhangramuffin' is a catchy term, it should be regarded as an artificial category which describes what is actually a very diverse net of different transnational musical trajectories. Reggae is in itself a multilayered musical style with many sub-genres that have developed across histories and geographies, from Jamaica to the United States and the United Kingdom and back, from ska and calypso to reggae, dancehall and various forms of Caribbean and European club cultures, from roots and conscious reggae[2] to dancehall in its many variations.

Similarly, bhangra can hardly be confined to one particular style or genre, but has been, since its emergence in the UK, characterized by diverse musical influences and practices. As has already been elaborated in more detail in Chapter 1, UK bhangra was a unique musical style which developed in the late 1970s, mixing elements from the Punjabi folk musical–style bhangra with Western instrumentation such as the electric guitar, bass, synthesizers and drum machines. The rhythmic, melodic and percussive elements of Punjabi folk music have continuously been combined with various musical styles such as reggae, dancehall, hip-hop and electronic music. These varieties have often been termed post-bhangra. Therefore, regarding the bhangra elements of bhangramuffin as the 'traditional' Indian part becomes clearly limiting when looking at the various syncretized versions of bhangra in the UK.[3] Furthermore, combining bhangra beats with synthesizers and other electronic instrumentation resembles 'similar syncretisms in other non-Western pop musics', as Peter Manuel emphasizes regarding the multiple musical intersections found in bhangra and bhangramuffin along local as well as global trajectories:

> The coexistence of Punjabis alongside West Indians (of both African and Indian descent) in places like Birmingham and Bradford has led to more eclectic sorts of musical cross-fertilisation. The 1980s and 1990s have witnessed the emergence of 'bhangramuffin' substyles, synthesizing Punjabi texts and folk rhythms with Jamaican reggae/dance-hall/raggamuffin declamation style, and also incorporating elements from rap and Hindi film music, and other ingredients randomly cannibalised from the global style pool. (Manuel 1995: 235–236)

It is important to note that UK bhangra and related music styles such as bhangramuffin are depicted as being specifically local, i.e. connected to particular places such as Birmingham and Bradford, where the music is mostly produced. Simultaneously however, they are portrayed as being part of a transnational and globalized music culture. This underlines the fact that South Asian and other diasporic musics cannot be compartmentalized as belonging to either the East or the West, or as being either traditional or modern. In the case of Apache Indian, this music's 'Asianness' is constantly negotiated on the level of the music itself, but also on the level of how this music relates to the here and now of urban Britain – and not as an Indianness of some distant past. In his conclusion of this analysis of Apache Indian's music, Manuel argues that Apache Indian's cut'n'mix aesthetic is characterized by a 'postmodern flavour' that 'foreground[s] a syncretic, depthless Indianness in a neutral media space' (Manuel 1995: 236). In Manuel's argumentation, 'Indianness', as an expression of the inherited culture, is dissolved and thus becomes a fragmented and rootless mass-mediated commodity (Manuel 1995: 234–235). This tendency might also too easily oppose technology, and especially digital technology, with postmodern mash-up culture, with pre-digital forms of music making as carrying a more solid authenticity. Although I am critical of Manuel's tendency to depict the global as a commodified and mediatized space in contrast to the local as an authentic and pre-mediated space, the idea that Apache Indian's use of Indian samples and beats result in a somewhat 'depthless' note is interesting and will be examined more closely in the following analysis. Rather than regarding this as a problem of global versus local, I claim that Apache Indian's affinity with sound system culture, his use of digital sampling as well as his vocal technique of toasting[4] are actually localized, through technological means of sampling and electronic music production, and firmly situated in the clubs and recording studios in which he works, while at the same time being part of a globalized and digitalized music culture.

Apache Indian has both attained the status of a musical innovator and has became the first British Asian artist to reach the top ten of the British pop and reggae charts. In 1993, he was signed to the major label *Island Records*, and his song 'Boom-Shak-a-lak' reached an unprecedented number 5 in the British singles charts (Hirani 2003). In the same year, his album *No Reservations* (1992) was released. My analysis will focus in particular on this album.

Apache Indian's music was also highly recognized in Jamaica and across India. As George Lipsitz highlighted in *Dangerous Crossroads*, Apache Indian's music and that for which it stands were perceived differently in different locations of the South Asian diaspora:

> Apache Indian's recordings enjoyed phenomenal sales among the diasporic Indian community in Toronto, largely because young Indian Canadians saw his use of bhangra as a sign of respect for Indian traditions. But when Kapur toured India he found that he had an image as a rebel because of songs like 'Arranged Marriage' that criticised the caste system, because he lived with but did not marry his Sikh girlfriend, and because his music adhered to Western rather than to traditional Indian standards of excellence. In England, Apache Indian's music became an important icon of unity between Afro-Caribbeans and Afro-Asians who had long been divided despite their common identification as 'Black' Britons. Reggae musicians in Jamaica welcomed Apache Indian as an artist worthy of respect and as an ally in their cultural and political projects. The Jamaican singer Maxi Priest contributed to Apache Indian's recording session at Tuff Gong Studios in Kingston by singing in Punjabi. (Lipsitz 1994: 15)

Taking into account the various transnational trajectories of Apache Indian's musical production and its perception, simple binaries 'traditional' versus 'postmodern' is not able to account for is work. Rather, it should be emphasized that Apache Indian 'took his art from the cultural crossroads he negotiated every day' in record stores, studios and the various places in which he performs his music (Lipsitz 1994: 130). As will be shown in the analysis of his sound practices, Apache Indian's transcultural sound practices are the result of transnational linkages of music culture, where he shares more with his fellow reggae musicians in the UK and Jamaica than with Indian heritage music, while simultaneously being influenced by the Indian music he was exposed to through his parents and the Indian community of Birmingham. In his music, Apache Indian negotiates the deterritorialized and discontinuous relationship between music and culture, and the imaginary dimensions of India and Britain.

The track 'Movie over India' from his album *No Reservations* (1992) 'paid tribute to the India that he had only visited once but knew well from the Indian films that his parents watched' as Manuel notes (1995: 130). On the one hand he translates fundamental linguistic idioms ('Say ick, thor, thin that a 1, 2, 3'), and on the other he acts as a cultural translator of Indian culture customs and habits – and this he does in the form of his Ragga chant, which runs over off-beats, and this tonal-linguistic level also becomes a dimension of this multilayered translation process. As will be shown in more detail with regard to his track 'Arranged Marriage' from the same album, Apache Indian's use of Punjabi lyrics are always contextualized in a way that the lyrical message is also conveyed to listeners who do not speak the language which seems to imply that his music is not primarily directed to a South Asian audience.

The track 'Calling Out to Jah' draws explicitly on notions of Rastafarianism and engages with his strong affiliations with Jamaican culture that is re-imagined in the context of Birmingham dancehall reggae. The track was co-produced with Jamaican conscious reggae artist and poet Jepther McClymont aka Luciano, and the lyrics deal with Rasta culture's potential to unite people across racial and ethnic boundaries. The two artists sing their stanza's alternately and repeat the chorus unisono: 'Calling Calling out to Jah – Calling out to the highest father/ Calling out to Jah – To mek every man come live together/I know a place where we can go – and I know a place to be free/And I know a place where we can go – let's unite and live in love and unity.' In his part of the lyrics, Apache Indian expresses the central idea of rastafariansim concretely in respect to his Indian background: 'Say whether African – or whether Indian/Remember Rastafari say the whole of we are one/Say whether you be black or white or whether you be brown/Say I and I come me come here so fe mek you settle down.'

Analysis of 'Arranged Marriage'

The following section concentrates on a more detailed analysis of Apache Indian's sound practices in the track 'Arranged Marriage'. The track came out as a single prior to its release on the full album *No Reservations* and reached 'the British music charts, Reggae Dance charts and the South Asian music charts simultaneously' in the year of its release (Dudrah 2007: 43).

The track opens with a dhol drum whirl (0'00–0'05). The dhol, a double-barrelled drum, with each drum skin pitched differently, is characteristic of bhangra music. The drum whirl is followed by a bhangra beat featuring dhol and tablas, accompanied by a melodic hook line featured by a flute sound (0'05). Dhol, tablas and the flute function as distinct bhangra key sounds. However, it is not a full bhangra tune which is unfolding here – instead, a bhangra tune's instrumental sequence was sampled and is played back four times in a loop (0'05–0'25). On top of this loop, Apache Indian utters his narrative vocals in street-style patois: 'Well the time has come fe the original Indian to get married ...' telling the audience that marriage for Indians is 'a pure, traditional business' which he is going to educate the listener about (Apache Indian 'Arranged Marriage', booklet).

The vocals function as a contrasting key sound to the bhangra sample, because they bear no similarity to the melodic lines characteristic of bhangra singing, which are usually sung in Punjabi, but are delivered in the fast ragga toasting style. Apache Indian's vocal style and the rhythmic structure of this section indicate that his narration forms a so-called introduction, an introductory note that is directed at the audience, which is typical for dancehall. Compare this, for instance, with dancehall tracks such as Dr Alimantado's 'Poison Flour' (1978) or Yellowman's 'Zungu Zungu Zungu Zeng' (1982) which have a similar song structure featuring a drum whirl, followed by a four-bar loop with a narrative vocal introduction, before the first stanza starts with a steady off-beat rhythm.[5] In Apache Indian's version, the dancehall reggae key sounds are further underscored by a reverb that was added to the mix. At the end of the intro section, an echo is added to the last couple of syllables of Apache Indian's vocals. Although the rhythm drops, the vocal echo stands alone – an effect which works as another dancehall key sound in the track (0'24). The echo also marks the transition to the first stanza which features an off-beat rhythm, accompanied by Apache Indian's lyrical vocals.

Regarding the specific recontextualization of bhangra and dancehall reggae in the opening part of 'Arranged Marriage', it is significant that the way in which the different key sounds interact marks a shift in the way they produce meaning. When Apache Indian's introductory ragga vocals come in, they are perceived against the background of the rhythmic and melodic bhangra patterns which were established at the beginning of the track. Although the bhangra sounds function as the dominant key sounds, this changes as the track proceeds, and the whole rhythmic structure of the opening sequence unfolds. Gradually, the dancehall sounds move to the foreground and create the fundamental rhythmic and vocal feel of a dancehall reggae track. This instance of shifting sounds creates a meaningful dissonance that adds a unique layer to the track. In the context of this analysis, dissonance is used not in the sense of disharmonic, which often has a negative connotation of inaccuracy, but in terms of a transitional sound practice, where differing sounds are dynamically intertwined and take on something new while remaining distinctive. In this instance, the specific juxtaposition of the sounds becomes key to generating difference, a difference which becomes audible when one sound is perceived in contrast to another one. Thus, at the moment the vocals come in, the bhangra sounds that were in the foreground, now shift to the background and become the base upon which the figure of the ragga vocals is perceived. This highlights the conjunctural relationship between bhangra and dancehall reggae sounds which 'ethnic' connotations engage in a transformative relationship rather than falling into binary frameworks.

Coming back to Apache Indian's intro lyrics, a question which should be posed here is: what is the role of the lyrics concerning the musical and cultural negotiations that are undertaken in this track? The ragga-inflected narrative seems to draw from sound system culture with regard to its entertaining mode combined with an educational goal. In his book *Sonic Bodies*, Julian Henriques refers to *There Ain't No Black in the Union Jack* (Gilroy 1991), in which Gilroy 'notes how the DJ aesthetic was "built around the pleasures of using exclusive or specialised language in cryptic coded ways which amused and entertained as well as informed the dancing audience"' (Gilroy 1991, cit. in Henriques 2011: 32). In 'Arranged Marriage', Apache Indian takes on the role of the DJ (i.e. the dancehall reggae singer, not to be confused with the disc jockey) to introduce himself and lay out what the track is about, while the cryptic nature of the track is derived from the staccato syllables and twisted syntax which brings language play to the foreground instead of textual clarity. The educational aspect is entailed in the message Apache Indian delivers in his introduction. It is directed at those who are not acquainted with the social practice of arranged marriages, and therefore not at an explicitly South Asian audience, but rather at a mixed dancehall audience. Apache Indian introduces himself as an 'original Indian', explaining to his audience 'the arrange marriage thing'. Taking into consideration the lyrical performance, however, he plays with the role of being an 'original Indian', while in fact deconstructing the notion of a 'pure' and 'authentic' Indianness in the context of a dancehall aesthetic. Moreover, the ragga style and patois-inflected lyrics works as a sound practice which creates a casualness with regard to the topic of arranged marriage, which is interesting also against the backdrop of the seriousness in which the topic is mostly dealt with by the British media at the time. Therefore, focusing on Apache Indian's lyrics in isolation would remove them from the performative context in which they take on significant layers of meaning that are not evident from the lyrical content alone. The interaction between the lyrics and their performance broadens the way in which they can be read. This is an aspect that is too often ignored in musical analysis, as Brackett highlights in his *Interpreting Popular Music*:

> Lyric analysis has often formed the starting-point for the analysis of popular songs. [...] However, [...] to analyse lyrics means not to abstract them from their context in a recorded performance; rather, it means to try to understand how lyrics and performances work to create a sense of a particular genre, a particular audience, and a particular relationship between performer and audience. (Brackett 1995: 77–78)

Although Brackett is mostly concerned with country music, his analytical approach is relevant with regard to other popular music genres as well. Moreover, his notion of 'recorded performance' is relevant here because recorded music is the focus of my study. It is precisely the performative dimension (in live performances as well as recorded performances) that is relevant when thinking about sound practices in general, or sampling practices or lyrical performance in particular, because it highlights the fluid nature of the interaction between the different elements in a track, rather than seeing them as part of a static structure.

Proceeding with the analysis of the track, the first, fifth and sixth stanzas are particularly interesting with regard to Apache Indian's lyrical performance. The lyrical performance complicates and challenges constructions of Indianness and Britishness through the transformative potential of the interacting key sounds that figure in the track. In the three exemplifying stanzas (0'25, 1'15, 1'25), the beat patterns are organized around straightforward reggae sounds, signalled by an off-beat played with a synthesizer, while the tabla pattern, which already accompanied the intro section, continues. Apache Indian performs the lyrics in an agitated ragga style featuring street-style patois interwoven with Punjabi words. In the first stanza, he explains that it is time 'Fe find one gal and to get marry', and seems to be the most natural thing to him that it will be a girl from India, as he expresses in the chorus: 'Me wan gal from Jullunder City/Me wan gal say a soorni curi [beautiful girl].' And the subsequent stanzas clearly indicate that it is a 'puthlee [skinny]' girl the song's protagonist (whom I do not wish to equate with the artist Apache Indian) is dreaming of, a girl who has 'the right figure' and 'in she eyes have the surma [kajal]' while 'talk the Indian with the patwa', evoking highly stereotyped image of male desire (for the lyrics and translations see Taylor 1997: 160–162).

Listening into the rhythmic inflections of Apache Indian's vocals as uttered in the stanzas cited above, their accentuation clearly follows the dancehall rhythm of the track. His pronunciation of the lyrics emphasizes the characteristic slang and patois sounds, something which is already notable based on the above transcription, namely in the written form of words such as 'gal', 'nuff' or 'patwa'. It is also significant that a syllable/a/is added to each line in the sixth stanza. Although this is not part of the actual lyrics, it functions as a phonological addition in order to yield the desired patois style and the rhythmic 'flow' of toasting.[6] In this way, the Punjabi words are organically interwoven with the dancehall beat and become Patois-inflected ragga sounds. It is at this point that the discussion above regarding the transformative potential of key sounds becomes clear: in addition to their meaning as Punjabi words, they also take on meaning *as sound*, and, more precisely, as a new sonic texture in the rhythmic flow of ragga toasting. However, although the Punjabi words are altered to fit the dancehall rhythm, their specific phonetic features add another signifying layer that does not fuse completely with the overall sonic texture of the track. In some instances, the Punjabi words are uttered not so as to engage in a smooth relationship with the patois-saturated lyrical performance, but in order to create contrasting key sounds. Here, Apache Indian exaggerates the distinctiveness of the Punjabi phonemes, thereby putting those individual syllables into the acoustic foreground. Two such instances are 'soorni curi' in the chorus and 'mortee curi' in the fifth stanza. These words are pronounced in a way that emphasizes the vowel sounds/ou/and/e/, creating a high-pitched voice that is rather atypical for Jamaican Patois and ragga singing style, and thus generating a mocking effect in the context of the track. This effect is even enhanced when Apache Indian transfers this practice to English words such as 'ugly' in the fifth stanza, placing exaggerated emphasis on the word final/i/of the Standard English word ugly. This in turn 'Punjabifies' the word, in order to match the pronunciation of the Punjabi words that end in/i/in the subsequent lines, i.e. 'puthlee', 'curi' and 'Punjabi'. Moreover, the vowel length is also extended, intensifying this exaggerating effect. In this way, the words take on an ironic connotation.

While the stanzas consist of a basic ragga off-beat, underscored with a tabla pattern, the chorus has a much thicker texture, featuring a thumping dub bass line (played with an electronic bass guitar), a full drum set playing a steady beat, and a tumbi, a high-pitched, single-string plucking instrument associated with bhangra. The tumbi is featured as another bhangra sound which functions as the dominant hookline of the chorus. The lyrics are uttered in the same ragga style as in the stanzas, only that the phrase 'me wan gal' is accompanied by a small group of males who sing along. The lyrical performance in the chorus effectively contrasts the lyrical content, in which Apache Indian (as the impersonated protagonist) articulates his search for a wife from Jalandhar (Jullundur refers to the name of the city during British colonial rule). While Apache Indian creates a romantic image of his potential future wife as beautiful, caring and lovable, the guttural exclamation of 'Me wan gal' creates a bold and ironic tinge to the image of the guy waiting to be married to a girl from India. Thus, the effect of Apache Indian's exaggerated lyrical performance creates a caricature-like, hyper-masculine counterpart which seems to reflect the protagonist's ambivalent relationship to the 'arrange marriage thing'.

This ambivalent relationship is not resolved in the track, as the last stanza makes it clear that the protagonist has a girlfriend whom he has to tell that he is going to get married (to an Indian woman, presumably). Although Apache Indian's thematization of the difficult and ambivalent circumstances of some young British Asians having to deal with expectations towards an arranged marriage, the track's lyrics are pretty much stuck in gender and ethnic stereotypes.

Notwithstanding that the whole textual narrative is constructed around stereotyped notions of gender relations, Manuel's reading of the chorus adds another, highly problematic shade of meaning when he describes the phrase 'Me wan gal' as 'an Afro-Caribbean grunting'; something that he understands as being used to caricature the Indian tradition of arranged marriage (Manuel 1995: 236). With regard to the sonic narrative of the chorus, I argue that the repetitive mode of 'me wan gal' and the patois-inflections firmly situates the track in the ragga/dancehall production culture. However, by identifying the phrase 'Me wan gal' as an Afro-Caribbean expression, Manuel falsely draws a direct connection from music to cultural essentialism. He actually constructs a notion of Afro-Caribbean masculinity as both aggressive and sexual. This is a stereotyped and reductive representation with which black people are often confronted in all sorts of popular discourses, music included.[7] It can be assumed that this interpretation has to do with the gender implications that are especially connected to reggae music and sound system culture, and the (pre) dominance of male producers. An additional case in point, which encourages readings such as Manuel's, is that there are in fact a number of dancehall artists who write misogynous and sexist lyrics and embody stereotypically masculine attitudes, an issue that has been debated by Manuel (cf. Manuel 1995) and others (Cooper 1995, 2004, Hope 2004). However, Manuel's reading is limited to constructing an opposition between assumed black sexual potency and the Indian tradition of the arranged marriage which, in contrast, is connoted as innocent. Apache Indian is situated in the middle of these two extremes in his indecision between libertarian male desires and the wish to adhere to an arranged marriage.

The problematic genderings in the track's lyrics are also underpinned in the ways in which female vocals are used in the track which features two distinct vocal parts by female singers, which evoke a further complication of the construction of gender and ethnicity in 'Arranged Marriage'. One of these vocal parts appears throughout the track (0'54, 1'42, 2'05, 2'44, 3'45) featuring female vocals singing a high-pitched melodic tune in a Hindi film music style with long sustained notes. Perceived against the dominant vocals of Apache Indian's ragga vocals, the female vocals seem to function primarily as another Indian-inflected instrumental sound which floats in and out of the track not interacting with the dancehall rhythm in any notable way. There is a way in which the two vocal sounds interact, however, and that is with regard to the gendered dimension of the male and the female voices. This also alludes to the performative and relational quality of key sounds as an analytical tool. While Apache Indian's vocals function as ragga keysounds when interacting with other ragga or bhangra keysounds, when the female vocals come in, the focus is shifted and a new engagement is generated between Apache Indian's male vocals which are perceived against the female key sound of the Hindi film music singer. Significantly, the female vocals do not correspond directly with Apache Indian's vocals and thus function as its evanescent, almost subliminal, 'other'.

The other vocal part that appears in the track further complicates the interaction of contrasting and conflicting voices in the track's sonic narrative. This vocal part comes in subsequently to the third chorus (1'45–1'54) in an instrumental part which differs considerably from the rest of the track (1'54–2'14). The tumbi, tablas and dhol are dropped, while the straight Western drum pattern and dub bass line continue as the basic rhythm. On top of this rhythmic ground, altogether new sounds come in: bits of male vocals are sampled and played back in a syncopated rhythm which evokes an aesthetic of 'scratching', which is related to hip-hop DJing and turntablism, creating a noise that is associated with hip-hop culture and turntablism.[8] Simultaneously, a female voice comes in singing a two-line lyric in a groovy fashion: 'Are you lookin' for love, or just a lover/'cause I can be one or another' (Apache Indian 'Arranged Marriage,' my own transcription).

Heard together with the basic drum beat and the scratching noises and sampled voice fragments, the female vocals which are sung in a way that sounds like American English, can be associated with the melodic style in hip-hop or modern r'n'b. The female Hindi film music vocal and the female r'n'b vocal feature in the same part of the track, creating a dissonant interplay of sonic signification which remains opaque.

I draw on Timothy D. Taylor's interpretation here in order to demonstrate how easy an analysis can be carried away by simple binaries such as male and female, if the listener takes these binaries as a given. In Taylor's reading of the same track, the Hindi film music vocal does respond, as from a distance, to Apache Indian's lyrical evocations. Taylor states that '[s]he shows up in the narrative but does not speak. She does, however, speak in the song itself' (Taylor 1997: 159). Taylor conceives of the female voice as the subject of desire Apache Indian sings about, when he utters the wish to marry a girl from 'Jullunder city' and suggests that the female vocal stands for 'the woman back in India who is waiting for Apache to come home' (Taylor 1997: 159). This interpretation is problematic for at least two reasons. Firstly, the Hindi film vocals are conceived as an expression of a particular kind of Indianness, as a romanticized and feminized image in which India is conceptualized as a distant and at the same time domesticated space. Secondly, Apache Indian is depicted as someone who is away from his 'home' in the Punjab, and who is caught in an in-between state, belonging neither here nor there. Concerning the relationship between the two female vocals, I do not concur with Taylor who conceives of the r'n'b vocals as a symbol of 'the European/American ideology of the love marriage' (Taylor 1997: 159) which is contrasted with the ideology of the arranged marriage symbolized by the Hindi film music vocal.

Again, a dichotomy of traditional India and modern UK is imposed onto the narrative of the track, not leaving much space for more subtle negotiations. I argue, instead, that the irony and ambivalence that is created through the sonic narrative of the track cannot simply be transposed on frameworks of 'in-between-cultures' or gender binaries.

However, although my analysis of Apache Indian's sound practices demonstrates a complex relationship of different sonic and cultural elements, in the case of 'Arranged Marriage', I argue that these sound practices actually fail to work around the limiting and prescribed notions of contrasting concepts that were noted above. Although it became clear that the different key sounds do not simply reflect prescribed cultural identities, there are a few instances in Apache Indian's sound practices which work with contrasts, especially with regard to the male/female connotations, which encouraged readings such as those by Manuel and Taylor.

What the analysis of 'Arranged Marriage' was able to do is to demonstrate that Apache Indian's affiliation to reggae music needs to be regarded not only as a musical preference or some kind of subcultural attire, but as a significant layer of his transcultural sound practices. Ultimately, his productions are clearly reggae productions more than anything else. Another aspect which highlights this fact are the remix versions of the track which feature as additional tracks on the CD single and are called 'Arranged Marriage (Indian Wedding Anthem Mix)' and 'Arranged Marriage (Ragga Mix)'. What makes a comparison of these two remix versions particularly interesting in the context of my analysis is to listen to how a special emphasis on, or an omission of, certain sounds alters the overall sonic narrative of the 'original' track. In the 'Wedding Anthem mix', the sounds which are associated with Indian music dominate: a full bhangra rhythm, tablas, tumbi and Hindi film music vocals. Solely Apache Indian's ragga vocals function as a characteristic ragga sound. A key sonic constellation which juxtaposes a bhangra sound and a ragga beat structure is the steady off-beat that accompanies the bhangra rhythm and features a tumbi sound (instead of a guitar or keyboard sound that would usually be used in a reggae track). Lacking the bass-saturated sounds that create the thick texture of the rhythmic ground of the album version,[9] the 'Wedding Anthem mix' comes across as awkwardly thinned out. The heavy ragga vocals are placed in contrast to the mid-frequency beat that sets the two levels – the vocal figure and the rhythmic ground – apart. The 'Ragga mix' 'works' better in this respect. In this version, all bhangra and film music sounds are omitted. The full ragga beat creates a minimalistic but bass-intense foundation with which the ragga vocals interact in a dynamic way. The comparison of the two versions illustrates that the fundamental spine of the track is based on rhythmic and sonic traits of a raggae dancehall production. The bhangra and Hindi film music elements are additives to a basic ragga dancehall track.

In this specific sound practice, the bhangra and Hindi film music sounds have primarily an *ornamental* function. In other words, rather than functioning as a *transformative* agent in the overall sonic narrative of the tracks, they remain static in a way, because they could easily be exchanged with other sounds, while the basic ragga dancehall structure would remain relatively unimpaired. And this is where Peter Manuel's notion of a 'depthless Indianness' that was discussed earlier in this chapter, actually has its point: Apache Indian's sound practices of cut'n'paste do not demonstrate a particularly 'deep' musical engagement with the possibilities of juxtaposing different reggae- and bhangra-related musical styles. Although Apache Indian's music is innovative because it has made some unprecedented musical connections, it is possible that the potential to develop these musical ideas further is lacking. Apache Indian's rootedness in reggae music is further emphasized when considering that 'Arranged Marriage' is actually quite an exceptional track in Apache Indian's musical repertoire. Although bhangra patterns are a key feature in some of his other tracks, most of his music is straightforward reggae dancehall, and the lyrics engage with ideas of Rastafarianism rather than with the situation of second-generation Indians in Britain. Moreover, a question that is relevant here is how Apache Indian's creation of bhangra-influenced reggae resonates with the recognition of the two musical styles in the contemporary (1990s) music press. Reggae was much more established as part of the mainstream pop culture in the UK in the early 1990s, and bhangra just became more visibly recognized in pop-musical contexts beyond South Asian communities. Being more firmly rooted in the reggae music scene, therefore, meant a lot more potential for success, and wider recognition across musical and cultural divides.

However, this conclusion concerning his sound practices should not be simply tied in with the Manuel's argumentation, who conceives of Apache Indian's music as representative of a 'depthless Indianness', as quoted earlier in this chapter.

Looking more closely at the musical influences of the album *No Reservations* as a whole, Apache Indian's music is a rich and multilayered mix of different sonic and verbal styles. He mixes reggae and dancehall beats and bass lines with samples from bhangra tunes, Indian classical music and Hindi film music and sings his lyrics in a ragga style (a fast version of reggae singing that is closer to rap). He uses Punjabi words which seep into his lyrics, which are a mixture of English and some lexicon from Jamaican patois that will subsequently be referred to as street-style patois in reference to the fact that aspects of patois are used in UK street slang.[10] The cover artwork of *No Reservations* reflects this mix of sonic styles on a visual level: it shows an image of Apache Indian wearing a style combining elements from US hip-hop, Rastafarian culture and British Asian street style – the latter not being a homogeneous style, of course, but his haircut represents a trend in the early 1990s among young South Asians to wear artfully shaved hairstyles. In the background is a paper-cut version of the Indian and Rastafarian flags.

Apache Indian's sound practices, the way he uses sonic and visual elements from different musical styles and interspersed with various (music-)cultural identifications (not identities) can more thoroughly defied as a practice of remediation. Following Jay David Bolter and Richard Grusin's definition, remediation refers to the logic of Derrida's (1981) account of mimesis, 'where mimesis is defined not ontologically or objectively in terms of the resemblance of a representation of its object but rather intersubjectively in terms of the reproduction of the feeling of imitation or resemblance in the perceiving subject' (Bolter and Grusin 1999: 53). Derrida's notion of mimesis is best transferable to the practice of sampling when he writes: '"True" *mimesis* is between two producing subjects and not between two produced things' (Derrida 1981: 9, quoted in Bolter and Grusin 1999: 53, original emphasis). Remediations refer here also to the potential meanings of sounds as they are further transformed in the context of the new musical track.

To emphasize the transcultural dimension of Apache Indian's sound practices, the Hindi film music that features in his tracks is a highly commodified popular music style and part of a transnationally operating music industry. Thus, the Hindi film music sounds in 'Arranged Marriage' do not become a postmodern simulacrum at the moment they are sampled and reappropriated to the track, but are rather already part of processes of globalized production and dissemination. The same is true for bhangra music, although in a slightly different way. For centuries, this Punjabi-derived folk music style only heard and produced only by a relatively small number of people in India and Pakistan, and was, even within the region of the Punjab, only one amongst many folk musical styles. Bhangra actually became popularized outside of the region of Punjab as the South Asian diaspora spread across various locations, including the UK, especially during the decolonization process. The distinct UK bhangra sound which emerged from the urban centres of the UK since the late 1970s was then transported back to India in some of its newly synthesized forms. Thus, it could be argued that the dhol drum which is featured in 'Arranged Marriage' is more characteristic of the

British context than the Indian one, and it would therefore be false to subsume these sounds under the 'other' category, if 'other' denotes a traditional India from the past.

Thus, the reappropriated fragments of bhangra and Bollywood sounds are remediated in the context of 1990s reggae productions which are tightly linked to Afro-Caribbean-derived musical developments, which actually reach back into the 1970s and can thus be regarded as part of a tradition of sample-based music which forms a continuum from reggae to dub and dancehall, to hip-hop, drum'n'bass and later to dubstep.

I argue that listening into Apache Indian's sound practices from a cultural analysis perspective demonstrates that his music should be conceived of as much a part of Afro-Caribbean diasporic music culture as it can be conceived of as part of a South Asian diasporic music culture that is intricately linked to the context of UK club culture. This is exactly how I perceive transculturality: as cultural formations in process, as part of 'entangled histories' (Chakrabarty 2000) which are generated across geographical confines as well as musical categorizations and cultural 'containers' (Hannerz 1996).

Drawing attention to the title of this chapter, re-fusing bhangra refers to the specific sound practices of sampling and lyrical performance which fuses sounds in a new way and thus transforms and recontextualizes their potential meanings, refusing to integrate into bhangra as a coherent genre. Re-claiming bhangra refers to the reappropriation of bhangra under the new premises of cut'n'mix as part of the creative texture of transcultural sound practices. Although Apache Indian's sound practices generate a complicating perspective with regard to conceptions of British Asian Music, and particularly bhangra, which restrict this music to an ethnic community, or to an ethnic culture, one could still claim that the subversiveness of his musical articulations is questionable, as a tendency was detected in Apache Indian's sound practices to reinforce cultural stereotypes particularly on the level of gender and ethnicity.

4

Demystifying Asianness: Asian Dub Foundation, *Community Music* (2000)

Not only has Asian Dub Foundation (ADF) enriched the British musical landscape through their distinct sound practice, characterized by a combination of diverse musical styles, they have also profoundly challenged preoccupations about South Asian music in the UK. From their 1994 debut album *Facts and Fictions* to their latest album *A History of Now*, they have continuously created a very distinct style that is crafted around dancehall rhythms, punk rock guitars, jungle breaks, sampled beats and melodies and dub bass lines, while the vocals are uttered in a mixture of Jamaican-derived ragga and US rap. Referring to a statement by bass player Aniruddha Das, Asian Dub Foundation wanted to 'demystif[y] the role of Asians in making music' (Huq 1996: 68). This chapter investigates how ADF's sound practice interacts with their critical intervention into discourses about South Asian culture and ethnicity, as well as broader issues of racism, social inequality and war.

In order to exemplify their sound practices, I will focus the analysis on Asian Dub Foundation's track 'Collective Mode' from their 2000 album *Community Music*. This example exhibits multilayered textures of aesthetic, cultural and political ideas interacting in a highly complex manner, making it a particularly informative selection for my analysis.

In order to perform an analysis, it is necessary to first contextualize their music. Their musical career started in 1993 and should be considered against the backdrop of the fact that there was a tendency for musicians with a South Asian background to be expected to play 'Asian' music, meaning Indian classical music or traditional bhangra, an assumption which Rupa Huq criticizes in her contribution to *Dis-Orienting Rhythms* (Huq 1996: 68). Huq argues that the wide range of musics that emerged from British Asian musicians from the 1980s onwards clearly refutes such essentialisms, and highlights the creative agency which counteracted this expectation. While British music consumers were often drawn to exoticized images of India, which involved sitars, incense sticks and yogi tea, these were attributes which had little to do with contemporary British Asian culture. Besides ADF, bands such as Hustlers HC, Kaliphz, Fun-da-Mental and Sister India are should be mentioned whose music had 'the potential to disrupt the Asian status quo' (Kalra et al. 1996: 149). Understanding themselves as musicians with a political and activist stance, Asian Dub Foundation have actively shaped new discourses on South Asian music in particular, and diasporic music in general, and expressed a critique of exoticizing images of and racist actions against migrants and post-migrants. Simultaneously, a number of cultural studies scholars who express explicitly leftist ideas started to focus on the music of these bands in order to acknowledge their subversive power and transformative potential.

In the context of this chapter the aim is to show how sound practices such as sampling and lyrical performance are used to create distinct new sounds, how sounds are recontextualized, and how this distinct form of musical appropriation generates new meanings. To exemplify their sound practices, the analytical focus will be on Asian Dub Foundation's track 'Collective Mode' of their 2000 album *Community Music*, in which the multilayered textures of aesthetic, cultural and political ideas interact in a highly complex manner, which makes it particularly productive for my analysis.

The sound practices of sampling, and the dynamic interaction of analogue and digital performance techniques, blur genre as well as ethnicized boundaries.[1] ADF's music is not electronic music in its strictest sense, nor does it fit into typical rock music schemes. Rather, it is electronically produced music and *track* music rather than *song* music. This means that the sonic narrative is created on a time line as well as in a vertical, multilayered space. The repetitive mode of track music allows more attention to go towards the layering and the three-dimensionality of the music.

Two specific sound practices will be analysed in this chapter. One concerns the use of samples and how they sonically recontextualize meaning and challenge binary frameworks of tradition and modernity. The other investigates, besides the lyrical content, the lyrical performance of rapper Deeder Zaman. With regard to these sound practices, a special emphasis will be placed on the interaction of the diverse musical styles which are featured in this track that provide the key sounds for aesthetic decisions, cultural negotiations and political agencies.

Bollywood sample

The sound practice that is analysed in this section concerns a specific sampling practice in Asian Dub Foundation's track 'Collective Mode'. The track begins with the sample of a Hindi film music tune which features a catchy melodic figure (0'03). When listening closely to the first eight bars, in which the Bollywood tune stands alone, other layers of sound can be recognized in the background which are only audible as a rather muffled background rhythm. This implies that the tune was sampled from a vinyl record, in which case the different sonic layers cannot be extracted and replayed separately. Looking at how the frequencies of that part appear in an equalizer it becomes clear how the sample was manipulated after it had been extracted from the vinyl record: the bass of the background rhythm was de-emphasized, while the Bollywood figure, which lies in the higher mid-frequency range, was boosted. Additionally, reverb was added so that the Bollywood figure clearly stands out.

To summarize, a complete section of the original recording was digitalized and transposed into the new musical context, and subsequently that section was manipulated with equalizers and filters to emphasize the melody line. Actually, the sampled sequence is only four bars long and has been looped, and runs through the whole introductory part (0'03–0'37). Therefore, this repetitive sonic figure does not simply quote the original recording, but was appropriated to form part of a new rhythmic pattern. Therefore, the melodic figure has at least two different functions. Firstly, it is a reference to a Bollywood record, and this reference is drawn due to the way in which the record is made audible in the sample. This is an example of 'hypermediacy' that Bolter and Grusin (1999) refer to in their book on remediation. The materiality of the medium is performed and becomes an integral part of the sampling process. Secondly, the repetitive figure created through the sampling and looping of a section of the Bollywood tune does not simply reflect the original recording, but was appropriated to form the fundamental part of an altogether new rhythmic pattern. Therefore, the Bollywood sample does not merely serve as a source for a catchy hook, but also forms the rhythmic base of the new track, to which all the other musical elements are added layer after layer: after the eight bars in which the sample stands alone, a snare ruffle (0'13) introduces a rhythmic section featuring a dub bass line and a hip-hop beat (0'16). Perceived against this new rhythmic ground, the Bollywood figure seems to float above the bass-intense rhythm, and the 'muffled background rhythm' which has been identified above, is completely swallowed up. Thus, the track is now clearly situated as a dancehall track, against which the Bollywood key sound is perceived.

In the following section, which still features the Bollywood figure (0'27), another Indian sound is interwoven into the sonic fabric: a sitar-style sound. The sitar-sound is neither played by a sitar, not is it sampled from a recording of a sitar – but it is actually played on an electric guitar on a single string in a Dorian scale so as to sound like a sitar. Furthermore, a short sampled lyrical fragment featuring the words 'You better get into the collective' provides a first hint as to what form the lyrical narrative will take. The last syllable of the vocal sample is caught in an echo reverb, adding to the track's ragga feel.

The use of reverberation effects adds to the sound's rich dancehall fabric. The tracks are supplemented with punk rock guitar riffs as well as the playing of single notes on the guitar in an amplified sitar-style. Additionally, the track is sped up by fast and syncopated jungle rhythms as well as the incorporation of bhangra and Hindi film music samples and samples from other 'non-musical' sources. It becomes clear that these different key sounds are not simply fused in a random manner, nor do they merge into one clearly definable music style.

Taking into account the sound practice of this opening section, it seems simplistic to think of the Bollywood tune and the sitar sounds as reflections of Asian Dub Foundation's traditional cultural heritage. Significantly, the Bollywood sound does not function here as a catchy ornament to lend the track an oriental twist, but functions as a creative and structuring element in the track's production process. The Bollywood sound does not simply reflect Indian culture, but instead becomes a key sound in a dancehall track by being transformed into a hookline.[2] Similarly, while the sitar sound provides a reference to Indian classical music, in its actualized form in the context of the new track, it becomes a key sound of the uptempo hip-hop beat of ADF's track.

As has been demonstrated, the rhythm pattern is a fusion of different musical influences in itself, as tabla and dhol sounds are woven into the rhythmic texture of the track. This sound practice is described by ADF on their website as follows:

> We would usually start by sampling drum loops but programme our own rhythms on top using individual percussive sounds. Also, we messed with the loops themselves so they weren't just playing their original rhythms and sometimes chopped them into smaller samples [...] Our favourite samples aside from jungle drum breaks were of course Indian percussion loops. (ADF 2008)

As an aside, ADF's bass player Aniruddha Das made a significant statement regarding ADF's sound practice and their self-conception, proclaiming, '[m]y favourite Indian instrument is the bass guitar', quoted in the epigraph of Sanjay Sharma's article on 'Asian Noise' (S. Sharma 1996: 32). This statement emphasizes the music's rootedness in the present, and his reference to the bass guitar, is a way of expressing an affiliation with dub and the Afro-Caribbean music tradition. By specifying 'Indian', the argument is taken one step further. It implies a refusal to accept the limitations set by journalists or scholars or music consumers regarding the definition of 'Indian' and what that includes or excludes. It implies the statement that because I am Indian, every instrument that I play becomes an Indian instrument. This implies a critique that instruments such as the electric bass guitar are defined as Western instruments and as such belong to Western culture, whereas the sitar and the tabla are bound to be Indian instruments and thus belong to a culture *from* India. This exclusionary opposition of Western and Indian culture is disrupted by Das' 'discursive' statement. It is an empowering statement which claims the freedom to re-define and transform culture. Significantly, besides being a critique of received cultural discourses, it is also an actualization of the concrete sound practice as a form of enacted cultural transformation.

Therefore, the meanings of ADF's music do not lie in a distant past. Rather, the multilayered meanings are generated in the here and now of contemporary urban Britain.

Arkanoid sound

Another instance which demonstrates how the use of sampling is used to recontextualize meaning is the very brief introductory section which precedes the track's intro. So let us press rewind and go back to the very beginning of the track which starts with a distorted sound that can be identified as a computer game sound deriving from the computer game called *Arkanoid* (0'00). Arkanoid is a computer game first released in 1986 that was developed for Atari and other home consoles. The game follows a simple scheme in which the player 'takes control of a paddle at the bottom of the screen and must use it to deflect a ball into rows of bricks at the top of the screen, thus destroying them and, eventually, clearing the screen to progress to the next level' (strategywiki.com 2012). If the player fails to destroy the bricks in due course, a distinct noise signals 'game over', followed by a short catchy melody that indicates 'start over again'.

The Arkanoid sounds are eight-bit sounds[3] and thus low-fi sounds which generates a specific 'tone' to it when transferred to ADF's track.[4] Strikingly, not only the Arkanoid sound is re-produced and transferred to ADF's track, but the whole narrative structure – 'game over' sound, pause, melodic figure – is transferred to the track's intro (0'00–0'03). In the context of the new track, the distinct Arkanoid figure is replaced by the Bollywood figure. Therefore, the Arkanoid computer game is used here as a narrative frame for the reconfiguration of the Bollywood tune. This sound practice deconstructs the Bollywood key sound as an 'authentic bit of culture from the past' and creates a form of difference which is situated in the present.

With regard to this example, one can conclude that the boundaries normally drawn between modern sounds and traditional sounds are rendered permeable through sound practices such as those of ADF. These sound practices challenge any claims of originality or authenticity. Instead, the sounds become culturally connoted raw material that is then reappropriated and re-imagined so as to enter into new musical and cultural engagements.

Lyrics

The following section draws attention the lyrics, which form a highly important part in Asian Dub Foundation's sound practice on the level of both content and sonic aesthetics. When the first stanza starts (0'38), the Bollywood hook and the sitar-style guitar are dropped, and the beat pattern is reduced to a minimalist rhythmic pattern, featuring a dub bass line and a drum beat to which reverb was added. The lyrics are uttered in an agitated style. In the vocal parts of the track, the voice of the singer figures as a new key sound in the rich dancehall texture of beats and bass line. It is articulated in a constant flow of street-style patois. Interestingly, although the lyrical message conveyed by the track is highly relevant to ADF's musical expression, it becomes obvious from the way in which the lyrics are performed that equal significance lies in its form of delivery. The way in which the words are uttered is clearly designed to fit the rhythm of the track, emphasizing the off-beat of the ragga beat patterns. This creates an immediacy and urgency to the performance that transgresses the confines of the textual message and calls for affective listening. The words are caught up in a dynamic flow, single syllables are swallowed or create a syncopated pattern, while the beat sets the continuous pace for the lyrical performance. In this way, the lyrics are opened up for further transformation and inspiration: they need not only to be understood, but also to be felt. However, before the lyrical performance is explored in more detail, it would be useful to first consider the lyrical content.

The track 'Collective Mode' is concerned with the situation of second-generation South Asian migrants in the UK, as well as the role music can play in the negotiation of this situation: 'For every opportunity we squeeze de last drop/Seeds sown inna de past and now we're reaping de crop/Yer, spreading de roots an we're no longer under-ground/Those dat turned away are now turning around' (ADF 'Collective Mode', this and all subsequent lyrics are quoted from the CD booklet). In these first lines, a great deal of recognition is awarded the first generation who made immense efforts in establishing themselves in the UK and in preparing the ground in order to provide their children with opportunities in the new homeland. This section also addresses British mainstream society's disregard of South Asian migrants. As people who are part of the upcoming generations, they feel responsible to live up to the opportunities they were given and make the best out of their lives in British society. The lyrics also comment on the fact that their situation has changed, and that they are more recognized than their parent's generation ('we're no longer underground'). The 'we' seems to be directed at the British Asian community. There is some kind of unity expressed here which situates the British Asian community in contrast to British mainstream society. However, this remains undefined.

The first lines of the second stanza deal with the significance of musical expression as a form of social participation and critique. Music becomes a tool to defend themselves against racial discrimination, as the lyrics go on: 'Homebeats and high-hats mightier than de sword' Music functions as a creative tool of cultural identification which reaches beyond ethnic and musical divides: While 'homebeats and high-hats' refer to hip-hop beats, 'version excursions' refer to Jamaican dub and dancehall, and 'breaks from abroad' might equally refer to jungle breakbeats or tabla samples, which are frequently used in ADF's tracks. The music also moves them into the position to re-narrate the untold stories – 'secret histories dat have never been told' – and thus rid British society of their ignorance and misrecognition – 'remove the blindfold'. Therefore, the lyrics can be read as a call for awareness of the history of South Asians in the UK as well as the writing of a new history.

In the third section of the stanza, their critical stance towards British media representation is explicit in their call to 'unscramble freaktalk displayed pon de front page' which refers to the way in which South Asians are represented mostly in terms of immigration issues or identity problems. This should be regarded in the context of the contemporary popular and music press coverage and the growing visibility of British Asian culture in these media. As the authors of *Dis-Orienting Rhythms* (1996) have stated, British Asians are constantly confronted with attributions which reached from those of problematization to celebration and exoticization. In the analysed track, ADF thus declare that these 'stories' have to be critically examined and demonstrate an urge to find their own ways of telling their story. Although British mainstream society is not explicitly addressed, the lyrics provide significant hints to ADF's critical stance towards British society, which seems to be represented by the government and popular/mainstream media. The members of ADF consider it crucial to 'examine de story before you tek de stage' – therefore, the critical negotiation of, and intervention into the politics of media representation seem paramount. In an interview with ADF's guitarist Steve Chandra Savale which I conducted in 2003, he comments on the ways in which the British music press, in particular, has tended to compare them to other bands in order to come up with stable categories. Although the music press was increasingly aware that bands such as Asian Dub Foundation could not be categorized as world music acts, they still seemed to gain some kind of control over the music:

> They want to control, find an angle, and they always need a reference, this is the worst thing, this is what destroyed music. I remember a journalist saying: Oh, I'd never heard music like you've done before, except the one that's like rage against the machine, and so I was into that militant rap thing. But isn't that a really great thing that it was a kind of music that you didn't hear before, because it was new to you. Why did you have to be focusing on the thing that you knew about, you know. I like to see music and hear music that I've never heard before, and be surprised by it, not knowing what it is. That's great! But the music press thinks the opposite. I mean British music press, they go on about Detroit 1975 where everybody wants to sound like the MC 5 and the Stooges and stuff, again, you know, I don't understand that. (Savale 2003, personal interview)[5]

In their development from an underground act to an acclaimed popular band, ADF were continuously confronted with the rigid structures of the music industry. In spite of their critical stance towards the music industry and the popular music press, in particular, they have not strictly denied the opportunities that the growing success of the band offered. However, they have not ceased to use these structures on their own terms, and have created the conditions under which they wanted to act, and were highly reluctant to be categorized. This determination was notably demonstrated by the decision made by John Pandit, ADF's DJ and sound programmer, to turn down the *Member of the British Empire Award* for their social engagement in ADFED. Pandit stated that he 'refused the award because of the "exploitation and colonialism" of the British empire and because "the existing honours system is archaic and shrouded in secrecy" ' (Lester 2003). This rejection was, above all, a symbolic act to demonstrate that they do not consider themselves to be representatives of the British nation. This should not be regarded, of course, as a reluctance to conceive of themselves as an active part of British society; nevertheless, they did not want the British government to be in the position of celebrating ADF as part of *their* efforts towards a multicultural society. This is related to ADF's critical stance towards the discourses of both the popular and music press to stage the band as the uniform voice of the second generation of British Asians. The ways in which their music was celebrated under marketable labels such as New Asian Kool did not resonate very well with the band members. Although this practice of categorizing and compartmentalizing music is by no means only done with regard to diasporic music, Savale's reaction, expressed in the interview quoted above, reveals a frustration which was audible in the music of a number of South Asian bands at that time regarding the constant ascriptions made by the popular and music press. Therefore, the activist stance put forward in their lyrics should be seen in light of their reluctance to fulfil what they are expected to do or to be. However, their lyrics should not be read as a one-dimensional 'struggle of identity' as South Asian migrants in Britain. Rather, they have emphasized their political agency in terms of social inequality and racism in general from the beginning. Their resistance is not restricted to their own local environment, or to a specific ethnic community. Their political engagement reaches well beyond that, as Hutnyk and others have demonstrated in *Dis-Orienting Rhythms* with regard to the participation of Asian Dub Foundation, Fun-da-Mental, or Hustlers HC in anti-racism movements and festivals in Britain, etc. Nevertheless, the agitated 'we' that is expressed does refer very specifically to a South Asian collectivity in some of their tracks, and a Bangladeshi community in particular. This was also an aspect which dominated some of the contemporary criticism of academics, mostly coming from left-wing cultural studies, who were concerned with how 'new ethnicities' were formed with regard to Asianness in the UK context (Hall 1992).

Negotiating ethnic identity

An interesting contribution to this debate dealing with notions of hybrid Bangladeshi identities has come from researcher Anirvan Chatterjee. In his article, Chatterjee comments on the specific renegotiations of Bangladeshi identity in ADF's music. Two former members of the band have a Bengali background, namely rapper Deeder Zaman (who left the band in 2003) and bass player Aniruddha Das aka Dr Das (who left the band in 2005 rejoining in 2013). Chatterjee states that 'While ADF is not a specifically Bengali band, their music draws upon Bengali history and culture, and meaningfully recontextualises it at the edges of diasporic Bengal' (Chatterjee 2000). He refers to ADF's song 'Naxalite' from their 1998 *Naxalite Culture Move* EP, which takes up the topic of the revolutionary uprisings in West Bengal in the 1960s and draws a link to 'modern day Britain, and to the reggae tradition' (Chatterjee 2000). The specific history of the Naxalite struggle is universalized, connected to all global movements for justice; in at least one concert, ADF members have dedicated 'Naxalite' to striking British dockworkers (Chatterjee 2000). It is important to note, however, that ADF hold a somewhat romantic perspective of the Naxalite movement with regards to its severely militant strands.

Another example which is given in this context is the track 'Rebel Warrior' that appeared on their 1995 album *Facts and Fictions*:

> 'Rebel Warrior', written in 1995, before the release of ADF's first album, is an anti-racist anthem directly inspired by the classic Bengali poem 'Bidrohi', by nationalist poet Kazi Nazrul Islam. Nazrul's 1920s poem told of a hero, a rebel warrior, offering up his poetic declaration of independence, an implied call to arms for an oppressed people. Dr. Das' rap/dub translates/transcreates its chorus from the original: 'ami bidrohi/I am the rebel warrior/I have risen alone/ with my head held high/I will only rest when the cries of the oppressed/no longer reach the sky/when the sound of the sword/of the oppressor/no longer rings in battle/hear my war cry'. Over 70 years after 'Bidrohi' was written, ADF's 'Rebel Warrior' neatly inverts Nazrul's equation, transforming a poetic assault on British colonialism in South Asia, to a sonic assault on the new internal colonialism, barriers against South Asians and others within Britain itself. (Chatterjee 2000)

Chatterjee states that with 'Rebel Warrior', ADF again draws inspiration from a text that is part of Bengali cultural history, and then recontextualizes its meaning with regard to contemporary neocolonial tendencies and racism. He emphasizes that the music plays a significant part in conveying these issues to a 'diverse Western audience' (Chatterjee 2000).

In his conclusion, Chatterjee makes a very strong point with regard to notions of specifically diasporic identities:

> The Asian Dub Foundation is clearly not Bengali as traditionally held. Its own composition is only partially of Bengali origin, disconnected from geographic Bengal, further mixed in with members of other desi backgrounds, and performing for an audience largely not South Asian at all. It is perhaps in light of this that it's all the more remarkable that ADF's music does not take Bengali (and more broadly, South Asian) culture for granted, but rather, takes the difficult road of meaningfully recontextualizing history, culture, and progressive values. This work, instead of being hidden within a single community in diaspora, has the capacity to convey unfiltered aspects of Bengali culture to a diverse mass audience. (Chatterjee 2000)

This is a very valuable reading of ADF's music, because it draws on the dislocation and discontinuity of cultural identities. What Chatterjee's analysis stops short of, however, is examining in more detail the significance of the other facets which seem to be equally important references for identification. As has been mentioned with regard to the different musical influences, the rap and dub influences are an integral part of ADF's cultural identification. I would not like to suggest that Bengali is not a highly relevant facet, but in this analysis, there is very clearly only one perspective taken – that of a Bengali identity. In ending with the statement that, 'Asian Dub Foundation offer up [a] compelling model [...] for living meaningfully Bengali lives in a confusing time,' the underlying concept of identity seems to be one of a stable, and unbreakable Bengali identity.

Chatterjee's analysis has further shortcomings, namely that it solely relies on the lyrical content while the music itself is largely dismissed:

> While the use of some South Asian instrumentation and scales is obvious, to the extent that the Asian Dub Foundation's music is Bengali, it is Bengali primarily in meaning, not in sound. (Chatterjee 2000)

I argue that this kind of reading clearly emphasizes the lyrical content as the prime measure for meaning formation. Sound is regarded by Chatterjee as an additional ingredient which is somehow disconnected from profound meaning formation. Moreover, in Chatterjee's conclusion, he somehow disconnects the transcultural potential of musical/lyrical meaning formation from Bengali identity. Bengali identity is represented as the essential inert condition from which the externalized 'confusion' is negotiated.

In this respect, it is paramount not to isolate the study of lyrics from the sound practices within which they are performed. It is important to mention what Lars Eckstein formulated with regard to his study of song lyrics; he asks: 'what happens when song lyrics (re)enter the aesthetics of post-Bhangra jungle and hip hop on the sounds of groups and artists like Asian Dub Foundation, Fun^da^Mental and M.I.A.?' (Eckstein 2010a: 248). Therefore, it is necessary to take the next step and consider not the lyrics only, but the lyrical *performance* as constitutive part of ethnic, national and transnational constructions.

In respect to ADF's sampling practice, it was demonstrated that their music does not simply display some South Asian instrumentation and scales which reflect their unambiguous cultural identity; their lyrical performance reveals, in fact, other significant aspects with regard to their negotiation of aesthetic principles, cultural conceptions and political stances.

Lyrical performance

Another significant aspect of the way in which Asian Dub Foundation challenges notions of homogeneity and renegotiates ethnicity is their lyrical performance, something which is already manifest in their language choice. The significance of language choice has been examined by Harris M. Berger and others in *Global Pop, Local Language*. In his introduction, Berger draws particular attention to the 'Politics and Aesthetics of Language Choice and Dialect in Popular Music', and this angle is indeed pertinent with regard to the lyrical performance of ADF, and the singer Deeder Zaman, in particular. I argue that his unique mix of English, street-style patois, Bangladeshi inflections and US-derived rapping is not a random accumulation of languages, dialects and slang, but should be regarded as constitutive of their multilayered sound practice as well as musical and cultural identifications.[6] Although Zaman uses English throughout, he obviously refrains from pronouncing the lyrics in received pronunciation (RP), but utters them instead in street-style patois, clearly linking the band to the continuum of Afro-Caribbean-derived music culture. Moreover, on his website, Deeder Zaman mentions the American rappers Chuck D and KRS1 as his most important influences for his rapping style. This is also interesting with regard to the specific implementation of US hip-hop in the UK. Here I would like to draw on David Hesmondalgh's study of urban breakbeat culture, in which he argues that the global dissemination of hip-hop culture has not led to a homogenization of hip-hop, but has gone through a process of emancipation in which elements of US hip-hop were reappropriated to local aesthetics, practices and cultural politics (Hesmondalgh 2001). Hesmondalgh states that the impact of US hip-hop in the UK was, with only a few exceptions, not one of imitation. In terms of content as well as accent, 'the drawl of the Brooklyn Badboys' as well as the 'carjacking, bitch-smacking lexicon of U.S. rap' seemed not very suitable for the black British youth who needed to find their own style (Hesmondalgh 2001: 91–92); and this would also be a style which differentiates them from the Afro-Caribbean British music scene. At least it seems significant that Zaman does draw a clear connection to US rap (rather than to ragga, which also definitively influenced his rapping style). In the context of Zaman's rapping style, his engagement with US hip-hop culture has resulted in the creation of a very unique style which integrates different musical influences and transfers them to the local context of contemporary London. At the same time, ADF's music cannot be regarded only in the local context, as it is rather transnational in scope, addressing topics of relevance to a number of places, from various locations in London to Bangladesh, and from Iraq to the United States and back. Moreover, the dissemination of their music has also from an early stage reached beyond the borders of the UK.

Moreover, a very unique layer is added through his Bangladeshi-inflected London accent. Therefore, taking into account the multilayered lyrical performance of Deeder Zaman, I argue that the languages, dialects and slangs that are used cannot be regarded solely from a linguistic point of view. Rather, the use of language has to be seen in relation to the music, and thus as part of ADF's specific sound practice. Thus, language choice and lyrical performance is an aesthetic strategy which reflects on, and is constitutive of, the larger musical and social context.

In this respect, coming back to Deeder Zaman's lyrical sound practice, his affiliation to rap is significant. Although ADF can be conceived of as 'consciousness rappers' in the tradition of bands such as Public Enemy, they reappropriate hip-hop by performing their rap differently through the use of South-Asian, Jamaican and London-specific inflections. In this way, they are 'challenging any claims to the inauthenticity of their involvement in Hip-Hop', which formerly had been connoted mainly as part of black culture, as Sharma aptly notes, adding that 'the syncretic nature of their Asian-inspired dub-Rap music [makes] new kinds of identities [available] that transgress and contest ethno-centric forms of cultural containment' (S. Sharma 1996: 48–50).

In 'Collective Mode', the beats and lyrics of the second part of the first stanza (0'50) are accompanied by a second guitar sound which features off-beat strokes, thus further supporting the dancehall feel of the track. The end of the stanza leads seamlessly into the chorus (1'12), which builds up to a thick sonic texture, supported now by the Bollywood hook which comes in again. The lyrics are sung in a melodic fashion and repetitively celebrate 'get[ting] into the collective mode'. While this stanza-chorus structure is repeated, there is one part which differs from the rest of the track (2'26), which features sustained synthesizer sounds as a bridge and a variation of the vocal melody of the third stanza, and is then followed again by the chorus. In the outro, all sounds get caught up in a centrifugal spin as if they were being played backwards – which refers to a *rewind*, until they finally implode into the Arkanoid-style 'game over' sound. In this way, the Arkanoid sample also has the function of working as a narrative bracket for the track as a whole.

Conclusion

Considering the ramifications for thinking about culture if we listen more closely to the sound practices of music, as far as the analysis of Asian Dub Foundation's 'Collective Mode' is concerned, it can be argued the Bollywood sample and the sitar sound that are used in the track are not simply representations of an 'authentic' Indian culture. Moreover, the Bollywood key sounds and the ragga key sounds have been recontextualized and transformed into an altogether new sonic experience. Katz speaks of sampling as a 'musical quotation' (Katz 2004: 138), but adds that there is a difference between digital sampling and traditional musical quotations in that 'traditional musical quotations typically cite works; samples cite performances' (Katz 2004: 141). In this sense, instead of creating a situation in which music is cited while the 'original' work remains intact, in ADF's 'Collective Mode' the sampled sounds are treated more or less independently from the sources from which they have been taken. They become the raw material for sonic intervention, exploration and restructuring. The various sampled sounds become part of a sound practice that can only be captured *as* performance, as a specific way of temporal recontextualization which cannot be re-inscribed into 'a work': the meaning of the individual samples lies in their performance and can no longer be authenticated in terms of their respective origins. Translated into the context of transcultural musical production and appropriation, and in consideration of my analysis of ADF's music, this resonates with Sanjay Sharma's claim that:

> This music's 'Asianness' is more than what its identitarian ethnic marker allows for; its alterity operates in the realm of untranslatable musical effects that are not reducible to the logic of representation and identity. (Sharma 2004: 415)

Consequently, it can be argued that ADF's sampling practice transgresses the boundaries of 'pure' musical traditions and fixed cultural identities.

As has been shown with regard to the previous case studies of Apache Indian and Asian Dub Foundation, exploring transcultural sound practices entails taking into account the ways in which new sonic constellations generate new cultural conceptions. As has been argued by Simon Frith, a very important precondition for this approach is that music is not a mere reflection of culture, or cultural identity, but that culture is generated through musical activity, and thus music making is understood as a *cultural practice* (Frith 1996).

'Always be a composer, not a player', suggested guitar player and composer Steve Chandra Savale on their website in 2006. This statement highlights his claim of creating something new, rather than only reacting to what is available within the boundaries of musical genre conventions. Due to their complex sound practices, their tracks push the boundaries of what is possible with musical structure, sound, lyrics and performance. Their creative process is not concerned with the essentialist notions of Indian music traditions. Rather, in terms of the music they use (from the old record collections of their parents as well as compiled sound archives on CD), they use it as sonic material which is appropriated in the context of their own tracks. Moreover, being a 'composer' not only refers to the musical realm, but also points to ADF's social and political activism – these different levels work together seamlessly in their artistic practice.

In looking at the concrete sound practices of the artists just mentioned, it is necessary to specify this general notion further. In the case of these artists, cultural practice is not restricted to any heritage culture or to the culture of an ethnic community, but is also musical culture, production culture: the concrete technologies of sound play a crucial role in the negotiation of culture. Thus, a cultural analysis of contemporary South Asian–influenced dance music in the UK needs to take into account the various references to Hindi film music,

Punjabi bhangra or Indian classical music as well as Jamaican dancehall, US hip-hop or UK jungle beats, and analyse them as part of a rich and growing sonic-cultural archive. In the chapter on Apache Indian, it is argued that his sound practices create a very concise notion of reggae culture which he puts into playful interaction with bhangra rhythms and Punjabi lyrics. With regard to this sound practice, the Punjabi lyrics cannot solely be described in terms of Apache Indian's Punjabi heritage, while the reggae beats are looked at in terms of his 'new' cultural identity. To investigate a specific sound practice which combines Punjabi lyrics with reggae beats as part of the same memory sound bank means accepting that culture is negotiated through music, and all the elements are constantly actualized and reinvented in the process of musical production. This also means that there is no inherent hierarchy along which elements can be said to be more important for the process of cultural formation.

With regard to Asian Dub Foundation's 'Collective Mode', this chapter demonstrated that in mixing South Asian inflected rap, jungle and punk, ADF's sound practice resists exoticizing images of Indianness and sonically generates their radical, danceable and activist stance. ADF's transcultural sound practice is derived from the specific location of London and creates a sense of community which draws from a common history of South Asians in Britain (and sometimes speaks explicitly from that position). At the same time, and more importantly, a community is addressed which is not divided by class or ethnicity and aims at uniting all people whose goal is to change Britain's politics of inequality, racism and violence. The locating of their music in London is enacted in ADF's sound practice which is based on a complex interaction of aesthetic ideas, cultural appropriations and critical thought; these forms of interaction will be further explored in the following case study which investigates the sound practices of M.I.A.

5

Sonic Fictions, Global Noise: M.I.A., *Arular* (2005) and *Kala* (2007)

In this chapter, I take up the notion of global ghettotech as a starting point for the analysis of the music of British Sri Lankan musician Maya Arulpragasam, also known as M.I.A. The term 'global ghettotech' is defined by Steve Goodman as 'an attempt to forge together a radically synthetic counter to "world music" that connects together the mutant strains of post-hip-hop, electronic dance music from the Planet of Slums, from kwaito to reggaeton, to cumbia, to dancehall, to crunk, to grime, to baile funk, and others' (Goodman 2010: 196). Although the term is associated with music, global ghettotech is not a valid description of a particular music style in general, nor of M.I.A.'s music in particular. And it might be productive for the analysis of M.I.A.'s music to counter the notion of global ghettotech with another connotation, that is, ghetto fabulous, a term which made it into the OED:

> ghetto fabulous n. and adj. orig. U.S. (a) n. an ostentatious or flamboyant lifestyle or manner of dress, associated with the hip-hop subculture and characterized as a marker of status in economically disadvantaged urban neighborhoods; (b) adj. of, relating to, or exemplifying this style (variously viewed approvingly or disapprovingly). (OED Second edition 1989; online version December 2011)

The various and contradicting connotations of the term will be used in the analysis to tease out the complexity of M.I.A.'s sound practices and their relation to controversial aesthetic, cultural and political discourses.

What does the word 'ghetto' in global ghettotech refer to? Historically, the word 'ghetto' referred to 'the quarter in a city, chiefly in Italy, to which the Jews were restricted' from the sixteenth century onwards (OED 2011). Ever since then, the term 'ghetto' has been widely used in connection with various locations and is sometimes also used simultaneously with 'slum'. In the context of this chapter, no direct relation can be drawn between M.I.A. and a particular 'ghetto' location, but there are instances in her music which link it with certain commonly accepted connotations of the ghetto and critical negotiations with these connotations. The notion of the ghetto that is important for my discussion of M.I.A. exceeds these historical definitions and focuses on the ghetto as a mediatized object of knowledge. This definition primarily regards the ghetto as a concrete space to which mostly poor people are allocated 'as a result of economic or social pressures'. However, in popular discourses, there are various characteristics that are attached to the ghetto. Depending on the media format (radio feature, music review), distributing channel (TV or special-interest magazine) or context (music, art, social issues, politics), characterizations of the ghetto range from 'run-down', 'filthy' and 'dangerous', to 'culturally diverse', 'inspirational' and 'underground' in terms of music culture. From a negative perspective, the ghetto is regarded as a space that is not freely chosen by its inhabitants, but that is allocated to economically disadvantaged people who are restricted to low-grade urban neighbourhoods with inadequate living conditions. Situated at the peripheries of urban metropolises, and, figuratively, at the margins of society, the ghetto is a 'forgotten' place where people are kept in an unceasing state of dis-belonging and non-citizenship. In the context of globalization debates, the globalization of the ghetto has been commented on by scholars such as Mike Davis who stated in *Planet of Slums*, a survey of the spread of urban poverty, that the development of mega-cities through the increasing influx in the urban centres, and the concomitant growth of slums is a phenomenon that is happening on a global scale and thus raises issues of how people are going to live together in the future under these changing conditions. This idea stands somehow diametrically to the image of the 'global village', a term coined by Marshall McLuhan that became a synonym for the decreasing size of the world through digital communication technology (cf. McLuhan 1962). The image of the global village includes notions of accessibility, convergence and mobility, while the notion of the global ghetto is of inaccessibility, dissociation and stagnation.

What is constructive about linking the controversies around the term 'ghetto' with M.I.A.? With regard to her person, there is a relation that can be drawn to M.I.A.'s life story. Born in the UK, Maya Arulpragasam returned to Sri Lanka when she was six months old, and had to flee the country after a few years with her mother and sister because of the Sri Lankan civil war that was going on at the time. The family resided in different (also war-torn, in part) countries before they eventually settled in London when Arulpragasam was ten years old. Here she was treated as an immigrant although she holds a UK passport, was put in special classes for foreign kids at school and grew up without being expected to do anything but integrate into the host society. This experience is shared by many migrants who are addressed in popular migrant discourses, mostly in terms of successful or failed integration, lost ethnic identities or problems with family structures and street violence. Therefore, although she has not exactly lived in a ghetto, the experience of being a refugee and of being a migrant to the UK does give her a background that she shares with many other migrants. It would be false, however, to confine her music to her life story, as if her sound practices resulted directly from her cultural and social background. However, there are instances in her music and specifically in her lyrics which explicitly reference some of the routes that she took that have influenced her artistic work.

Continuing with the analysis of the arbitrary meanings of the ghetto, particularly in pop-cultural discourses, there is a more positive perspective which celebrates the ghetto as a 'lifestyle' that is 'associated with the hip-hop subculture and characterized as a marker of status in economically disadvantaged urban neighbourhoods', as provided by the OED (OED Second edition 1989). The notion 'ghetto fabulous' is clearly associated with the opportunity to escape the economic and social stagnation and to turn 'being from the ghetto' into a cultural capital of street-credibility, physical attractiveness, artistic creativity, and new-richness. Moreover, the ghetto is here no longer clearly associated with a 'slum area', but with 'economically disadvantaged urban neighbourhoods' more generally, which does not necessarily refer to areas situated around the city centre, but within it.

In relation to M.I.A., the notion of 'ghetto fabulous' resonates in her cover artwork when she 'wraps' war imagery like guns and bombs in stencilled pop artwork, or prints a picture of a group of young black males with bare breasts, golden chains around their necks and dollar signs on their caps. At the same time, M.I.A.'s visualizations are not adaptations of the typical gangsta-rap image proposed by artists such as US-based rap star and producer 50 Cent. M.I.A.'s cover artwork, lyrical booklets and homepage always evoke a provocation of stereotyped images and at the same time an avoidance of consistent and predictable messages. At the same time, it might be argued that the lifestyle of her commercial success has allowed her to live a life on the 'fabulous' side of things, and the stylish and outspoken pop-persona that she has created for herself, as well as creating music videos with acclaimed producers and engaging in musical collaborations with people from the Global South, and especially people living in precarious and/or war-torn conditions, does also have some clear resonances with the 'ghetto fabulous' image which she also deconstructs in her (art)work.

More specifically, the term 'global ghettotech' confines the contrasting connotations of the ghetto mentioned above and links them to two other terms: a music-specific notion of technology signified by 'tech' (as in the electronic music style *techno*, although 'tech' refers to electronically produced music styles more generally) and the notion of the global (in terms of global exchange and the dissemination of music in general, and music files such as MP3s or online platforms such as *SoundCloud*[1] in particular). In this way, the technology-oriented notion of the global village is synthesized with the various notions of the ghetto and thus suspends an alleged division between the ghetto and digital/mass technology. The assumption that people from disadvantaged urban neighbourhoods do not participate in the global exchange of ideas, information and culture is contestable. Global ghettotech emphasizes the microeconomic structures and pirate practices which sidetrack the global juridical and economic norms set, for instance, by the World Trade Organisation (WTO).[2] More specifically, global ghettotech refers to the music that is created at the peripheries of Johannesburg, San Juan, São Paulo, Kingston and London.

What is significant about this discussion with regard to M.I.A.'s music in particular is the link that her sound practice draws to emerging musicians and producers from the global South who have been part of transnational and globalized music production. This marks a general shift away from the old world music paradigm in which '"the West" [imposes] itself on the "periphery"' as Martin Stokes argues in his article on musical globalization (Stokes 2003: 301). While the world music concept mostly implied that established record companies and eager producers attempted to promote Afro, Asian and Latin American music as authentic reflections of the respective heritage culture, there have been processes which sidestep the essentialist cultural politics and exoticizing marketing strategies of Western music industries. As Thomas Burkhalter states in reference to Kolland, 'nowadays, modernity and the zeitgeist emerge poly-centrically through exchange between the global north and the global South' (Burkhalter 2010). Musicians and producers have increasingly created what could be called vibrant microeconomics which fundamentally counter the cultural and economic logics of the Western music industry. The received sonic borders between the margin and the centre shift when marginalized sounds become disconnected from their assigned 'original' locale and get multiplied in globalized networks of blogs and shared online channels. It would, however, be limiting to think of the development of new musical styles as a mere result of technological developments. Rather, as Jace Clayton highlights, the newness of this development can be regarded as being generated in a 'feedback loop between technology and emerging music' (Clayton 2009). On the other end of the spectrum, some strands of these styles have already become part of the workings of the 'mainstream' music industry and thus have also been utilized by more socio-economically privileged producers and consumers – they thus have 'moved to the centre', so to speak. Therefore, as Marshall et al. suggest with regard to reggaeton, but which is equally valid for funk carioca and kwaito, it is precisely because of this partial connection with mainstream cultural production that the development of these styles resulted in a more 'profound reordering of mainstream and margin, center and periphery' (Marshall et al. 2009: 3).

In this way, depicting these musical styles and their various modes and multiple locations of production, perception and dissemination as 'global ghettotech' underscores its potential 'to forge together a radically synthetic counter to "world music"' as Goodman claims (Goodman 2012: 196). When the term 'global ghettotech' was coined by self-described 'techno-musicologist' Wayne Marshall on his blog in order to emphasize the inherent link between electronic music from the global North and the global South, he remarked that the critical implications of the term had often been neglected by other artists and promoters in favour of its either romanticized connotations or 'edginess' (as a stylized and commodified form of resistance):

> Another name for world music 2.0, in this regard, might be 'global ghettotech' – a term I floated on my blog a few years ago, hoping its implicit critique would be clear. Surprisingly, it has since been unironically embraced by a number of artists and entrepreneurs across Europe and the Americas. The ghetto remains a major signpost in this new world, but its romanticization or exploitation as a signifier of edginess, especially by those not of it, will always create tensions. Teamed with a recent embarrassment of tropical tropes and neo-tiki motifs, it's almost enough to return us full circle to hearing the world as kitschy exotica rather than the noise next door. (Marshall 2010)

For the purpose of this chapter, it is precisely the contested and arbitrary nature of the term that makes it productive for the analysis of M.I.A.'s sound practice which plays with exoticizing imagery and its deconstruction.

It is not surprising that musicians such as M.I.A. and Thomas Wesley Pentz, also known as Diplo (who was the co-producer of M.I.A.'s *Arular*), have embraced musical styles such as reggaeton, funk carioca and kwaito and incorporated elements of these styles into their own productions, since their danceable rhythms and rough aesthetics resonate well with the aesthetic realm of urban dance music styles such as UK garage and grime. However, there is no one-to-one imitation of musical styles such as reggaeton or funk carioca in M.I.A.'s tracks. As will be shown in the analysis, elements of these styles are recontextualized in M.I.A.'s production, and in this process, new meanings are generated, new styles are created and new issues are raised.

M.I.A.'s affiliation to musical styles from the global South plays a crucial role in her music by expressing specific aesthetic, cultural and political ideas. It is not irrelevant in this context that reggaeton, for example, is itself the product of various spatial trajectories and transcultural mixing and reappropriation. Reggaeton can be defined as a mixture of 'reggae, hip-hop, and a number of Spanish Caribbean styles and often accompanied by sexually explicit lyrics and a provocative dancing style known as *perreo* (doggy style)' that derived from Puerto Rico (Marshall et al. 2009: 1, emphasis in the original). The authors suggest that it is necessary to investigate the overlapping histories of production, perception and mediation in order to reveal the interrelated as well as differing musical, social and political dimensions of reggaeton.

The following part of this chapter will focus on the tracks 'Sunshowers' and 'Bucky Done Gun' from M.I.A.'s 2005 debut album *Arular*, and the subsequent section will analyse 'Paper Planes' from M.I.A.'s 2007 album *Kala*. With regard to these tracks, the aesthetic, cultural and political particularities of M.I.A.'s sound practice will be investigated. While the overall focus is on her sampling practice and lyrical performance, the lyrics and the cover artwork, as well as selected music videos, will be taken into consideration as well.

'Sunshowers'

M.I.A.'s track 'Sunshowers' was released as a single with XL Recordings in London in 2004, prior to the release of the debut album *Arular* which came out on the same label. The focus of this analysis will be on two specific sound practices in particular, as they are crucial to the track's sonic narration. One concerns the creation of the basic beat pattern, and the other the lyrical performance. These specific sound practices will be investigated in relation to the lyrical content as well as with regard to the diverse intertextual references that are made. All these aspects are important in order to understand M.I.A.'s sonic fictions.

The basic beat pattern at the beginning of the track 'Sunshowers' consists of three single, syncopated bass drum hits featuring a high-pitched conga sound (0'00–0'03). What is significant about this syncopated beat pattern is that it differs from the *four-on-the-floor* beat of most dance music tracks, nor is it similar to syncopated beats that are known from dance music styles such as jungle and drum'n'bass. In spite of its imprecision, the flamboyant description of the 'lurching, roughed-up slappy-clappy beat' by Robinson in his review of M.I.A.'s music, as quoted in the introduction to this study on page 5 (Robinson 2006), draws on a specific effect that is characteristic for the sound practice analysed here.

To start with, this sound practice is a specific alteration of the *son clave* pattern. The son clave is a very concise pattern which is usually played with wooden sticks called claves or with a cowbell. The son clave consists of two repeated 4/4 measures featuring two hits in the first measure, three hits in the second measure. In 'Sunshowers', it is not the whole pattern that is used, but only the first three hits, creating the following pattern:

one two [gap] three | one two [gap] three

Therefore, only the first three hits of the full son clave are used and then repeated in M.I.A.'s track. In this way, the clave rhythm is transformed into a fragmented beat in which the gaps don't mark a part of the groove, but become an element of disorientation and give a feeling of being 'off the track'. This cut'n'paste practice produces a special kind of syncopation that was created by M.I.A. with a Roland MC-505 drum machine.

The other sonic element which is dominant in this sound practice is the synthesized conga-sound mentioned above. The sound was created with a Roland MC-505 drum machine which is known for producing raw and inchoate sounds. The conga sound was actually used here to substitute a bass drum sound, which in dance music would usually be the sound to feature as the leading sound in the basic beat pattern, with its warm sub-bass, deep-vibrational sound. In contrast, the conga sound which is featured here has little *sustain* and sounds dry and is unusually high-pitched.

It is precisely the juxtaposition of the clave rhythm and the synthesized conga sound that creates an affinity with reggaeton. Although reggaeton has many different musical shapes, as mentioned above, there are characteristics which make it recognizable: the syncopated rhythm mixing African-Latin beats with rough, synthesized sounds. In the sound practice described above, it is therefore a reggaeton key sound which plays a significant role in M.I.A.'s track.

This reggaeton key sound, consisting of a fragmented son clave and a synthesized conga sound, is looped and continuously runs through the whole track, while some other sonic elements fade in and out. After the first two repeats of the initial basic beat pattern, M.I.A. starts rapping her lyrics (0'04), accompanied only by the reggaeton key sound just described. After two more repeats, the rhythmic pattern is accompanied by a snare, situated in the [gap] right before the third conga hit (0'16).

The 'Sunshowers' lyrics are uttered by M.I.A. in a way that follows the syncopated rhythm of the track: 'I bongo with my lingo/Beat it like a wing yo/ From Congo to Columbo[3]/Can't stereotype my thing yo' (M.I.A. 'Sunshowers', this and all subsequent lyrics are quoted from the CD booklet).

The lyrical performance adds another narrative layer to M.I.A.'s sound practice. Besides generating linguistic meaning, the lyrical performance generates meaning *through* sound, through the specific way in which the lyrics are uttered. The pronunciation and 'flow' of M.I.A.'s vocals is characterized by elements of Jamaican Patois and a singing style which is oriented towards ragga dancehall and rap.[4] M.I.A. takes up rhythmic patterns of the reggaeton beat and interacts with them in a smooth and dynamic fashion. The effect of this lyrical performance is that the fragmented and syncopated beat starts to groove. However, rather than being left to work as a completely 'grounding' element, the natural flow of the voice was disturbed in the post-production of the recording: the vocal track was doubled and slightly set apart in the stereo picture and thus shifts from right to left and back again (most clearly perceptible when listening to the track with headphones). The effect of this is that the listener's ear cannot rest on the singer's voice, but is kept in check by this unsettling listening condition.

All the elements seem to be in constant motion – jumping, dancing, refusing to be tied to one place. Therefore, the relationship between vocals and beat can be conceived as a communicative act, in which vocal and beat figures are engaged in a dynamic process of rhythmic negotiation. While the vocals in many reggaeton productions are oriented towards US American rap, M.I.A.'s vocal style shows attributes of African-Caribbean-derived ragga, which plays a significant part in London's dance music culture.

The lyrics of 'Sunshowers', rather than being a completed script which the lyrical performance has to follow, are the result of a performance that is specifically vocal. The lyrics are themselves sound-oriented, which becomes clear from the way in which the words are chosen and how they are modified in order to fit the performance. There is a high proportion of words in the stanzas which end in /o/, although the words do not usually end in *o*: words which end in *er* are changed into *o*, as in *fingo* (0'22) and *surrendo* (0'28). If the line does not end in a word that is malleable in this way, the syllabus *yo* is added as a suffix.

The sonic narrative that is created through M.I.A.'s lyrical performance actually resonates in the lyrical narrative as well. The first lines, 'I bongo with my lingo and beat it like a wing yo' can be read as a comment about the way she treats language: they imply her claim of creating her own type of expression that is not restricted by a specific, locally or culturally confined code. The following lines, 'from Congo to Columbo, can't stereotype my thing yo', underscore the fact that she speaks a language which is derived from multiple places and media and cannot be constricted to one formula. M.I.A.'s playful exaggeration of the vocal possibilities also transgresses any claims of either some kind of 'street' realness or ethnic authenticity.

On the level of the lyrical content, notions of ethnicity and exoticism are negotiated. Looking again at the lyrics of the first part of the track quoted above, they deal with cultural stereotypes. The lines 'I salt and pepper my mango' construct and comment on M.I.A.'s Sri Lankan identity. M.I.A. narratively constructs an exoticized identity for herself through the image of the mango. At the same time, a critique of this image is implied: the way in which the mango is 'seasoned', that is, how exoticized identity is dealt with, is articulated as being a matter of her own choice, in the same way as 'shoot spit out the window', as the following line has it. Significantly, in drawing on the image of the mango, she does present herself as different, because she is aware that people in the UK usually refrain from salting and peppering mangos before enjoying them – which is in fact the way mangos are usually sold in the streets of Sri Lanka. In this way, a form of strategic essentialism is at play in the construction of a difference in order to demonstrate the arbitrariness of essentialized constructions. This arbitrariness is demonstrated by another connotation of 'salt and pepper' (0'12–0'14) when understood as a reference to female US rap group Salt'n'Pepa, who were tremendously popular in the 1980s and early 1990s. The significance of this reference becomes even more obvious when listening to the track's version 'Sunshowers (Diplo Mix)' which was released on M.I.A.'s mixtape *Piracy Funds Terrorism*, featuring the beat from Salt'n'Pepa's 1987 hit 'Push It'. This reference emphasizes her connection to hip-hop, as it is processed through the framework of UK urban music culture. Rather than representing a particular US version of hip-hop, her rapping style reappropriates elements from US hip-hop into her own track.

The overall attitude of the track is one of self-assuredness and being in charge, not only in terms of various 'ethnic' identifications, but also in terms of the negotiations of gendered attitudes. The stanzas demonstrate an explicitly bold and audacious attitude that resonates with 1970s female punk bands such as the X-Ray-Spex and The Slits, as well as female rap singers and producers such as Salt'n'Pepa, or more recent ones such as Missy Elliot, who have counteracted stereotypes in many different ways, most of all in relation to the received idea that female singers should be soft-spoken and modest.

Another significant intertextual reference which prominently features in M.I.A.'s 'Sunshowers' is the 1976 song 'Sunshower', a catchy love tune from New York soul/disco band Dr. Buzzard's Original Savannah Band. The instrumentals of Dr. Buzzard's 'Sunshower' are sampled and adapted to M.I.A.'s track and arranged in such a way that they accompany the syncopated reggaeton beat of M.I.A.'s track. The 'warped Haitian guitars and splintered percussion' (Wheaton 2005) collide with the rough and syncopated beats. The dynamic that is created here between Dr. Buzzard's catchy tunes and the edgy beats found in M.I.A.'s track can be regarded as programmatic for M.I.A.'s sound practices. While the original is a love song, M.I.A. creates a version in which the dreaminess of the song's melody is used only in order to contrast it with lyrics that evoke conflict and a subtle threat. While the sunshower in the original helps to create the romantic setting for a date, the sunshowers in M.I.A.'s version conjure up images of bullets falling down instead of raindrops, and images of love relationships are substituted with images of snipers. M.I.A.'s version of the chorus is sung by guest singer Nesreen Shah and might remind the listener of a modern r'n'b track – if the voice wasn't processed with so much compression that the singer's voice sounds slightly technoid and artificial.

The recontextualization of Dr. Buzzard's Haitian guitars and the nostalgic feeling they invoke are used as a contrast to the roughed-up vocals and lyrics.

The following 'Sunshowers' lyrics continue this narrative form as they weave their way along the syncopated rhythmic pattern, with two more choruses being inserted (0'53–2'23).

While the perspective elaborated above with regard to the first three stanzas can be read as a critical negotiation of ethnicity, gender and politics from a personal and self-reflexive perspective, a more overtly political perspective is constructed in the latter part of the track which is more difficult to disentangle. This perspective deals with a critical view on gun crime ('I checked that mouth on him/Fucking checked that gas on him'), as well as with issues of the war on terrorism, racial profiling and sweatshops. The lyrics deal with the tracking down of someone who has been connected with a criminal/terrorist act because he was seen 'with the MU.S.LIMS'. The reference to *Newsweek* ('He's made it to the *Newsweek*') locates the story in the US context. The situation of a person is depicted who works in a factory in which 'he does Nike'; this refers to the company's worldwide production sites in places such as South Asia, the United States, Canada, Italy and Mexico. It is paramount not to attempt to assemble the references, story fragments and images that M.I.A. creates in these lyrics into a complete jigsaw puzzle. The pieces will not fit together, and gaps will appear. Another reference which stirred controversy is the provoking line in the first part of the track saying 'Like P.L.O. I don't surrendo'.[5] This line caused MTV to ban the track, and probably also helped to complicate her visa application when was she was supposed to record her new album, *Kala*, in the United States.[6] The controversies created in the lyrical narration cannot be translated one-to-one into activist claims, and there does not seem to be an explicit political agenda. M.I.A. has repeatedly stated that her lyrics reflect her own confusion and inner conflicts, and has claimed that she wanted to make people start to think and ask questions about what is going on around them. The evocation of arbitrary and unsettling images is what characterizes many of M.I.A.'s tracks, as far as her lyrics as well as the cut'n'mix technique of her sound practices are concerned.

A note on the final part of the track: the last section of the track features a 'scratching' noise that is a reference to the practice of turntablism in which the DJ moves the record in a way to create rhythmic noises. The scratching noise that was electronically re-created accompanies the beat pattern of the last section of the track. However, it does not seem to interact with the overall rhythmic structure of 'Sunshowers', but stands oddly beside the rhythmic track, as if added by accident. The track then simply ends with the scratching noise standing alone, an arbitrary sound, as if the DJ were just walking away from the turntables while carelessly brushing the record one last time.

What becomes clear from my analysis of the various sound practices in 'Sunshowers' is that M.I.A.'s specific sonic fictions are created in a complex and contradicting interplay of sounds, rhythms, lyrics and lyrical performance. M.I.A.'s particular use of syncopation, recombination and sonic twists transgress pop music conventions as well as exotic formulae by exaggerating their stereotypical forms.

'Bucky Done Gun'

'Bucky Done Gun', also released on M.I.A.'s debut album *Arular*, is an uptempo track that is highly influenced by a funk carioca track by Deize Tigrona called 'Injeção' which is mentioned in the CD booklet. Deize Tigrona is a funk carioca musician from São Conrado in Rio de Janeiro. Funk carioca (also known as baile funk outside of Brazil) is a musical style which has developed in the favelas of Rio de Janeiro as a mixture of Miami Bass, drum machines and sexually explicit lyrics.

M.I.A.'s adaptation of 'Injeção' is particularly intriguing since it allows a detailed discussion of the ways in which sonic and lyrical elements from the funk carioca track are reappropriated, and of how the sound practices that are involved in this process generate diverse and contradictory notions of race and gender. In comparison to 'Sunshowers', in which only partial elements from other songs were recontextualized, the adaptations of 'Injeção' to 'Bucky Done Gun' are much more comprehensive.

The rhythmic pattern featured in Deize Tigrona's 'Injeção' is characterized by syncopated beats that are arranged in a stop-and-go modus with huge gaps in between. This rough aesthetic, characteristic of funk carioca, is transferred to 'Bucky Done Gun' in a similar fashion. Moreover, the prominent hookline of 'Injeção', which features a sample of the horn section of the *Rocky* theme 'Gonna Fly Now' written by Bill Conti in 1976, is adopted by M.I.A. (0'17–0'23). Finally, besides the rhythmic and sonic similarities of the two tracks, there is a poignant similarity in the overall vocal gesture of the two singers in regard to their outspoken, defiant and provocative rap.

What clearly distinguishes the two tracks, however, are the lyrical contents. The lyrics of Deize Tigrona's 'Injeção', sung in Portuguese, are about a visit to a doctor who gives her an injection that she describes as painful, and that makes her scratch him. However, the way in which this situation is described is highly sexist and problematic, because there is an implied equating of the injection with penetration. Furthermore, the horn section of the Rocky theme 'Gonna Fly Now' highlights the imagery of a muscular, sexually potent hero. The narrative is based on the perspective of male desire, while the female protagonist is depicted in an ambivalent state between naivety, helplessness and attraction. Sexually charged lyrics can be found in many funk carioca tracks, and their sexist tendency figures in tracks by both male and female singers. As Senekowitsch has pointed out in her study of funk carioca in Rio de Janeiro, however, it is important to regard these ascriptions in the wider context of media, politics and public debate, and to take into account both the depictions of this music culture and the self-definitions of funk carioca musicians (Senekowitsch 2010: 150). Funk and hip-hop musicians from the favelas are often marginalized and seen as outsiders, while the people active in funk carioca regard the 'baile', the dance, as a place of sociality which crosses social and racial boundaries (Senekowitsch 2010: 150–151). In this context, the energetic beats and explicit lyrics are arbitrary because they also function as a way to counter the climate of suspicion and criminalization with which people of the favelas are faced. Senekowitsch emphasizes that the emergent music culture which developed with regard to funk carioca was seen as a threat and was responded to with a reinforcement of distance and suspicion, as she states in reference to Ivana Bentes:

> The criminalization of funk in Rio de Janeiro was only a symptom of the fear of the social and cultural rise of the groups of young people from the periphery who were taking over the market. The success of this funk and hip-hop movement resulted in a confirmation of the continuously negotiated, indiscriminate and decontextualized relationship between crime, poverty and violence. (Bentes 2004: 75, quoted in Senekowitsch 2010: 152–153, my translation)[7]

In contrast, the lyrical content of M.I.A.'s 'Bucky Done Gun' goes in a different direction (0'24), dealing with gun crime or some form of militant action. However, the lyrics also deal with a sexual relationship between a man and a woman. Regarded in relation to Deize Tigrona's track, the sexually provocative attitude of 'Injeção' is partly taken up in 'Bucky Done Gone', but in M.I.A.'s version this provocation functions as an intensifier for her politicized lyrics. Moreover, while the lyrics in 'Injeção' construct the female protagonist as a 'passive' figure, the female protagonist in 'Bucky Done Gun' is much more in charge of the situation.

Compared to Deize Tigrona's vocals, M.I.A. sings her lyrics in a much more melodic and groovy fashion, while Tigrona's lyrics are uttered in a very rough and almost piercing way. Therefore, while taking up the confrontational attitude of funk carioca, M.I.A. approaches this style with a 'smoother' connotation that is more affiliated to reggae dancehall aesthetics. This also has a tangible effect on the way in which the lyrics are perceived: although they are addressing violence, due to the way that they are performed they cease sounding serious and complicated and become catchy and accessible in a pop/dance music context.

This last point is significant also with regard to the dissemination of M.I.A.'s track in Brazil. 'Bucky Done Gun' was actually broadcast on MTV Brazil and the national radio stations. While at that point in time funk carioca hardly got any airplay, M.I.A.'s track was played and eventually reached the Brazil music charts. Deize Tigrona's success with 'Injeção' was in no way comparable, although the two artists performed some concerts together in São Paulo. While locally produced funk carioca was largely ignored by the mainstream music industry and criminalized in popular discourses, delivered by M.I.A. it entered the charts through the back door – as a form of global pop.

'Bucky Done Gun' music video

The aesthetics of the 'Bucky Done Gun' music video create a narrative that is completely decontextualized from the lyrical content and instead focuses on stereotyped connotations of the gloomy ghetto and shallow sexiness. The imagery of the roughness and provocativeness of the funk carioca style seems to be directly equated with 'ghetto fabulous' aesthetics. The video shows M.I.A. in a rough neighbourhood, dancing while rattling at a wire mesh fence, shaking her hips and singing her lyrics into the camera. M.I.A. is presented here in a pose which diverges from the transgressive power of her sound practices and reduces her to the image of a female background artist in a hip-hop video by a gold chain–laden rap star. This comes as a surprise, and even more so when considering her desire to correct the tendency exhibited by some journalists of assuming that she did not produce the tracks on *Arular* herself, which she reflects upon in retrospect in an interview with the music magazine *Pitchfork*:

> If you read the credits, he [Thomas Wesley Pentz, also known as Diplo] sent me a loop for 'Bucky Done Gun,' and I made a song in London, and it became 'Bucky Done Gun.' But that was the only song he was actually involved in on *Arular*. So the whole time I've had immigration problems and not been able to get in the country, what I am or what I do has got a life of its own, and is becoming less and less to do with me. And I just find it a bit upsetting and kind of insulting that I can't have any ideas on my own because I'm a female or that people from undeveloped countries can't have ideas of their own unless it's backed up by someone who's blond-haired and blue-eyed. After the first time it's cool, the second time it's cool, but after like the third, fourth, fifth time, maybe it's an issue that we need to talk about, maybe that's something important, you know. (Thompson 2007, quoting M.I.A.)

While the 'Bucky Done Gun' music video does not resonate at all with the playful and critical agency of M.I.A.'s sonic fiction, there are other examples which demonstrate a much more convincing visualization of her musical ideas. The music video for 'Galang' (another track on *Arular*) is particularly significant in this regard, because it uses cut'n'paste techniques such as collage and stencilling, a technique that is similar to digital sampling. In the video, M.I.A. is shown dancing in front of a canvas, looking straight into the camera. On the canvas behind her, animated stencils and drawings of war imagery appear and disappear in fast-changing sequences. The war imagery corresponds with M.I.A.'s politicized lyrics while the pink, yellow and blue stencil art makes the tanks, bombs and guns she sings about seem less threatening. The intensive play of movement and colour, and M.I.A.'s steady gaze into the camera, make the spectator's gaze cling to the repeating visual cues. The effect is actually a much more confrontational one than in 'Bucky Done Gun', in which the ghetto aesthetics result in a distancing relationship to the singer/actor.

The cut'n'mix technique of the 'Galang' music video is also similar to other forms of M.I.A.'s visual art, and particularly so with regard to the artwork of the album covers and lyrical booklets. As far as the cover artwork of *Arular* is concerned, the stencil techniques and colourful collages of tanks, bombs and guns are mixed with photographs, Tamil and 'peace' symbols. M.I.A.'s artwork creates an aesthetic counterpart to the grim contents of the lyrics. Along with the sound practices, the visuals generate a contrasting relationship of catchiness and roughness that evokes frictions and dissonances which transform stereotypes and generate complex transcultural constellations.

'Paper Planes'

'Paper Planes' was released on M.I.A.'s second album *Kala* in 2007. While the track addresses stereotypical representations of immigrants, it is based on a song by British punk band The Clash, 'Straight to Hell', from their 1982 album *Combat Rock*, as well as on a 1992 hip-hop track by US rap group Wreckx-N-Effect called 'Rump Shaker'. These intertextual references are significant with regard to both the sonic and the contextual constellation that they create.

As *The Clash* is one of the most popular British bands connected to the development of punk music in the late 1970s and early 1980s, referencing them in a UK production means alluding to collective memory. It might thus be more relevant to think about the musical and, importantly, the political background of this band than is the case with some of the other references that feature in M.I.A.'s music. Without wanting to overemphasize the point, it is significant that M.I.A.'s 'Paper Planes' sonically quotes the song 'Straight to Hell' in particular, as it expresses a critique of social injustice, deals with the shutting down of steel mills in northern England and addresses the racism suffered by immigrants to the UK. The song is also about transnational concerns, such as issues concerning the Vietnam War. Another affinity can be discerned with regard to The Clash in their support of political activism and the use of combat iconography on their record sleeves.

The sampled sequence of 'Straight to Hell' which M.I.A. uses in 'Paper Planes' consists of a bass line accompanied by a guitar, both instruments simultaneously playing a monotonous and straight rhythm, sixteen single strokes in a four-quarter-note pattern (0'00–0'10). This sequence is looped, creating a steady beat that runs throughout the track, while in The Clash's version, this sequence is only played at the beginning of the track as an intro. With the repeating mode, together with an additional bass drum and some added reverb, the punk key sound is transformed into a downbeat electronic dance music track.[8]

A distorted guitar sound floats above this rhythmic pattern, which is also part of the sampled sequence of 'Straight to Hell', but in the context of 'Paper Planes', it sounds as if it were created by a synthesizer.

M.I.A.'s lyrics are uttered in a softly articulated rap, the melody winds itself easily around the beat patterns and echoes the monotonous vocal style used by The Clash's singer Joe Strummer. The vocals consist of three stanzas with a simple, repetitive melodic structure: 'I'll fly like paper get high like planes/ Catch me at the border I got visas in my name' (M.I.A. 'Paper Planes', quoted from CD booklet). While the rhythmic pattern of the track also runs through the chorus as a persistent rhythmic spine, the chorus features an altogether new sound practice. The chorus is influenced by Wreckx-N-Effect's track 'Rump Shaker', already mentioned above. Wreckx-N-Effect is an American rap group, and the track 'Rump Shaker' actually reached number 2 on the *Billboard* Hot 100. This track is perceived as controversial, having been criticized for its sexist attitude, and thus fits into the 'ghetto fabulous' aesthetics that can be found in numerous hip-hop music videos presenting the male 'hyper-sexual' rapper surrounded by scantily dressed women whose only function is to look sexy. The lyrical-rhythmic structure in 'Rump Shaker' is transformed from: 'All I wanna do is zooma-zoom-zoom-zoom/In a boom-boom/And shake your rump'

(Wreckx'N'Effect 'Rump Shaker', my transcription) into a similarly structured phrase in 'Paper Planes', which in this case, however, deals with a stereotyped conception of immigrants:

> All I wanna do is [bang-bang-bang-bang]
> And a [ker-ching]
> And take your money.
> (M.I.A. 'Paper Planes', my transcription)

While in Wreckx-N-Effect's version, the 'zoom' and 'boom' clearly relate to fantasies of sexual intercourse, the [bang] and [ker-ching] create a more complex sonic fiction. The lyrics of the chorus are sung by a children's choir that was recorded in Brixton, which takes up the link to The Clash (who sang about the Brixton riots in another song), and situates the sound practice in a London neighbourhood where people with a migrant background still face forms of social exclusion and racism on an everyday basis. The children's choir multiplies the voices of those who are faced with the stereotyped and irrational image of migrants, one which depicts them as coming to the host country in order to (violently) take the money and the jobs from the natives in order to get rich on a country to which they don't belong. However, the meaning of the lyrics is not confined to the UK, but is also related to the United States, where parts of the *Kala* album were produced. In addressing visa issues, the paper planes themselves become a metaphor for visas which 'fly like paper, get high like planes', imagining what it would be like to cross national borders in this very easy way – which is actually visually acted out in the music video, when a swarm of paper planes flies across the Hudson River.

The significant point about this sound practice is that the lyrics 'zoom' and 'boom' in 'Rump Shaker' are articulated verbally, while in 'Paper Planes', the [bang] is a gunshot sound, and the [ker-ching] is a cash register sound. Thus, in 'Paper Planes', the sound practice in the chorus becomes significant through the use of everyday sounds as meticulously placed instruments which create the section's rhythmic pattern. Moreover, besides functioning as a rhythmic pattern, the sounds interact meaningfully with the lyrics featured in the chorus. In this way, the sounds do not have a clear indexical meaning. The gunshot sounds in 'All I wanna do is [bang, bang, bang, bang]' and the cash register sound in 'And [ker-ching] And take your money' are arbitrary. The particularity of the sonic in contrast to the linguistic narrative is that it evokes a different kind of associative repertoire. Taking the cash register sound as an example, this sound has very specific sonic characteristics which do not evoke the same images as the word 'cash register' does. The [ker-ching] has a jingly and rattling sound quality which evokes the image of a heavy, iron register with huge protruding keys that is opened with a handle. This sound does a lot more than indicate 'cash register' – it sounds out a mixture of boldness and the playfulness of a music box. In connection with the lyrics, which address a stereotyped and irrational image of immigrants, the sounds have special connotations. In this specific sound practice, the [bang] and the [ker-ching] become a warning, an instigation and a parody, all at the same time.

Listening to the sound practice in this way, it is hard to grasp the programme managers' intention when M.I.A. was invited to perform 'Paper Planes' on the *Late Show with David Letterman* on CBS in 2008. In preparation for the performance, the gunshot sound was substituted with a less sharp and pervasive sound that was closer to hitting the snare drum of a drum kit. As can be observed based on M.I.A.'s reaction on stage, she wasn't even informed about this change in advance of the show. When the chorus was played for the first time, she was in the middle of dance moves, and incredulously turned around to the DJ when the soft popping sounds resonated instead of the [bang, bang, bang, bang]. What makes this incident so telling is, firstly, that the [bang] was actually perceived by the programme managers as an isolated sound symbol with exactly one chain of meaning: [bang] = gunshot = threat. Secondly, the sound's meaning as artistic performance was denied.[9] Thirdly, in this manner, the artist M.I.A. was repudiated. Although she was invited to perform, there was a restriction as to what, how and how loud she was to perform. In this way, the contrasts (that are part of M.I.A.'s artistic strategy) were blurred, the sonic performance spoiled, the artist disarmed. The very issue of her criticism – immigrants being too loud, too dangerous, too envied for what they have achieved – was projected back onto herself. The hardly perceivable sounds [plop, plop, plop, plop] say: we want you, but we want a pre-selected bit of you, we want the 'interesting-because-different' bit and the 'controllable-because-pacified' bit.

Significantly, this ignorant handling of M.I.A.'s artistic practice was perpetuated with regard to MTV's release of a version of 'Paper Planes' that was manipulated in a similar way (Lamb 2008). The question that needs to be raised in this context is whether there is a specific gendered implication at work in these restrictive measures. Thinking of the sheer amount of rap music tracks, mostly produced by male producers, that feature gunshot sounds, explicit and often sexist lyrics and bold 'manly' attitudes seem to be completely acceptable.

However, these tracks fit very nicely into the 'ghetto fabulous' aesthetics and often lack the underlying critical edge that qualifies M.I.A.'s sound practices in 'Paper Planes'.

Conclusion

To summarize the particularities of M.I.A.'s sound practices, there is a special kind of friction that is created in linking exoticized sounds with urban dance music beats and a unique lyrical performance. On the rhythmic level, qualities of syncopation, reduction and gaps are emphasized. In this way, the beats become key sounds in the creation of an unstable base sound in relation to which the exoticized sounds are perceived. In 'Sunshowers', for instance, the bongo sound that features in the basic beat is an exoticized key sound because it is commonly associated with African-Cuban culture. However, in the context of the track, it is doubly deconstructed. Firstly, by functioning as the bass drum in a very reduced beat structure, it becomes detached from the received repertoire of African-Cuban beat patterns (such as cumbia, son, samba or others). Secondly, the sound itself references the earthiness of a bongo sound that is usually created through the specific materiality of its wooden or fibreglass shell and a deerskin screw-tensioned drumhead. However, since the bongo key sound is produced with a drum machine, the sound is a synthesized imitation of a bongo sound. Its synthesized quality is enhanced by the way in which the sound is manipulated: there is very little sustain and no 'natural' reverberation that the bongo drum would usually create when played manually. Therefore, the interplay of sonic, technical and performative aspects is constitutive of this transgressive sound practice.

As was demonstrated with regard to 'Bucky Done Gun', the sound practices that are found here create specific forms of musical and cultural reappropriation. It would be too simple to regard M.I.A.'s referencing of 'Injeção' as mere quotation. As was mentioned in theory Chapter 3, sampling as a form of musical quotation is not only quoting a sound from another source. Rather, as Katz suggests in *Capturing Sound*, sampling is most notably a '*performative* quotation' (Katz 2004: 149, original emphasis). This is particularly relevant when looking at the piece of sound that was quoted from 'Injeção', namely the horn section of the *Rocky* theme 'Gonna Fly Now' that was written by Bill Conti in 1977. The horn section sample in M.I.A.'s 'Bucky Done Gun' is not a simple representation of the

Rocky theme, it is instead a performative quotation referencing a context (Deize Tigrona's track) in which the horn section had already been remediated. The different musical pieces, Bill Conti's 'Gonna Fly Now', Deize Tigrona's 'Injeção' and M.I.A.'s 'Bucky Done Gun' do not simply share the same sampled melodic figure, the horn section, like an artefact (that is, a produced thing) with one fixed meaning. Rather, all three artists perform a specific version of the horn section (that is, they are producing subjects), and these sound practices create three different sonic fictions.

With regard to the overall perspective of my study of transcultural sound practices, the *cultural* analysis of M.I.A.'s sound practices works on a number of levels. For instance, 'Sunshowers' and 'Paper Planes' permit us to analyse the ways in which cultural identities and stereotypes are negotiated. Significantly, M.I.A. does not only use exoticized sounds that are connected to her Sri Lankan heritage, but freely uses other exoticisms to create her dissonant and transcultural sonic fictions. In the comparison of 'Bucky Done Gun' with Deize Tigrona's 'Injeção', the way in which different gendered identities are renegotiated and transformed was explored with regard to the lyrical content as well as the lyrical performance. Lastly, 'Paper Planes' was investigated to look into how M.I.A.'s sound practices juxtapose politicized messages with catchy rhythms to create complex and inconclusive sonic fictions.

Therefore, M.I.A.'s sound practices constantly work around stereotyped constructions of cultural identity in general, and those surrounding her person and her political agency in particular. Her growing popularity as an artist and someone who openly expresses her opinion about controversial issues has resulted in an increasing awareness of her power – artistically and politically. The politicized fabric of her lyrics and music, along with her resistance against the ignorance of the rights of the Tamil minority in Sri Lanka – which she expressed on her Myspace page and on other internet platforms – brought her the honour of being declared one of the most influential people by *Time* magazine in 2009. The comment that accompanied the list sounds simple, almost naïve, but actually touches on an important point: 'The great thing about her is that she doesn't have some global plan. She just has things she cares about and is interested in, from all over the world' (Jonze 2009). It sounds naïve because it could lead the reader to think of her in terms of the artist-as-genius, strolling the world for inspiration. The point it touches, however, is the note about lacking a 'global plan' – with regard to her artistic work and sound practices it was demonstrated in this chapter how she refuses to construct an inherently consistent sonic fiction, or political agenda.

The drawback of this *Time* magazine award was, however, that media coverage increasingly focused on her political and 'pop' persona rather than on her output as a musician, something which had been noticeable right from the beginning of her musical career, when the main interest circled around her experiences of the Sri Lankan civil war and her refugee status in the UK. The more recent controversies around her person reached another peak after the release of a music video for the single 'Born Free' of her latest album /\/\/\Y/\(*MAYA*, 2010), made by Romain Gavras. The video deals with a killing raid chasing 'redheads' – an allegory of the arbitrariness of violence and the convertibility of the roles of 'who is to blame'. Once more, press coverage focused on the alleged violence of her art and the question of her personal authenticity.[10]

Listening to M.I.A.'s sound practices, however, means thinking beyond 'the conventional reception habits of popular music audiences' and attending to 'the private, political and artistic spheres of *production*' (Eckstein 2010b: 37, my emphasis), as was demonstrated throughout this chapter.[11] The aesthetic decisions M.I.A. takes create multilevelled ideas which cannot be harmonized in any simple manner. The specific ways in which M.I.A. deals with ethnic, gender and political aspects are integrally linked to the specific ways in which she utters her lyrics, combines different rhythmic elements, performs a sampled melody. The 'glue' which holds all these different aspects together is the sound, processed through technological tools and performed through practices of cut'n'paste, fragmentation, contrast. However, the glue does not create a homogeneous mass. The noisy often meets the sweet, the rough is contrasted with the catchy, and this creates a sound practice which generate shifts, inconsistencies and gaps.

Finally, I come back to the term 'global ghettotech' which was proposed at the beginning of the chapter as a starting point for the analysis. There are several instances which have demonstrated constructive links between M.I.A.'s sound practices and the arbitrary connotations of global ghettotech. One such instance concerns M.I.A.'s reference to Wreckx'N'Effect's 'Rump Shaker', a track that is saturated with the sexualized and sexist attitude of a number of mainstream hip-hop acts which are oriented towards the aesthetics of the 'ghetto fabulous'. It could be argued that M.I.A., by implementing the characteristic lyrical-rhythmic structure of this highly popular track, simply capitalizes on its popularity and recognizability and in this way reproduces the 'ghetto fabulous' aesthetic, including its sexist connotations. My analysis in this chapter points to another direction: although the 'ghetto fabulous' does resonate in 'Paper Planes', in this version the 'ghetto fabulous' connotation has a completely different function. It is used here to embellish the immigrant figure that she creates in staging him/her in a typical gangsta attitude, which enhances the parody effect of the bad and dangerous immigrant. Analysing M.I.A.'s sound practices against the connotations of global ghettotech has thus proved a useful tool for linking the relevant sonic and lyrical aspects of her music to the controversial implications of the term, and highlights the complex and arbitrary meanings generated by M.I.A.'s sound practices.

6

Performativity, Technology and the Body: Nathan 'Flutebox' Lee, *Flutebox* (2011)

Live Performance

When Nathan Lee enters the stage, the audience falls silent. He starts playing the flute in a lucid, melodic fashion, featuring Indian classical scales. Standing alone in the middle of the huge stage, he appears introverted and almost fragile, his eyes are lowered, and his body only makes small movements, not more than a shy nod of the head, creating little vibrations in his shoulders. The sound is crisp and fills the entire concert space; the sound waves are processed by a reverb, enhancing the Queen Elisabeth Hall's capacious architecture. Then, after a breath of a pause, Lee starts playing the flute in a completely different way: using a lot more breath, and pressing the air through his half-closed lips into the mouthpiece of the flute, he produces thudding, syncopated beats which make his whole body vibrate. The vibration is transported into the floorboards and out into the room, the thick sonic texture becoming the substance that puts the audience under Lee's spell. Just when this energetic rhythmic explosion reaches the audience and makes them burst into cheering, Nathan drops the beat and returns to the melodic, caressing tune, smoothing down the frenzied sound waves he had created.

The room falls silent once again, only the melodic tunes remain audible. But this time, it's a different kind of silence, as the reverberation of the thundering rhythm is still tangible, if not audible, hanging in mid-air in the space between the artist and the audience. In fact, the reverberation of this sonic situation has created an atmosphere of expectant tension, as if a pact has been made between those who have been witness to it. Against the background of this new auditory awareness, the melodic figure's sonic experience is intensified and sounds even more lucid and transparent. After a short sequence of melodic song,

Lee switches modes again, charming out pounding beats from his instrument and thus eagerly fulfilling his promise of rhythmic bliss. From treble to bass, highness to lowness, crystal to rubble, the rhythm expands and unfolds in a frenzy hip-hop pattern, generated through the heavy beatboxing Lee applies to his flute. The sound has a thick texture, making the air vibrate. Now the sonic effect is reversed: while the flute's transparent melody fades into the background and becomes only a thin string of remembered affect, the presence of the pounding beats has occupied the entire space, unifying the bodies in collective celebration of the rhythm, like a shared heartbeat. Eventually, when Lee finishes his performance, the audience pays tribute to this sonic whirlwind with loud and extensive cheers and shouts.

Liveness

This description of Lee's performance at Queen Elisabeth Hall is an attempt to make the particularities of live performance tangible for the reader. These particularities seem to form around specific relationships: the relationship between the musician and the audience, the relationship of the sound waves and the architecture, the relationship of body and mind. All of these relationships play a role with regard to questions of cultural analysis concerning listening conventions, cultural resonances and sociocultural settings.

If these complex sonic and cultural constellations are taken into account, what exactly is a sound practice? As will be elaborated in this chapter, sound practice refers here to Lee's playing technique, i.e. the specific way in which he plays the flute. Another sound practice that will be analysed here is, therefore, the way in which 'liveness' becomes an integral part not only of his live performance, but of the process and product of Lee's studio recording, namely his 2011 EP *Flutebox*.

There are at least three features of liveness which are fundamental to Lee's sound practice: its physicality, immediacy and intensity. Physicality refers to the playing technique that is performed through his body. However, it also refers to his flute playing not only as a form of sound production, but also as a form of sound-reproduction – for instance, in the use of reverb in order to enhance the space in which he is performing, or the reproduction of hip-hop-related beat patterns that are applied to the flute. Immediacy refers to the way in which Lee creates a feeling of spontaneity and unpredictability. Although Lee did not improvise freely in the performance described above, his way of playing evoked the feeling that the music was created at that very moment. In this way, the audience understands and re-enacts the creative process while listening; this in turn connects them to the music in a way that resounds differently than would the effect of a flute player playing from sheet music. There is an immediateness in Nathan's performance, and a special presence. The physicality and immediacy also has an effect on the audience, which interacts with the artist physically and verbally in a kind of feedback loop.

The particular dynamic that is generated in the interactive relationship between the artist and the audience can be described as intensity. The way in which a certain kind of energy and intensity is created that is capable of creating a bridge between the artist and the audience was described by Mark Butler in his analysis of the performance of a live DJ:

> Intensity, more than any individual musical factor, is the glue that holds a set together. Although the DJ must manipulate the intensity level in a way that makes sense within the conventions of electronic dance music, within the context of live performance, intensity remains contingent upon the audience's interaction [...] Ultimately, [...] the sense of coherence associated with a well-done DJ set derives from an integrated mixture of 'purely musical' compositional choices and on-site physical responses. (Butler 2006: 254)

This description of the DJ set is comparable to Lee's performance with the flute in that it resembles the way in which Lee 'manipulates the intensity level' using different and contrasting modes while playing the flute. This quality of 'liveness' is also reproduced in Nathan 'Flutebox' Lee's recorded pieces, as will be discussed below in the analysis of his *Flutebox* EP.

The flutebox technology

My description of Nathan Lee's live performance is relevant as a starting point for the cultural analysis of Lee's sound practices in general, and his flutebox technology in particular, because it makes it possible to grasp the intimate relationship between the sonic, physical and cultural coordinates of his performance that challenges conceptions of music as mere reflections of culture.

One aspect which can be immediately recognized with regard to Lee's live performance is the contrasting relationship between two different modes in which Lee plays the flute. While one is very clearly related to classical music featuring Indian sounds, the other is related to a rather unconventional engagement with the flute and features bass-intense, hip-hop-related sounds. In order to disentangle the particularities of this sound practice, a closer analysis of what I call *flutebox technology* is required.

Flutebox technology can be framed based on two main features: on the one hand, flutebox technology refers to a precise *playing technique*, and on the other hand, it refers to a complex *sound practice*. Technique refers to the specific art of playing the flute; sound practice refers to a set of techniques and practices that generate a distinct sound and style. First of all, the precise *playing technique* refers to the way in which the flute is played, which refers also to the properties and architecture of the instrument itself. The concert flute is a transversal, side-blown instrument which consists of an embouchure hole and sixteen tone holes that are opened and closed with keys and regulate the pitch; it usually has a 3.5 octave range. To generate the tone, the embouchure hole in the flute's mouthpiece is not completely enclosed by the mouth; rather, the player blows a stream of air over the transversal hole. The frequency and intensity of sounds are controlled not only by the closing of the finger holes, but also by the direction and intensity of the air stream. In the realm of Western classical music, there is a specific repertoire of sounds and sonic qualities which are conventionally produced with the flute. In his article on 'extended techniques' of flute playing, composer and sound artist Matthew Burtner states that the lack of extended playing techniques in Western classical music lies in:

> the concept of unity in Western classical music performance, and the ideal of uniformity in the areas of pitch and dynamics. This uniformity is upheld by the notion of virtuosity, a concept generally referring primarily to dexterity of pitch and applied ubiquitously to all instruments. (Burtner 2005)

Thus, the concert flute commonly features tones in the high-frequency spectrum, if one thinks, for example, of the bird character in Sergei Prokofjew's 'Peter und der Wolf'. In Indian classical music, a number of flutes are used which are also characterized by high frequencies. For example, the bamboo flute is often used in classical music: the bansuri features predominantly in the Hindustani music of Northern India, while the venu or pullanguzhal is played in the Carnatic music of Southern India (Dutta 2008).

The crucial point with regard to Lee's flutebox technology is that he extends the conventional playing technique and thus provides the instrument with new sonic characteristics. This practice as such is not exceptional, since musicians have experimented with and extended the possible playing techniques of the concert flute since the early decades of the twentieth century at least, and across the boundaries of musical styles such as classical, modern, jazz and pop.[1] Nevertheless, what does make Lee's extended playing technique unique is both the use of beatboxing techniques, and the singularity of this specific practice in the context of contemporary urban dance music. The specificity of the sound practice of beatboxing in itself lies in the way in which sounds and rhythms are produced using mouth, lips, tongue, nasal passage and throat in order to imitate the particular sounds of a drum set, or other instruments such as the bass, and thus create the illusion of polyphonic music (Stowell and Plumbley 2008). In fact, beatboxing could be regarded as an extended technique in and of itself, extending the sonic and technical repertoire of vocalization through expressions such as panting, hissing, sucking or blowing breath through pursed lips. Unlike the limited repertoire of a bass drum, snare drum or hi-hat in a conventional drum set, a wide variety of different sounds can be created with the body. In beatboxing, the whole body becomes an instrument, a resonant body, and this therefore highlights the unique voice of each individual beatboxer. Moreover, beatboxing can also incorporate 'singing, vocal imitation of turntablism, the simulation of horns, strings, and other musical instruments' as Egyptian beatboxer Farah Abdellatif notes on her blog (Abdellatif 2009).

Fluteboxing, then, is a term Lee invented himself for this particular technique which implies a combination of flute playing and beatboxing: Lee creates rhythmic patterns with his mouth, while at the same time sending his breath and the guttural sounds he makes through the transversal hole of the flute. The fluteboxing technique thus extends the sonic and technical repertoire of the concert flute. In contrast to the sustained, airy, high-frequency flute sounds which feature in the melodic parts of his performance, when using the fluteboxing technique, the streams of compressed air which hit the transversal hole of the flute produce short thudding and low-frequency flute sounds. In so doing, Lee adds bass to the flute, while creating multi-rhythmic and polyphonic beat patterns. In this way, the flutebox technology is a transformative technology: first, it adds new frequencies and timbres to the conventional flute sound. Second, it reinvents the instrument by synthesizing new sound practices and musical repertoires. Third, it challenges the boundaries of musical styles: the confines of classical music are transgressed by applying the beatboxing technique and thus connecting it to the realm of hip-hop and urban dance music. At the same time, the typical characteristics of beatboxing and hip-hop music culture are extended by a different repertoire of sounds unique to the flute. Looking at this particular playing technique, one that is realized at the intersection of musical styles, technical conventionalities and sound qualities, fluteboxing needs to be listened to not solely as an extended playing technique, but as part of a wider framework encompassing this playing technique: a specific sound practice.

Thinking of fluteboxing as a specific sound practice in the context of urban dance music becomes relevant when looking at Lee's connection to hip-hop culture mentioned above. As far as the specific musical and cultural context of beatboxing is concerned, there is a much older tradition of vocal percussion forms which precedes the hip-hop-related form of beatboxing and can be traced back to the 1930s, 'the era of swing, jazz and barbershop music' (TyTe and Defenicial 2010). The imitation of instruments became an integral part of the rhythmic and timbral fabric of jazz music:

> 'Scatting' was used as jazz singers improvised harmonic and vocal scales over solos or instrumentals. This was the first mainstream look at what would become vocal percussion, and later beatboxing. Singers would sing made up words such as 'doot', 'wawp', 'bapadoo' and many others, effectively imitating the sounds of the two most common instruments in their music, saxophones and trumpets. (TyTe and Defenicial 2012)

Beatboxing, as it is still practised today, derived from 1980s urban music culture in the United States and Chicago, the Bronx and LA in particular, and is a practice which was adopted in many parts of the world, including the UK.

It is important, therefore, not to confine certain sound practices or playing techniques to one particular musical style, but to acknowledge the transformative potential of different sonic 'modes of production', as Théberge notes in *Any Sound You Can Imagine* in reference to the musicologist Blacking:

> Such statements beg the question of the nature of the relationship between musical instrument, sound, and idea. They also demand a more thorough consideration of a complex set of issues ranging from the intimate, physical relationship between performers and their instruments (and, not incidentally, the social relations between performers, composers, and engineers as well), to the role of instruments in the definition of musical genres and in musical change, and to broader theoretical issues concerning technology as a 'means' of production versus technology as a 'mode' of production. (Théberge 1997: 158, quting Blacking 1977)

Fluteboxing as a technology of the self

Beatboxing was a vital part of Lee's musical socialization and identification as a musician, as he told me in an interview I conducted with him in Brixton in 2008. He grew up listening to hip-hop, and started rapping and beatboxing in his teens. When he started playing the flute in his mid-twenties, he therefore approached it through his knowledge as a beatboxer and jungle MC. However, his musical influences were not confined by hip-hop; he was equally drawn to jazz and soul:

> My first influences were my friends. We all used to listen to a lot of jazz, a lot of drum'n'bass, to hip-hop, reggae, Indian music, everything really, and I just put it into the flute. (Lee 2008, personal interview)[2]

Lee uses his flute to tease out the different, contrasting sounds and rhythmic variations that are found in the aforementioned musical styles. It was only after he had already devoted himself to flute playing that he started taking lessons in Western classical music, and his practice in Indian classical music was taken up at an even later stage:

> And then I learned Indian classical, went over with MTV to India, and played with people in the desert, in Rajasthan, played with people in Bombay, in Poona and Delhi, and played with all these musicians and that helped me a bit, I mean, playing Indian music is like an ocean. I only just scratched the surface. But I am trying a little thing and mixing it with Western music. (Lee 2008, personal interview)

Lee's fluteboxing technology makes the cultural conception of the concert flute approachable as a conception which emphasizes the contrasting relationship between the characteristic sounds in Indian classical music and hip-hop. As was noted above, Lee's live performance in the Queen Elisabeth Hall performs Indian classical key sounds and hip-hop key sounds in such a way that the contrasting relationship between the different sonic qualities are emphasized. At the same time, Lee's performance moves beyond a mere 'staging of difference'. His performance is an example of a transgressive practice which reconceptualizes the instrument, as well as the conventional playing technique of the instrument, and thus challenges the performance traditions that have formed around it.

In the process, fluteboxing becomes a resource for Nathan Lee's personal identity formation. In her article 'Music as a Technology of Self', Tia DeNora studies the motivations and effects of musical experience, stating that '[m]usic is an active ingredient in the organisation of self, shifting mood, energy level, conduct style and the mode of attention and engagement with the world' (DeNora 2000: 61). She claims that:

> Music is a material that actors use to elaborate, to fill out and fill in, to themselves and to others, modes of aesthetic agency and, with it, subjective stances and identities. This, then, is what should be meant when we speak of the 'cultural construction of subjectivity' – and this is much more than an idea that culture underwrites generic structures of feeling or aesthetic agency as is implied in so many post-structuralist writings and by musicologists trained in semiotic analysis of texts. (DeNora 2000: 74)

Reading Lee's flutebox technology against essentialist discourses which regard music as a mere reflection of ethnic identity, it can be argued that the relationship of 'self and other' is reversed with regard to the assumption that his link to Indian music must be the most basic influence with regard to his own work as a musician, while the influences from British music culture are additional influences. Lee's music does not reflect some kind of traditional Indianness only because his mother is Indian. The way in which Lee approached playing the flute in the first place fundamentally challenges any such assumption. Lee's sonic technology of fluteboxing should instead be seen as part of a specific sound production culture that is rooted in urban dance music, incorporating sound practices such as sampling, turntablism, MCing or beatboxing. Culture is only constituted in the process of music making, and is influenced not merely or primarily by the 'traditional cultural heritage' of the musician, but also by actual musical preferences and diverse cultural and social affiliations.

In our interview, Lee described his practice in the following way, 'I've made the flute more aggressive, I put more bass in it. People have played the flute for years, I made it more angry-sounding' (Lee 2008, personal interview). Thus, fluteboxing becomes part of a specific 'technology of the self' (DeNora 2000), a specific sound practice, in which the instrument is re-invented by taking on some of the characteristics that Lee creates. This also works the other way around: as Lee poignantly formulated it in the same interview, he sees fluteboxing as a way to 're-invent oneself with the instrument' (Lee 2008, personal interview). The instrument, or, more precisely, the sound practice developed with the instrument also works as a tool for Lee to re-invent himself as a subject. He takes up new tools and techniques along the way, and thus, new sonic constellations emerge, new sound practices are forged. These new sonic constellations always have several dimensions, as Tia DeNora discusses in the following passage about music as a social practice:

> As a sonic medium happening over time, and also configuring time (Hanrahan 2000), music is a material of social ordering and social imagination. As such, understanding how music operates and what it does illuminates the otherwise too-often tacit bases of action, consciousness, and subjectivity. (DeNora 2008: 158)

To regard fluteboxing as a sound practice means listening to fluteboxing as a sonic technology, and as a social practice. With regard to the latter, a very important facet of Lee's flutebox technology is jamming, that is, playing together with a variety of musicians with different cultural and musical traditions and practices. From the beginning of his career as a flutebox player, he engaged in musical collaborations with various musicians such as the tabla player Hanif Khan, the beat boxer Wandan or the rapper Skrein. One could say that jamming is indispensable to how he 'writes' his music – namely through improvisation, and in jam sessions with fellow musicians.

Technology, liveness and recorded music

Lee's flutebox technology is not only significant for his live performance, but also for the recorded production of his EP *Flutebox*. The particularities of his recorded performance and the specific nature of his 'liveness' will be analysed in the following sections. The first track on Nathan 'Flutebox' Lee's EP is simply called 'Intro', and its function as an intro, rather than as a full track, is also implied in the track's length of a little less than two minutes. Significantly, this track features several cues that evoke the start of a live performance. This becomes audible right at the beginning of the track, commencing with the vocals of Kevin Amarfio, a black British hip hop MC also known as Mystro, performing a microphone check, and an introduction of the musician at the centre of attention, namely Nathan 'Flutebox' Lee: 'One/One two/One two/Ladies and Gentlemen/Introducing to you/Nathan Flutebox Lee' (Nathan 'Flutebox' Lee. 'Intro', my transcription). While the microphone is indeed checked for loudness and level balance, sometimes by repeatedly saying the words 'one two, one two' in the live music context, the 'mic check' has also become part of an aesthetic and stylized strategy of rap and hip-hop performances in which the MC takes on the role of the 'master of ceremony' (which is, suitably, what MC stands for).

Underlying the vocals, and throughout the first sequence of the track (0'00–0'22) several instruments are audible which also sound like they are in the process of preparing for the actual musical performance: a random drum whirl, a sequence of triplets on a concert flute, some low-frequency noise from a keyboard sequencer, a few notes of the upcoming melodic theme, also played with the flute. There are two short instances in which the fluteboxing sound comes in, as a fragmentary rhythmic pattern (0'10, 0'22). However, the intro is not attempting to create the illusion of a 'real' live performance, as there are several features in this sequence that clearly divert from what a recording of a live performance would sound like: this sonic scenery actually consists of a composition of different layers of samples (the MC's voice and all the instruments that feature in the recording) that were cut and rearranged so as to form a thick fabric of melody and rhythm. The samples are faded in and out, and reverb is added. Rather than being a random arrangement, the different sonic elements form a rhythmic structure in and of themselves, albeit creating a fragmentary and unfinished effect. The fact that it is recorded and that the sonic reproduction is manifest in the intro turns 'liveness' into an aesthetic effect.

On the last word of Mystro's vocals, 'Lee', the second sequence of the intro starts with the playing of a bass, accompanied by a flute melody, a beatbox pattern and a jazzy drum kit (0'23–1'05). In addition, a low-frequency synthesizer sound oscillates through the track and lends it the feel of an electronic dance music track. Moreover, the rhythmic pattern also includes the sound of inhaling breaths (0'33, 0'55, 1'18). These are instances where inhaling becomes another effect of liveness and immediacy, while at the same time being worked into the rhythmic structure of the sample-based track.

The third and last sequence of the 'Intro' (1'06–1'30) eventually introduces Lee's first fluteboxing part that sits on top of the sonic layers featured in the previous sequence. The intro ends with the low-frequency synthesizer sound standing alone.

Dog

In my analysis of the *Flutebox* EP's second track, 'Dog', special analytical attention is given to the way in which Lee's flutebox technology becomes a particular structuring element in the complex sonic composition of the track. In this case, Lee's flutebox technology becomes an agent in a sonic transformation that challenges conventionally drawn boundaries between musical styles and different cultural expressions. This track particularly exemplifies some of the aspects that were raised in the description provided above of Nathan 'Flutebox' Lee's live performance. As was pointed out, a contrasting relationship is created between the two different modes of Lee's playing of the flute – that is, the mode of playing in a melodic and airy way, mostly producing tones in the high-frequency spectrum, and the other, 'flutebox technology' mode, creating thudding and bass-intense notes by applying the beatboxing technique to the flute. This very basic principle is taken up in 'Dog' as well, but in the context of the track, this contrasting principle becomes even more complex. Here, the flutebox technology is transformed into a tool for transgression through different musical styles, playing techniques and 'electronic' production techniques.

In this instance, the overall structure and arrangement of the track is significant. It consists of a number of sections that are divided by a break in the form of complete silence that lasts for approximately one second. Each of these breaks marks a shift towards a different constellation of sounds and rhythms, or a different constellation of playing modes. In the course of the track, these shifts also mark transgressions between different musical styles. In the end, the track cannot be pinned down to one particular musical style. Therefore, the flutebox technology, itself a multilayered and multimodal sound practice, becomes an inspiration for other sonic and musical transgressions that characterize the specific sound of the *Flutebox* EP.

The first section of the track (0'00–0'30) features a dynamic interaction between the flute and the viola, which both play in varying modes. While the viola starts playing the basic melodic theme, the flute comes in after a few seconds (0'06) as if approaching from the background and slowly working itself into the foreground with staccato-like sounds produced by sending short breaths through the flute's embouchure hole. These airy tones build up in intensity, while the viola repeats the melodic theme. Subsequently, after a break of complete silence that marks a transition to the next part, the flute is in the foreground playing the melody line that was played by the viola, while the viola continues playing in the background, in a delayed mode that is created through playing sustained notes that extend the shorter notes played by the flute. The interaction between the two instruments works in a call and response way in which each instrument takes up melodic or rhythmic cues from the other instrument. Broadly speaking, there is a resonance with jazz improvisation aesthetics. These aesthetics are counteracted, however, by a sub-bass tone that is played by a synthesizer, creating a vibratory base to the melodic part. At the end of this section, just before the next break, the flute stands alone, introducing the transition into the fluteboxing mode by transforming 'thick' and saturated tones into 'thin' and sharp ones.

After the break (0'31), a flutebox solo comes in (0'32–0'44). This section not only marks a shift in the playing mode from flute melody to flutebox, but also establishes sonic characteristics that allude to grime track aesthetics. In the second part of the section, the fast and syncopated rhythmic pattern created by the fluteboxing technology is accompanied by a heavy and creaking bass line that turns into a full grime pattern in the section that follows the next break (0'46–0'48).

In the following section (1'00–1'28), the arrangement of the first sequence is repeated, featuring the dynamic interplay of flute and viola. In this part, thudding breath sounds are added in short intervals, forming part of the underlying beat pattern. The sonic and rhythmic constellations are then further varied, including flute, viola, drums and bass. Afterwards, rapper Skrein performs a rap which corresponds to grime beat patterns (2'53–3'39).

After another round of the track's basic theme (3'40–4'08), the last sequence is introduced (4'09–4'39), featuring an instrumental wind-up in which the sound of inhaling breath is accompanied by the rapper's voice: '[drag]/uh/that tastes good/haha/[drag]/yeah/[drag]/yeah' (Nathan 'Flutebox' Lee 'Dog', my transcription). This last portion evokes the image of someone enjoying marijuana, which has an ironic effect that invokes a rupture from the seriousness that is often expected from a 'proper' musical recording. The criss-crossing of different musical styles and genres is reflected in this spontaneous form of musical performance that is usually reserved for the live performance, but that here becomes a structuring and stylistic element of recorded music production.

Interlude

The track 'Interlude' suitably describes not another full musical track, but a spontaneous situation that occurred in the recording studio. The track begins with a few notes on the flute played by Lee and a few chords played on the piano in a random, and seemingly directionless mode. What is significant about this interlude is the communication that occurs between the two musicians, or, more precisely, between the verbal and sonic utterances. The following transcription of Nathan's direct quotes and the sonic utterances of pianist Maquenzie (in square brackets) illustrates this call-and-response:

> Do those [two chords, abrupt cut, then silence]
> Do those other ones, Ross, don't, like, let's do the, let's
> jazz [single chord] one's yeah the more
> that one yeah man
> [two chords].
> (Nathan 'Flutebox' Lee 'Interlude', my transcription)

After the last two chords, and after a silent break of a fragment of a second, Lee and Maquenzie start playing a piece together, the flute sounds accompanying the piano sounds. The fact that this 'Interlude' is included in the EP is another instance of liveness as a structuring element in the sonic narrative of the recording.

Cover art

The EP cover and four-page booklet is designed to place the presentation of the music in a hip-hop context. The front cover shows the EP's title, *Flutebox* in golden lettering, as in a logo. The symbolic attributes of the design are clearly assigned to old school hip-hop aesthetics, featuring curved letters and a crown on a black background, as well as a crown that sits on top of the logo, and a speaker membrane that substitutes the title's 'o'. The only other 'design' element is the 'Parental Advisory: Explicit Content' stamp, a label that is used by record labels in order to mark explicit lyrical content in sound recordings.

The portraits of the artist Lee which feature on the second and third pages of the eight-page booklet further underscore associations with the 'dark' and 'edgy' connotations of hip-hop as a ghetto culture, being shot in black and white in a narrow alleyway with brick walls that rear up at each side. One photograph stands out in particular; it depicts Lee glancing in the camera with narrowed eyes while placing the flute between his bared teeth like a belligerent dog defending his stick. The following two pages of the booklet are covered with a collage of more than one hundred photographs depicting Nathan Lee at various ages and accompanied by friends, family and fellow musicians. The collage can indeed be regarded as displaying the multiple musical, social and cultural networks of which Lee's *Flutebox* EP is a product. This multiplicity also resonates in the music. However, as was demonstrated in the analysis, the investigation of sonic narratives requires different approaches in order not to reproduce the music-as-cultural-reflection paradigm. Hidden under the part of the CD case which carries the CD, a recipe for 'South London Daal' is displayed in curved handwriting that might be a reference to Lee's familiarity with Indian food. The music and the recipe bear no obvious relation. But in cooking a dish, like in recording a record, the ingredients and the techniques have to go through a process in which the different elements form a chemical, or a sonic bond, and the result remains opaque (although there is an aspiration of something) until the dish, or the composition is actually finished and can be tasted, or listened to.

Conclusion

To conclude, this chapter argues that, rather than being confined to fixed musical and cultural conceptions, Nathan Lee's sound practice produces ruptures that transgress the boundaries of musical traditions, listening conventions and cultural conceptions. As was demonstrated in this chapter, trying to attach a stable notion of Indianness to Nathan 'Flutebox' Lee's music in order to establish it as a prime marker of his musical expression would mean to artificially maintain an outdated model of cause and effect: because Lee has an Indian cultural heritage, his music is an expression of that heritage. The previous examples have demonstrated that this model, one based on binary oppositions such as traditional and modern or East and West, is not applicable to the complex sound practices of transcultural electronic dance music in the UK.

What differentiates Lee's sound practices from those of Apache Indian's, for example, is that the question of how Indianness is negotiated in Lee's music requires a subtle way of listening. In the analysis of Apache Indian's music, samples from Bollywood or Indian classical music functioned as *sonic ornaments*, that is, sounds that had Indian connotations that were 'staged' in the new musical context of reggae dancehall tracks. Moreover, Apache Indian's sound practices, including his lyrical performance and lyrics, constructed a dialogic relationship between Indian and British sounds, languages and vocalizations. While these sound practices emphasize a contrasting relation of 'music' and 'culture', which partly had the effect of reinforcing binaries and partly worked as a transgressive practice, this kind of framework does not apply to Nathan 'Flutebox' Lee's music.

Instances in Lee's sound practices in which Indian sounds become part of the sonic fabric of the music always need to be regarded as part of the development of musical ideas, and should not primarily be seen as markers of an 'Indian' cultural expression.

It was therefore useful to analyse Lee's flutebox technology, as this playing technique and sound practice emphasize the permeability of different musical styles, conventions and practices that transgress cultural essentialisms. In appropriating beatboxing techniques for the flute, Lee applies bass to the high-frequency orientation of the classical repertoire of flute sounds, and in this way dissolves the essential link that is conventionally postulated between musical styles and their technical means of creation. The bass that is added to the flute through the beatboxing technique becomes a key sound in applying the 'classical' attributes of the flute, and the Indian scales that are played, for a hip-hop context.

Especially in the context of the studio recordings of the *Flutebox* EP, the relationship between a 'real' instrument and 'electronic' music production is complicated even further, as the flutebox sounds become part of the electronically arranged grime beat patterns, and fragments of the flute sounds are sampled and played back as overlapping layers of sound in the tracks.

Moreover, as was demonstrated with regard to the recordings, the opposition between 'liveness' and 'recordedness' is dissolved. 'Liveness' is represented in the studio recordings as an aesthetic strategy which firmly situates the music on the *Flutebox* EP in the context of hip-hop music culture.

From the perspective of a cultural analysis of Nathan 'Flutebox' Lee's music, this case study challenges any analytical approach which tries to pin down this music's 'Indianness', neither can it be captured as taking place in a hybrid 'third space' (Bhaba 1994) of cultural negotiation. Instead, the notion of transcultural sound practices connotes here an engagement across and through a variety of sonic repertoires that works with materialities and intensities, rather than specific cultural connotations.

7

The Sonic Politics of Place: Dusk + Blackdown's *Margins Music* (2008)

This chapter explores the relevant sound practices in *Margins Music*, the 2008 album by London-based producers Dan Frampton, also known as Dusk and Martin Clark, also known as Blackdown who form the production team Dusk + Blackdown. A particular focus lies on the way in which South Asian sound samples become the raw material in the producer's creation of a diverse and multilayered, yet distinct sound and problematizes the use of South Asian sounds by white British producers. Without aiming to provide a universal answer to this question of aesthetics and ethics in South Asian dance music, this chapter explores the complicated relationship of sound practices, sonic materialities and politics of place. I understand the materiality of sound in the way it is conceptualized by Peter Wicke, who emphasizes the difference between recorded sound, that is sound that is produced as part of a studio production, and sound in the live performance, as decisive in the creation of contemporary popular music:

> In the studio, it is not only music-making, but also the material in which this is executed, the sonic materiality of the music, that has been undergoing profound modification. By this is meant not merely the various technical interventions that may be made into the sound character, such as modifications of the frequency using an equalizer [...] or the technical synthesis of sounds. What is meant, in a much more fundamental sense, is the way in which the physical parameters of sound are connected with the aesthetic parameters of the music - in brief, the way sound is conceptualized as music-making material. (Wicke 2009: 147-148)

The album is greatly influenced by contemporary UK dance music styles - grime and dubstep in particular - which create the backbone of all the tracks on the album. Another focus of analysis is how Dusk + Blackdown's use of interview footage and environmental sounds create the substance for a sonic reconfiguration of place which locates the music in urban space and, as I will argue, generates specific notions of London's geographic and social coordinates.

The concrete sound practices in Dusk + Blackdown's music will be investigated against the backdrop of the commentary on the focus on ethnically defined urban dance music. Georg Gatsas, an artist and journalist who has been documenting South-East London's grime and dubstep scene, argues that in contrast to African-Caribbean music styles such as dub and dancehall which entered London's dance music scene in the 1970s and 1980s, Drum'n'Bass of the 1990s, and particularly Grime and Dubstep of the 2000s, grew increasingly independent from the music's cultural heritage in Jamaica and became genuinely linked to London:

> Grime, Dubstep and Funky are soaking up the acoustic legacy of preceding generations like a sponge – this time without any hierarchical cultural divide or hype, straight from the streets of South London, places like Croydon, Brixton and Camberwell. This music is dynamic, confident, and is constantly redefining itself: hybrid Dancefloor, impossible to ethnically categorise, thuds with deep bass vibrating in the equality of the present. The producers are usually not much older than 20, and all have their own distinctive styles. They bring their own unique mix of influences, their individual way of working and their own idiosyncrasies into play. (Gatsas 2009)

With regard to the various statements of musicians, producers and club-owners I interviewed in London in 2008, I agree with Gatsas' observations concerning the fluidity of the grime and dubstep scene which seems less concerned with ethnic boundaries than with the drum and bass orientation as a common denominator. South Asian sounds feature in dubstep productions by producers of various cultural backgrounds, not only British Asian, examples of which are Horsepower's 'Sholay (Epic Mix)' (2004), Loefa's 'Indian Dub' (2004), DJ Wonder's 'Asia' (2004), Kode 9's 'Sub-Kontinent' (2004) and Kode 9 and The Spaceape's 'Fukkaz' (2006). This means not to oversimplify the music's various cultural, social and aesthetic practices and politics by simply stating that this music has become universal and non-hierarchical. What makes Gatsas' point relevant with regard to the questions investigated in this chapter is the fact that these emergent music styles are based on a common ground that can be called, with dubstep producer and scholar Steve Goodman, 'dub materialism', signified by the ubiquity of the sub-bass. As Goodman put it in an interview I conducted with him in 2008:

The bass holds it all together, it's like the glue, literally the glue that holds anything together so you can throw in whatever sounds you want. I always think of it as a big blob, like a huge big blob, that's the bass, and you can just throw things into that blob, and what holds all of these different elements together is this big blobby sub-bass sound. (Goodman 2008, personal interview)[1]

Therefore, while being aware of the embeddedness of urban dance music in African-Diasporic music culture, rather than overemphasizing the 'African-Caribbeanness' or 'Asianness' of the music, the use of bhangra or Bollywood sounds has become part of the urban dance music repertory beyond ethnic confines. However, a differentiation needs to be made between the concrete sound practices that create sonic discourses beyond 'hierarchical cultural divide or hype' (as noted above in Gatsas' quote) and the discourses about new musical talents and musical styles, which still tend to play the exoticism card. Dubstep producer Sara Abdel-Hamid, also known as Ikonika, reminds us that non-white artists do still have to work against ethnicizing (and gendered) categorizations which do not have anything to do with the music itself. This is made clear in the following statement she made in an interview with *The Guardian*:

'Some little blog called me the M.I.A. of dubstep', she snorts. 'Is it a Hounslow thing or to do with the colour of my skin? It's not the music. People have called me a Muslim producer because of my surname. I'm not even a Muslim. Would they call Skream a white, male, Christian producer? I hate this "first lady of dubstep" shit. Do they think I go around consciously thinking about my gender? I'm trying to see the funny side of it, though'. (Macpherson 2010, quoting Ikonika)

Therefore, Dusk + Blackdown constitute one facet in the loose assemblage of dubstep artists who pursue very different artistic and cultural strategies.

'Darker Than East'

The following analysis investigates the sound practices in the opening track of Dusk + Blackdown's *Margins Music*, 'Darker Than East'. The auditory footage which the track is based on was recorded by Martin Clark during his visit to the studio of East London grime crew *Roll Deep*, a group of MCs and DJs that was founded in 2003.[2] Clark conducted an interview with one of its members,

DJ Target, in front of the studio building, and these recordings were used for the production of this grime track.

'Darker Than East' begins with an amalgam of speech fragments and ambient noises that immediately evoke a rich world of imaginations for the listener: a group of young men, somewhere in the street, in random conversation – cheerful laughs, boisterous shouts, car noises. Most of the words are incomprehensible, because they are interrupted by other comments or are too far off in the background, to the effect that the listener gets immersed in a multilayered sound-bubble rather than being concentrated on a specific noise or comment. When listening more closely, the presence of the recording microphone becomes audible through the wind that creates a rustling noise on its surface. Against the background of this sonic scenery a sonorous male voice comes in (0'15), addressing the listener directly, speaking closely into the microphone so that the sound gets slightly distorted. Simultaneously, a police siren is wailing in the background: 'Where we are right now, there's a police siren running perfectly in the back-ground. We're in Wilehouse, it's – it's called Limehouse, we've been around here for years since we were little nippers running around doin' water fights' (Dusk + Blackdown 'Darker Than East', my transcription).

Subsequently, this statement is repeated, and this time the lyrics are accompanied by a bass line (0'28). The bass plays sustained notes which are located on frequencies of around 60 Hz. These very low frequencies which are referred to as sub-bass in dance music terminology are particularly characteristic for the darker side of grime and dubstep. Only now, as the bass comes in, it can be realized that the vocal footage becomes part of a musical track, and the speaker becomes a vocalist. The speech sample and the voices and noises in the background now noticeably indicate a rhythmic structure which matches the rhythm of the bass line. This indicates that not only the quoted statement was sampled, but the whole sonic scenery which is introduced at the beginning of the track is already a complex composition of sampled speech. The raw audio footage that had been collected was cut into pieces and then put together again differently in order to form a sound collage with a particular rhythmic structure. The sound collage is fourteen seconds long and was looped – and this loop runs through the track as its persistent rhythmic spine. Moreover, the length of the loop exactly matches the length of the sampled statement. The effect of this specific sound practice of layering everyday sounds and speech is that the sampled speech conveys meaning not primarily as linguistic content, but as part of a sonic narrative which is constituted as rhythm. It is in the way in which the audio footage is recontextualized and manipulated that a specific notion of liveness and dynamic interaction between speech, noise and spatiality is evoked which could not be captured in the uncut version of the original audio footage. Here I come back to the reference I made in Chapter 3 with regard to Mark Katz' claim that: 'Sampling is most fundamentally an art of transformation. A sample changes the moment it is relocated' (Katz 2004: 156). Following this thought, the statement that is derived from interview footage is transformed into song lyrics through its recontextualization in 'Darker Than East'. Moreover, to come back to the evocation of liveness in 'Darker Than East', the sound practice of sampling also transforms spatiality in altering the dynamics between speech and music through a new rhythmicization of sound.

As far as the content of the lyrics is concerned, they deal with a specific place in which police sirens belong inherently to the everyday soundscape. Narrating his lyrics from a 'we'-perspective, the speaker seems to be part of the group that is heard in the background. 'We've been around here for years' indicates that the place is familiar, and, 'since we were little nippers runnin' around doin' water fights' describes the familiarity amongst the people who live in the area. The place is explicitly called both 'Wilehouse' and 'Limehouse'. While Limehouse refers to the Southeast London district, Wilehouse is a chosen name, re-naming the official designation of the district. This re-naming is significant, because it constitutes more than mere wordplay. Rather, Wilehouse is saturated with very specific experiences and incidences that are connected with the area. The reference to wildness indicates the roughness of Limehouse, an area often connected with poverty, gang politics and police violence. Moreover, the re-naming is an act of creating a strong sense of collectivity and community. As such, wildness also indicates solidarity and power of those who belong to this specific area. Later in the track (2'37), the lyrics continue:

> The postcode is E14 [...] this is called Wilehouse, it used to be Limehouse, but because things are so wild around there, it just had been called Wilehouse [...] W.I.L.E. – WILE-house [...] The police are not sure, they come 'round roll six up. (Dusk + Blackdown 'Darker Than East', my transcription)

This part of the lyrics further emphasizes the deep connectivity which is established with the area. The reference to E14 depicts more than just the postcode; it expresses a strong identification with the area and a precise knowledge about how things 'work' there. Knowing about Wilehouse can be conceived of as a form of subcultural capital,[3] because it is acquired insider knowledge which is hidden in the double meaning of Wilehouse and further encoded through the use of street slang (wile instead of wild). The re-naming is thus an act of knowledge production and thereby creates a sense of owning the place: 'It used to be Limehouse' emphasizes that the place is no longer owned solely by the official representatives of the district. In this sense, 'The police are not sure, they come 'round role six up' signals the uncontrollability of the area – which further enhances the value of belonging to those who control the area in their own terms. Therefore, while Limehouse denotes a geographical place, Wilehouse connotes a socially located place.

Proceeding with the analysis of the track, the sampled statement is looped a second time and then faded out so that the sound-collage stands alone again, accompanied by the bass line and a grime beat pattern. The beat consists of a bass drum and a clap playing a minimalistic pattern characteristic for grime tracks. Subsequently, the grime pattern is enriched by other musical elements. The grime pattern becomes the dominant sound, while the sound collage of speech and street noises increasingly shifts to the background. Only here and there, its more prominent sound figures, such as the background comment 'let me answer my call', stick out.

Taking into account the rhythmical and repetitive form of the sound collage, other more evanescent spatialities are created. As the spoken words are interwoven into the dynamics of a musical track, the words are perceived as melodic rhythm. The lyrics increasingly merge with the background sound collage with every new repetition. When at the beginning of the track, a scene was created in which the listener could trace very tangible spatial signposts – the announcement of the name of the place (Limehouse/Wilehouse), police siren, background chatter – the repetition has the effect that the scene becomes increasingly intangible and abstract for the listener. The recognizable background chatter becomes accentuated rhythm, the spoken words become sound. Rather than listening to a linear story of a distinct geographically situated place, the listener is somehow caught in a feedback loop of noises and rhythms. The repetition has the effect of foregrounding the rhythmic and melodic attributes of the track which opens up an imaginary space for the listener which is no longer delimited by the tangible coordinates of Limehouse/Wilehouse.

With regard to the sampling practice and the complex recontextualization of noises and speech, this track displays a creative reinterpretation of the connection between sound, music and spatiality. In this regard, following Lipsitz's notion, a specific poetics of place is created in 'Darker Than East': the reference to 'Wilehouse' does not simply represent a geographically locatable place, but becomes an imagined space which is unstable and evanescent. In the context of the aesthetic practice pursued in producing the track, the sonic references to a specific place become the raw material of a musical idea. This aesthetic dimension is complemented by a sonic politics of place in which street sounds are aesthetically formed so as to amplify the street-credibility of the acclaimed Roll-Deep crew, an aspect which probably was also intended to help the artists Dusk + Blackdown to raise their own credibility.

The opening track 'Darker Than East' can be regarded as an entry point to the album as a whole. Bass-saturated sounds, dark frequencies, street slang and urban dance music rhythms are emphasized throughout the album, and thus the South Asian-inflected sounds which feature in 'Kuri Pataka', for instance, are perceived against the background of this specific sonic fabric, as will be demonstrated in the following analysis.

'Kuri Pataka' (The Firecracker Girl)

The track 'Kuri Pataka' (The Firecracker Girl)' begins with a sample of a Hindi tune[4] featuring a male singer uttering his lyrics a capella. The voice sounds clear and lucid: 'Koyee aakhe pariya dhee rani/Chaal eh dhee mathvaale/ Koyee aakh bagaarh licencee eh koyee rifl dhunaree' ('Kuri Pataka', text printed in CD booklet). The a capella sample, which runs for thirteen seconds, is accompanied by sparsely applied single strokes of a bass creating a gloomy melody. Each stroke of the bass is echoed by a delicate synthesizer sound. This section is repeated, and percussive elements are added to the track (0'14). The percussion features tabla breaks and a syncopated bass drum.[5] While the first impression is that the bass and beats follow the rhythmic structure of the vocal sample and thus function as mere accompaniment of the vocal track, it can be recognized by the end of the second line that the rhythm of the vocal part does not match exactly with the consistent beat that the bass has introduced and which now clearly creates the rhythmic lead. In the next part, the vocals are repeated, and subsequently another short vocal sample of the same Hindi tune is added (0'28), accompanied by a melodic figure that is played by a tumbi:[6] 'Vee fare odhaa fookah na jaavay' ('Kuri Pataka', text printed in CD booklet).

The sequence which features this short vocal functions as a bridge from the previous vocal part to the following instrumental part. For this purpose, a very small sequence of the tone that sits on the last syllabus [ay] of the short vocal sample was cut out and looped to the effect that the tone is extended as if the singer held the tone for a long time. It becomes clear that the tone is not held naturally because it will run through the track for forty-six seconds at exactly the same pitch (0'30–1'16). The looping of the tone on [ay] causes a superficial vibrato, and a reverb has been added which further alienates the voice of the singer from its 'human' connotation. Thus the sampling and further manipulation of the Hindi tune can be regarded as an act of transformation in which the human voice is transformed into an instrumental sound in a dubstep track. This sonic transformation also generates a narrative shift in the track from a characteristic song structure to a dance music track. Subsequently, the beat pattern consisting of tabla and bass continue, while a heavy sub-bass sound is added (0'48), which marks a further shift towards dubstep aesthetics.

However, there is another twist to the heavy sub-bass sound that was just mentioned. This sound was not generated by plug-in synthesizers, as might have been expected from a straightforward dubstep production. Rather, the string section of a Bollywood tune was sampled, and the strings were pitched down to the sub-bass level (0'48). At this sub-bass level, the strings are no longer identifiable as strings, but sound much more like a synthesized bass. The underlying Bollywood tune only becomes audible a few bars later, when the bass frequency is decreased again and the melodic line of the original strings (re-)emerges (0'57). This instance demonstrates another transformative shift, in which the characteristic sonic feature of the Bollywood strings, the high pitch, is manipulated and thus no longer functions as a Bollywood key sound. Only when the pitch is gradually reconstructed, the sound regains its recognizability as Bollywood key sound. What is significant about this sound practice is that the shift from Bollywood to dubstep and back is staged in an almost transitionless way – the exact moment when Bollywood key sounds become dubstep key sounds is hardly detectable. Listening to the track in this way, the idea of 'bass materialism' becomes tangible which Steve Goodman develops in his book *Sonic Warfare*. Bass materialism implies the construction of a 'vibrational ecology' centring on low-end frequencies (Goodman 2010). With regard to grime and dubstep production culture, bass materialism can be regarded as the core principle of this sound practice which is constituted of the affective and material quality of frequencies. The way in which the Hindi vocal is cut, looped, and layered in 'Kuri Pataka' demonstrates the *musical* engagement with the sample as sonic raw material, rather than an engagement with a particular

Indian musical tradition. Here, the practice of the 'dub materialist' becomes comparable to the practice of a scientist who works very closely with the sonic material as the core fabric, and the filters as the experimental tools. In this sound practice, the Hindi sample is processed through the aesthetic and technological practices of contemporary London dance music. In this way, it takes on 'some of the character of its new sonic environment' (Katz 156). It becomes a key sound which functions as a specific sonic facet of the dubstep track. This effect is further emphasized in the following section in which the sample is repeated again, this time accompanied by a rhythmic pattern featuring a whole drum kit, as well as tablas and a bass line. When, suddenly, the sound of rewinding magnetic tape comes in, this signals a break that is followed by an altogether different sonic sphere, as the following analysis demonstrates.

There is another significant sound practice in 'Kuri Pataka' which marks another notable shift in the sonic composition of the track: The voice of Farrah Jarral, a British Asian singer from London, is introduced, singing a melodic vocal. The vocal features sustained notes, which effectively slows down the track, and the added reverb effect causes a widening of the 'virtual' musical space. Against the background of the sustained melody which works as an Indian key sound, short fragments of Teji's vocals are added to the mix. Rather than being faded in and out, the lyrical fragments have a 'cut-off' and 'edgy' quality which is known to be created in the scratching practice which relates to old-school hip-hop and the art of turntablism. This sound practice generates a syncopated rhythm which counteracts with the sustained notes of the vocal melody. In comparison with the beginning of the track, where the a capella Hindi tune constructs an Indian key sound, in this part of the track, it is transformed into a hip-hop key sound. The listener's attention no longer rests on the sample's 'Indianness', because the fragmentation of the sample lacks any phonetic similarity with the Hindi lyrics, and, more importantly, the attention remarkably shifts to the sound practice itself, namely the production aesthetic of scratching.

Another aspect becomes evident when considering the relationship between the female vocals and the lyrical content of 'Kuri Pataka' (The Firecracker Girl)'. In the previous part of the analysis, the lyrics have been treated only with regard to their musical function, and not with regard to their content. This is also due to the fact that they are in Hindi and therefore not accessible to non-speakers of Hindi. However, a translation of the lyrics into English was added in the booklet. In the lyrics, a woman is described as 'the queen of the angels/she has a sensuous walk', but of whom one has to be aware because 'getting involved with her is as dangerous as owning an unlicensed double-barrelled shotgun' (Dusk + Blackdown 'Kuri Pataka', lyrics printed in booklet). It is also an image which resonates with Bollywood movies in which the female protagonist 'entices the boys/and they lose their hearts to her'. In translating the lyrics, their quality as sonic 'raw' material is further questioned, as every linguistic translation also has a cultural, and in this case probably a rather culturalistic, dimension. As I learned from my interview with Martin Clark (whose stage name is Blackdown, as was already mentioned above), the translation of the lyrics was made by a friend's grandmother, who was able to understand the form of Hindi that is used in the tune which relates to traditional Hindi poetry. A question which is relevant concerning my analysis is how these lines function in the context of the present track: although the lyrics can be said to derive from a specific Hindi poetry tradition, the imagery which is evoked in the lyrics about India resonate well with popular music from the 1970s and 1980s, by the Beatles and other bands who used Indian melodies in order to construct images of women as attractive, exotic and dangerous creatures (cf. The Beatles' 'Norwegian Wood'), much like the image that is established in the lyrics of the Hindi tune in 'Kuri Pataka'. Connecting the lyrical content of the Hindi tune with the female vocal of Farrah, the construction of exoticist imagery is emphasized through the ephemeral quality of the vocal sound. Significantly, the female protagonist sung of in the lyrics does not have her own voice: 'the boys watch her closely,' but from a distance, while 'she' remains inarticulate. Unlike the various dissonances and discontinuities which are created with regard to the male vocal sample, there is no notable twist that productively reworks the formulaic function of the female vocal in the otherwise multifaceted and hybrid sonic narrative of the track.

In 'Darker Than East' and 'Kuri Pataka' (The Firecracker Girl), complex sonic fictions are created in treating Indian key sounds as part of the production culture of grime and dubstep, which challenges the cultural politics of Indianness and Britishness. I argue that 'bass materialism' bears the potential of hybridizing fixed notions of Indianness by treating Indian key sounds as part of the sonic fabric of bass culture. Sampling practices play a key role here in dislocating sounds from their 'original' connotation and transforming them into an imaginary 'poetics of place'. However, 'Kuri Pataka' also shows that within the context of urban dance music, orientalisms may still surface when Indian key sounds are used, for instance, so as to construct images of Indian women as exotic, sensuous and dangerous, and thus ethnic and gendered stereotypes are reinforced.

'Rolling Raj Deep'

A more interesting and inventive sound practice is developed by Dusk + Blackdown in working with an archive of sounds found on Bollywood records. The notion to conceive of sampled sounds as sonic raw material is particularly remarkable with regard to the sound practices in Dusk + Blackdown's track 'Rolling Raj Deep'. The track is entirely created from more than forty samples that were extracted from different Bollywood records that Martin Clark bought in a record store in West London's district Southall. The sound fragments were recontextualized and manipulated so as to form an altogether new track. In this track, some samples that are used consist of longer sections that can be identified as sound fragments relating to Bollywood music, while others are manipulated beyond recognition. The rhythmic pattern that the track starts with, for instance, is recognizable as a Bollywood beat featuring dhol and tabla drums (0'00). However, the sample is looped and repeated almost throughout the whole track. Rather than unfolding as a full Bollywood song, it remains in this repetitive mode and thus functions as the basic layer of the track which becomes an amalgam of various other layers of sound. Other Bollywood key sounds feature at different points in the track, such as a fragment of a string section (0'21), a male Hindi vocal (0'48) and a female Hindi vocal (1'58), signalling a liminal and obscured presence of the musical source(s). There are other instances in the track which feature sounds that are taken from the Bollywood records as well, but that are manipulated in order to become recognizable within a completely different musical repertoire. This is audible in a section of the track in which sounds are processed through a filter and manipulated in such a way that a monotonously pulsating, creaking sound is created resulting in a dark sonic connotation (0'07–0'41). In another section, different string samples are rearranged in such a way that they generate a completely new melodic composition (2'02–2'29). The high-pitched strings are looped and re-looped, layered and re-layered, and additionally pitched so that they start to sound like the repetitive, hypnotic and trance-like acid-house productions that started to developed in the UK in the mid-1980s. In another section of the track (2'37–3'13), some Bollywood samples were pitched down so as to tease out their sub-bass frequencies, which makes them function as dubstep key sounds. Dubstep key sounds means here sounds which have features that are characteristic in dubstep.

This example demonstrates a specific way in which the boundaries of sounds that cite musical works, and sounds that are entirely electronically created are blurred. In 'Rolling Raj Deep', the sound practice of sampling creates a complex and dynamic interplay of Bollywood and dubstep key sounds: The catchiness and cheerfulness of Bollywood tunes is transformed into the nagging and dragging messiness of slowed-down drum'n'bass tracks.[7] The sonic narrative is characterized by inconsistencies and unforeseeable turns which re-imagines Bollywood music through the sonic, technical and performative practices of electronic dance music. However, the sound practice of sampling in 'Rolling Raj Deep' does not respond to the Bollywood tunes as a clear reference to the horn section of the *Rocky* theme 'Gonna Fly Now'. Rather, the track is constructed in a seamless way which is guided by the idea of a 'dub materialist' dance track. The Bollywood samples become key sounds in realizing this idea. Therefore, any attempt to trace the snippets of sound back to its source is simply impossible. They become audible only in an already electronically reproduced and mutated form.

In this way, the sounds that are extracted from the Bollywood records are key sounds that are different from other key sounds that were analysed so far. In M.I.A.'s 'Bucky Done Gun', for instance, which is an adaptation of a song by Deize Tigrona, the sample of the horn section of the *Rocky* theme 'Gonna Fly Now' that features in Deize Tigrona's track is reappropriated in M.I.A.'s track as a clear and recognizable reference which can be traced, if so intended, in numerous other pop music productions. The sonic narrative created here is based on the key sound's recognition value and its specific sound practices of recontextualization. In contrast, the samples that are used in Dusk + Blackdown's track defy any recognition of or fixation to a specific song. In this way, the key sounds in 'Rolling Raj Deep' also defy any characterization as sonic ornaments, that is, static sonic signifiers. They are, unlike Apache Indian's use of Hindi film music vocals which have an 'ornamental' effect, transgressing any culturally specific or orientalist fixations.

The poetics and politics of place

In this chapter's analysis of Dusk + Blackdown's music, the particular *production culture* was highlighted. Here, production culture was primarily used to depict the aesthetic repertoire (i.e. sub-bass sounds and syncopated beats) and technological tools (i.e. sampling and filtering) that feature in the music. In order to elaborate the poetics and politics of place this production culture conveys, it is also worth further contextualizing the mediatedness of the Indian key sounds which feature on *Margins Music*. The point with this is to demonstrate that the keynote sounds do not have a clearly delineable 'origin' in India, but that they are already remediated and dislocated previously to their appearance in the sonic repertoire of Dusk + Blackdown's production. Four examples are emphasized to illustrate this:

1) The track 'Kuri Pataka' (The Firecracker Girl) is based on a Hindi folk tune with the same title which was recorded in a studio in the Punjab. Martin Clark bought this vocal from VIP records in Edinburgh, a company which cooperates with the studio in the Punjab and specializes in distributing recordings of a variety of Indian songs to producers in the UK. As Blackdown explained in my 2008 interview with him, it proved difficult for him to get to know the singer's name, as the Punjabi studio hires singers and musicians who are mostly not represented by a music label or music publisher. The names of the singers are usually not announced. Moreover, as most of the songs that are recorded are often only orally transmitted folk tunes, they are regarded as non-copyrighted works.[8] However, Clark wanted to include the singer in his credits, since he features so prominently in 'Kuri Pataka', and, after some difficulties, he finally got hold of the singer's name, Teji, through VIP.

2) The tumbi which features in 'Kuri Pataka' was played by Kush Arora, an Asian-American musician and producer from San Francisco who has worked across diverse genres such as bhangra, dub, punk and various electronic music styles. His music is also led by an interest in Punjabi-derived musical traditions, and he plays the stringed tumbi as well as the algoze flute (Nachmann 2009). The recordings of the tumbi were made at Martin Clark's studio in London, and samples from this recording session were then cut, looped and filtered in order to fit into the track.

3) The track 'Rolling Raj Deep' is based on more than forty samples of Indian Bollywood records which were rearranged and manipulated so as to sound like an electronic dance music track. The Bollywood records which feature on 'Rolling Raj Deep' were bought from a record store in Southall, an area of London which is primarily inhabited by the Punjabi and Sikh community. This area is also regarded as one of the birth places of British bhangra music, and this is where the term 'Southall sound' was coined in order to depict this emerging new music scene. Moreover, it is also the place where the first Asian British radio station, Sunrise radio,

was established. The ABC music shop, where Martin Clarke bought the Bollywood records, also played a crucial role from the 1980s onwards in distributing Indian music (From Bollywood to bhangra and classical music) and Bollywood films to their Southall neighbourhood. When Bollywood sounds became popular in mainstream hip-hop and r'n'b productions, US producer Timbaland went to this store in order to buy stacks of Bollywood records.

4) Guest singer Farrah Abdellatif, who features in 'Kuri Pataka' (The Firecracker Girl), 'Con/Fusion' and 'Iqbal's Groove', grew up in London with her Punjabi parents. In an interview with Melissa Bradshaw, a journalist who has been documenting London's dubstep scene from its beginnings in 2005, she describes her approach to Indian music and notes that it was through a childhood friend that she was exposed to Indian classical music:

> I don't have any training in classical Indian music I just knew that scale because when I was little my best friend, who is Sri-Lankan Tamil used to have classical Indian singing lessons. And they have this instrument, I don't know what it's called but it has this sort of frequency knob on it and it emits the sounds of a stringed instrument, and it goes 'bong bong boonggg boonggg',[9] and that's the backdrop to all their scales. We used to muck about with it and try and beatbox over it and whatever, and she taught me some of the scales of what she was learning. And that particular one always stayed with me. (Bradshaw 2008, quoting Jarral)

What these examples illustrate is that there is a transnational dimension to the process of sonic mediation, which cannot be confined to a binary relationship between India and England. Dusk + Blackdown do not, in any straightforward way, engage with Indian music as a homogeneous and traditional corpus. Rather, they deal with remediated, dislocated and fragmented notions of Indian music and culture. Therefore, rather than trying to trace the meanings of the Indian key sounds in their Indian heritage, it is much more productive to explore the various nodes to which these different key sounds are linked, and how this linkage adds to the production of specific meanings. In the context of *Margins Music*, these multiple linkages become part of the creation of a specific, imaginary notion of London – this soundtrack of London actually consists of various soundtracks which interact in this sonic fiction.

It is significant in this context how Bradshaw sums up a comment Martin Clark made in an interview she conducted with him:

The point he made to me was that as such he could never really have any encounter with 'the east' except as something purely fantastic; but nevertheless he experienced the presence of 'the east' in London on a daily basis. (Bradshaw 2008)

The point that is made in the above statement is relevant with regard to the imaginary sonic fictions of Dusk + Blackdown's production. Rather than judging the tracks on the album as 'authentic' expressions of Indian culture, the tracks create sonic fictions which include sonic *versions* of culture which are neither purely Indian nor purely British, and which are received through the production culture of contemporary London dance music. There is a specific 'poetics of place' (Lipsitz 1994) which is created on *Margins Music* with regard to London – the album is compiled so as to be perceived as a soundtrack of London. London becomes an imagined space in reference to which the musical ideas are localized, and thus realized.

However, this does not mean that the product that emerges from this engagement is per se replete of any 'orientalist' or exoticizing connotations. To deal with Indian key sounds is always also to deal with their embeddedness in postcolonial imageries, although the musical outcome might not be restricted to these imageries. This will be further explored with regard to the conceptualization of the album by Dusk + Blackdown in general, and the visual and textual presentation of the album's booklet in particular. There seems to be a divergence between the sound practices and the visual and textual presentation of the music, which is significant in terms of its (im)possibility of creating a more fluid conception of culture, place and ethnicity.

Visual and textual conception of *Margins Music*

The following section analyses the visual design and textual content of the album cover and booklet of *Margins Music*. This is pertinent with regard to Dusk + Blackdown's album in particular, because there is a very specific narrative that is established in its visual and textual presentation, which also interacts with the music on the album.

The amount of space that is given by Dusk + Blackdown to the 'packaging' of the album differs significantly from the majority of electronic dance music albums which are usually characterized by a minimalistic design and hardly any accompanying text. The focus is mostly on abstraction, not on substantiation.

In the case of *Margins Music*, however, the booklet comprises twelve pages, including front cover, pictures, texts, credits, the lyrics of 'Kuri Pataka' in Hindi and an English translation of these lyrics. The main text can be read as instructions to the listener concerning the journey through the tracks of the album, and London respectively.

The cover of the album shows a food stall in front of a grocery store filled with fruit and vegetables: red and green peppers, broccoli of a different shade of green, black aubergines, orange clementines, pale red tomatoes, light green salads and yellow lemons. The photo is shot at nighttime. The street is illuminated by white neon light tubes attached to the blinds above the stall. Only tiny bits of the dark London sky are shown. Far off in the background leaning towards a telephone booth are two young men in dark parkas, white faces against dark tarmac. They are Martin Clark and Dan Frampton, the producers of *Margins Music*, looking towards the camera from the far end of the picture.

The pictures which feature in the booklet were all shot at dusk, dawn or at night, showing London street corners, yellowish lit fronts of housing estates, a smashed telephone booth, a street sign marking Croydon, vacant overground stations. Two pictures show displays of Bollywood films and variations of peas as they can be found in Indian grocery stores. Shattered between these pictures of street sceneries are some which show persons, mostly young men wearing baseball caps and hoodies. A close-up of a young woman, the singer Farrah Jarral who features on *Margins Music*, is shown in front of a shop selling saris. The pictures are arranged so as to appear randomly pinned to a wall. There is a text spreading across two pages, divided by three pages of pictures and holding the handwritten headline 'keytext' which begins with the following words: 'Beyond the corporate finance of the city, the anodyne bars of the West End and the affluent riches out west [...] a different city emerges, a mesh of disparate groups and communities, visible but unseen, vocal – in countless vibrant accents, languages and dialects – but unheard, vital but unrecognized by the centre' (Dusk + Blackdown *Margins Music*, printed in booklet).

The text is written so as to invite the listener of the album to a journey through the city, along particular coordinates: from the centre to the margins, from the 'riches' to the 'edges'. Throughout the text, the journey to 'another London' is represented in an interplay of oppositions which all seem to relate to the core binary of centre and margin. In the above description, the day seems to belong to the centre, while the margins only become visible, and audible, at the break of dawn. The 'corporate finance' that belongs to the centre is opposed to 'a mesh of disparate groups and communities, visible but unseen, vocal – in countless vibrant accents, languages and dialects – but unheard, vital but unrecognised by the centre.'[10] The presence of different languages and accents is presented as an expression of a cultural diversity that is located at the margins, revealed only in the gloominess of the night. While 'corporate' identifies a homogeneous cultural entity, 'disparate' points to cultural diversity, and dis-unity. Here the dichotomous relation between centre and margins becomes a hierarchically inflected relation; the economic hierarchy of the 'riches' and the 'edges' is shifted towards a social one, where the people at the margins are characterized as 'unseen', 'unheard', and 'unrecognized' by those who allegedly belong the centre. Moreover, on both the economic and the social levels the overall division is being made along the lines of an ethnicity that seems intricately tied to marginality and otherness. This juxtaposition of cultural diversity and the margins of the city is further emphasized in the subsequent part of the text as an intrinsically sonic experience for the listeners of the journey through the London of *Margins Music*: 'By night, the city comes alive with sound: raw slang, dialects, clanking trains, sub-bass waves and rebel radio frequencies' (Dusk + Blackdown *Margins Music*, printed in booklet). In this section of the text, the margins are represented as an inspiring place, full of life, and full of creative potential embedded in the sounds of voices from the street, urban noises and messages from pirate radio stations. The listener is invited to explore the richness of 'the forgotten edges of the city' under the guidance of the album's tracks, which crack open this normally hidden place.

The following section of the text names the stops of the sonic journey through London which can be traced along the album's track list. While the stop at Limehouse is represented through the track 'Darker Than East', London's British Asian diaspora is represented through subsequent tracks such as 'Kuri Pataka' and 'Rolling Raj Deep'. The problem with creating a musical topography of London in this way is that the musical influences which form the key sounds of the tracks are no longer understood as points of departure into complex sound practices. Rather, the journey is constructed along points of destination which represent distinct cultural spheres. These cultural spheres are continuously marginalized through their segregation from the centre.

If the album was listened to solely through the filter of what the album's booklet suggests, this would actually result in a rather simplifying and reductionist way of listening that would turn Indian key sounds into reflections of cultural spheres which are firmly allocated to geographically fixed and marginalized positions.

Although the textual narrative attempts to open the listener's ears for a more edgy version of London, the actual narrative strategy employed in the booklet has a reverse effect: the music resounds as if from a distance, the complexity of the sound practices recedes, while the 'oriental' key sounds evoke stereotyped cultural depictions – or, in other words, they seem to convey an all too neat 'translation of cultures'.

Part Three

Thinking Sound as Cultural Transformation

8

Conclusion – Transcultural Sound Practices in British Asian Dance Music

This study started with a critique of the discrepancy between the diversity of musical developments in South Asian dance music in the UK and the one-dimensionality of the popular media and music press coverage of these musics in their depiction of South Asian sounds primarily as signifiers of a fixed notion of ethnicity (through musical categories such as *world music*, or through an overemphasis on the ethnic origin of British Asian musicians). This critique was not confined, however, to popular discourses, but extended into the realm of academic discourses as well. The way in which diasporic music is discussed within cultural studies, for instance, is often by taking up terms and concepts that circulate in the music press and using them as if they were self-evident categories. The concept of world music is a telling case in point in this regard, because it tends to reproduce territorialized and ethnicized notions of culture. Other terms have been coined which try to encompass the digital and globalized forms of musical production and dissemination, such as world beat, fusion or global ghettotech. While these terms generally encourage more complex perspectives on culture, in some contexts they are still used in a way that relies on the same (neo)orientalist rhetorics. Furthermore, using established musical styles as meaningful categories is also limiting when, for instance, hip-hop is per se regarded as subversive, or folk music is regarded as traditional, without recognition of the particular modes and multiple sites of production, reception and dissemination of these musics. Therefore, as was elaborated in detail in Chapter 2, the various developments and mutations of South Asian sounds in urban dance music and the complexity of British Asian cultural negotiation require a critical and inventive thinking that is found neither in pure discourse analyses, as often conducted within cultural studies, nor in the neologisms of pop music criticism.

The questions which I posed at the end of the second chapter will be recapitulated in the following section:

What kind of critical and inventive thinking is required to take the various developments of South Asian dance music to the domain of cultural studies? What sonic particularities are emerging which demand and incorporate new ways of thinking *through* sound rather than about music? How can a capacity be developed for listening differently and more thoroughly to the transcultural sound practices of these musics?

These questions were approached through the perspective of sound studies and auditory culture, which is itself an interdisciplinary field of study, as was demonstrated in Chapter 3. My analytical engagement emphasizes sound and listening as constitutive to the formation of culture. Significantly, the analytical tool that I developed in order to investigate transcultural urban dance music is constructed based on two fundamental claims. One claim is that the sonic particularities of transcultural urban dance musics need to be investigated in terms of how they incorporate new ways of thinking *through* sound rather than merely *about* music. Another claim is that culture – and that has been at the core of cultural studies endeavours since its emergence – is something that is learned rather than inherited, and something that is done rather than given. Taking into account these two claims, I chose to work with the concept of *sound practices* as a key idea that I elaborated in my study in order to emphasize sound as an activity, and to understand *doing sound* as a specific way of doing culture. This conceptualization of sound practices is particularly relevant for a cultural analysis of sound and music, as it understands sound practices as a form of analytical intervention that moves beyond approaches to music which see it as a mere reflection of a seemingly homogeneous culture.

The question that immediately arose, then, was how the concept of transcultural sound practices was to become a workable tool for analysing music. In this regard, the concept of transcultural sound practices that was developed in the theory chapters needed to be further specified concerning the *concrete sound practices in a single musical track*. To think through the concept of sound practices in the restricted space of a musical track required taking into account all the different elements in the track which *do* sound, and techniques and practices which are used in order to do sound, or do something with sound, respectively.

An important aspect which was necessary to consider was that my analysis aimed to focus on the workings of sounds of different sources, and diverse cultural and musical traditions, techniques and practices in South Asian dance music in the UK. Therefore, the goal was to find ways to listen to South Asian sounds differently from those readings that treated South Asian sounds as fixed cultural artefacts that either reflect the ethnic origin and traditional culture of a musician, or represent some sort of hybrid, subversive or rebellious cultural identity. To emphasize how these sound practices in South Asian dance music become part of *doing sound*, I propose the idea of **key sounds**, which work as an analytical tool to identify key moments in a specific sonic constellation of a musical track, or a musical performance, in which the meanings of certain sounds are negotiated and transformed. This sonic constellation might include elements of different South Asian and other musical traditions and techniques, but the analytical goal would not primarily be to discern where the sound comes from, but rather how, for instance, the sound of a sitar is recontextualized, cut, looped and manipulated, and how this key sound generates an alternative sonic narrative in the track. Therefore, analysing key sounds means listening to a musical track as a moment of *sonic fiction* (cf. Kodwo Eshun's *More Brilliant than the Sun*) that is created through a specific form of layering sampled sounds, a certain lyrical performance or a revealing way in which an effect was applied to a sound.

In order to recapitulate the findings that resulted from this, the following paragraphs will provide a summary of the relevant conclusions.

With regard to the chapter on Apache Indian, three sound practices in particular were identified in the track 'Arranged Marriage' in which different sounds function as key sounds in generating different and contrasting sonic fictions. One sound practice concerns the intro of the track which features a particular interaction between a bhangra sample and ragga vocals. In this sound practice, the bhangra sample constructs a reference to bhangra music, characterized by a dhol drum beat and a woody flute melody. However, this bhangra sound is not a stable signifier, since the way in which the sample is looped results in a new repetitive rhythm and cut-up melody line. Therefore, although its basic traits remind the listener of a bhangra track, the sound is reshaped in the context of the intro of 'Arranged Marriage'. In its recontextualized form, the sampled and looped bhangra sound becomes a key sound by working as a hookline and repetitive beat pattern in the track's intro. As soon as the ragga vocals come in, which are *toasted* on top of the looped sample, it becomes clear that the bhangra sample was manipulated in order to work as a rhythmic base for the ragga vocals. The ragga vocals carry the characteristic traits of a typical 1990s reggae dancehall production that are created through the spoken singing, the use of patois elements in the lyrics, the agitated toasting style and the reverberation that is added to the vocals. These ragga sounds are the dominant sounds in the intro as soon as they come in, while the bhangra sounds shift to the background. The bhangra sample was thus refashioned as part of a particular dancehall production culture. Therefore, in this sound practice, the bhangra sound is transformed from a bhangra reference into a background loop of a dancehall reggae intro.

The second sound practice that is telling in Apache Indian's 'Arranged Marriage' is not confined to a small section of the track but concerns all the lyrical parts that are sung by Apache Indian. The specific sound practice consists here of his lyrical performance: a mixture of English, some lexicon from Jamaican patois and Punjabi. The Punjabi words which are used are interwoven in the ragga-style singing, and thus are integrated into the *flow* of the ragga beat. Significantly, through emphasizing and exaggerating the phonetic particularities of the Punjabi words, and especially the vowel sounds /ou/ and /e/ in words such as 'soorni curi' and 'mortee curi', they become key sounds in altering the sonic fabric of the ragga vocals. The specific phonetic features of the Punjabi words add another signifying layer that does not fuse completely with the dominant ragga-style sung phonemes like /a/ in words such as 'gal', 'nuff' or 'patwa'.

The third sound practice that is significant in 'Arranged Marriage' concerns the female Hindi film music vocals that feature almost randomly throughout the track. Sections of the Hindi film music vocals were sampled and accompany some of the instrumental and vocal parts without actually interacting with the other sounds. Rather, this sample somehow floats above the sonic ragga base in a detached and static way. The film music vocals become key sounds in generating a static form of difference that is perceived as detached from the dominant reggae dancehall sounds of the track. Therefore, in contrast to the transformative function of the bhangra key sound in the track's intro, the Hindi film music vocals function as a kind of *sonic ornament*. The concept of sonic ornament signifies that a key sound remains relatively static and does not interact with the other sonic elements in a dynamic and transformative way. In its function as a sonic ornament, 'Indian' sounds become particularly predestined for orientalist or stereotypical implications. The Indianness of the Hindi film music vocals are primarily perceived as a cultural artefact, rather than being part of a complex cultural practice.

To sum up, a key sound can have different functions within different sound practices. It can have a transformative function which results in a complication of the sonic narrative of the track. It can also function as a sonic ornament in creating a static idea of an 'Indian' sound. It is important to emphasize that a key sound is not identified by a sound's *internal* characteristics. Instead, the relevance of the analytic category of key sound is understandable only if the key sound is regarded as part of a specific sound practice, that is, a specific and complex sonic constellation which takes into account its sonic, technological and performative aspects.

As was shown, an analysis of sound practices goes beyond the question of how Apache Indian's Indian cultural identity is reflected in his music, and instead asks how a distinct musical production culture creates the basis for Apache Indian's musical engagement with Asian sounds. Apache Indian's sound practices are embedded in his affiliation with reggae music culture, as the analysis has demonstrated. His sound practices create a stronger bond with dancehall *production culture* than with any alleged Indian *heritage culture*. Therefore, sound practices have the capacity to forge new transcultural sonic relationships which defy any simple fixation on ethnic identity.

In Asian Dub Foundation's 'Collective Mode', sampling practices and lyrical performance are particularly important sound practices that negotiate the relationship of music, politics and ethnicity. One sound practice concerns the intro of the track and the way in which a tune that was sampled from a Bollywood record determines the pitch and dynamic of the whole track. In this instance, the sampled and looped section of the Bollywood tune is transformed into a hookline, and is in fact the fundamental rhythmic spine in the rich sonic fabric of 'Collective Mode'. This sample interacts with the other musical elements that feature in the track such as a dub bass, punk guitars, dancehall beats and the rap of the singer in a dynamic way. Dynamic in this context refers to the fact that the Bollywood sample does not work as a mere sonic ornament which lends the track an oriental twist. Rather, the sampled melody line is treated like an instrument in its own right that is an integral part of the whole composition of the track. Moreover, the specific *materiality* of the Bollywood record becomes part of the performance. In the sampled sequence, the frequencies were manipulated in order to bring the high-pitched melody line to the foreground. In spite of the pitching, the other instruments which feature in the Bollywood tune are still audible as a muffled background rhythm that is perceivable only at the beginning of the track when the sample stands alone. This specific sound practice generates a form of 'hypermediacy' (Bolter and Grusin 1999), which means that attention is drawn to the medium itself, in this case the sound of the recording that was pressed on vinyl. The listening experience of the Bollywood tune is generated through the framework of the medium. The affect that this sound practice of hypermediation has is that it defies notions of any alleged authenticity of the Bollywood tune in the first place. If it were to be assumed that an 'original' tune was copied and transferred to the new track, this assumption would be rejected due to the emphasis on the process of mediation and remediation of the Bollywood recording.

Comparing the sample of the film music vocals in Apache Indian's 'Arranged Marriage' with the Bollywood sample in ADF's 'Collective Mode', there is a remarkable difference with regard to the function of the two key sounds. While the vocals in 'Arranged Marriage' function as a sonic ornament and thus only take part in a restricted form of interaction with the basic reggae dancehall production, the Bollywood key sound in ADF's track is involved in a more far-reaching musical engagement between different sonic repertoires in the track and the creation of new musical ideas.

A different form of remediation was demonstrated with regard to another sound practice in Asian Dub Foundation's 'Collective Mode'. This concerns the reference to the popular 1980s Arkanoid computer game sound that features in the track. What is significant here is that the computer game melody was not sampled from the auditory track of the computer game, but the Arkanoid melody was reproduced with a sequencer in order to sound like the actual game sound. The sounds that were chosen needed to have some attributes of the Arkanoid sounds. It would not have had the same effect if it were just the melody that was reproduced – the attributes of low-fi sounding were taken into account in the reproduction process as well. While the reference to the Arkanoid computer game remains recognizable to those who shared in the hype of the game in the mid-1980s, this key sound has a transformative function in mutating the computer game sound to become an integral rhythmic element in ADF's track. The Arkanoid sound becomes the key sound that links the track's intro and the first stanza and initiates a *breakdown* that disrupts the rhythmic pattern and thus marks a transition to the following vocal part. It is precisely due to its performance in the track as a breakdown that it is doubly remediated, so to speak, in creating a specific dancehall key sound: the latter part of the Arkanoid sample sounds like the *rewind* in a sound system performance. Therefore, the Arkanoid sound becomes a key sound that does not simply add another 'cultural tag' to the track. Rather, the Arkanoid sample becomes a key sound in a specific production culture that works across different media in linking computer games with music sequencing and dancehall production aesthetics.

With regard to ADF, the main goal of this study was to draw attention to the specific forms of sonic recontextualization and remediation by which Bollywood, as well as computer game sounds, becomes the key sounds in the generation of complex musical narratives which expand essentialist notions of culture. Moreover, Asian Dub Foundation use sounds and stories that refer to different media formats and thus different narrative versions of the past in order to raise issues that are current. The aim is not to reveal a past that was lost, but to understand and to rethink the present. ADF's sound practices create sonic fictions that transform the ways in which the past is controlled and fixed.

The analysis of M.I.A.'s sound practices emphasized the artist's use of sounds of different genres associated with the global south, and how they amplify M.I.A.'s politically loaded lyrics that deal with issues of immigration, gun crime, surveillance and war. Particularly with regard to the transnational repertoire of sounds and intertextual references she draws from, M.I.A.'s sound practices can be read as inherently transcultural sonic fictions. In the analysis of 'Sunshowers', the intertextual reference which prominently features here is the 1976 song 'Sunshower', a love tune from New York soul/disco band *Dr. Buzzard's Original Savannah Band*. The instrumentation and vocal melody line of *Dr. Buzzard's* 'Sunshower' are adapted to M.I.A.'s track. The Haitian guitars and soul-oriented vocals are reappropriated to the rough reggaeton beat and audacious vocals of M.I.A.'s track. The exotic connotations of *Dr. Buzzard's* 'Sunshower' become key sounds in underlining the fracture and syncopation that M.I.A.'s version creates. This sonic fiction is created as the working fabric for negotiating cultural stereotypes and the experience of being under surveillance that are thematized in the lyrics. As she raps about mangoes and sweatshops, M.I.A.'s music freely alternates between different 'exoticisms' constructed around Sri Lanka or those created in the music of other bands she draws from in order to convey her dissonant and transcultural sonic fictions.

The significance of M.I.A.'s use of sounds from the global south is demonstrated in her track 'Bucky Done Gun' which is based on the track 'Injeção' by funk carioca musician Deize Tigrona from Rio de Janeiro, Brazil. Rather than producing a mere imitation of the track, elements of 'Injeção' are recontextualized by M.I.A. in order to generate a new style and raise other issues. The prominent hookline of 'Injeção', which features a sample of the horn section of the *Rocky* theme 'Gonna Fly Now' written by Bill Conti in 1977, is adopted by M.I.A. This is another example of how the sound practice of sampling becomes a tool for remediating sonic material from different media contexts. The sample of the horn section in M.I.A.'s 'Bucky Done Gun' is not a simple representation of the Rocky theme, but is instead a performative quotation referencing a context (Deize Tigrona's track) in which the horn section had already been remediated. The different musical pieces, Bill Conti's 'Gonna Fly Now', Deize Tigrona's 'Injeção' and M.I.A.'s 'Bucky Done Gun' do not simply share the same sampled melodic figure – the horn section – a musical form (that is, a produced thing) to which one fixed meaning can be attached. Rather, all three artists perform a unique version of the horn section (that is, they are producing subjects), and these sound practices create three different sonic fictions. The sexually explicit lyrics which feature in Deize Tigrona's track and are characteristic of many funk carioca productions are taken up by M.I.A. However, while Deize Tigrona's lyrics are blatantly sexist in constructing the female protagonist as being exposed to violent male desire (in the guise of a doctor giving his patient an injection), M.I.A.'s lyrics evoke different ideas that cut across and play with, not only 'ethnic', but also gendered and sexualized identifications. When she sings 'Do you like me vulnerable/I'm armed and I'm equal', her vocalization resonates with female punk attitudes by bands such as *The Slits*. Therefore, the way in which different gendered identities are renegotiated and transformed needs to be explored as an interplay of lyrical content, sound practices and vocal performance.

To conclude, the aesthetic decisions taken by M.I.A. create multilevelled sonic fictions which cannot be harmonized in any simple manner. The specific ways in which M.I.A. deals with ethnic, gender and political aspects are integrally linked to the specific ways in which she utters her lyrics, combines different rhythmic elements and performs a sampled melody. The outcome is a multilayered sound, processed through technological tools and performed through practices of cut'n'paste, fragmentation and contrast. The noisy often meets the sweet, the rough is contrasted with the catchy, and this creates a sound practice which generate meaningful shifts, inconsistencies and gaps.

As far as Nathan 'Flutebox' Lee's sound practices are concerned, the analysis highlights some aspects that are not emphasized as much in the other case studies. The sound practices that are of fundamental importance to Lee's music are his inventive technique of playing the concert flute – which he termed *fluteboxing* – and the aspect of live performance. With regard to the fluteboxing, I demonstrated how this sound practice is part of a complex sonic technique. On the one hand, the way in which Lee combines flute playing with beat boxing is inventive in that it actually reinvents the instrument by adding new and unconventional sounds to it. The thudding beats that are produced sound unlike the classical sonic repertoire of the concert flute. On the other hand, this technique should not be seen as restricted to the instrument itself, but rather as extending the discussion of Lee's specific sound practice to the basic production culture in which his music is embedded, one that is grounded in jungle and grime, highly bass-oriented and geared towards live performance. His experience of beatboxing and of being a jungle MC in pirate radio shows before he began playing the flute highly influenced the way he has treated the concert flute, the way he has composed tracks with his flute and the way in which he has performed his music live and in the studio. Moreover, listening to hip-hop and jungle, as well as jazz, blues and Indian and European classical music, this knowledge of a wide range of musical styles and genres always worked as a sonic archive he drew from for his own work as a musician. Thus, the particularity of Lee's sound practice lies in the interaction of a specific playing technique and the wider production culture he is part of – which also creates a specific sonic fiction – own which 'tells' stories about how his tracks are really only created in the studio – which become part of his recorded music: jamming with fellow musicians, and creating a 'live' atmosphere while recording, must be regarded as a constitutive practice of Nathan Lee's musical creation.

A particular sound practice was analysed that is significant on his recorded EP and concerns the transposition of aspects of liveness and jamming into the recording process. Of particular importance is the interplay of the flute and a violin which features in the track called 'Dog'. The flute and the violin sounds interact in a *call and response*, in which the violin answers to the flute melody. There are several instances in his recorded tracks where an aesthetic self-referentiality becomes audible with regard to liveness and jamming. This is evident in the first track of the EP which is called 'Intro' that commences with the vocals of the singer and beatboxer checking the microphone and introducing the artist to an imagined audience and thus creating a 'live on stage' situation. Another instance is the very short track called 'Interlude' in which Nathan engages in a musical–verbal interaction with the piano player, sorting out which song to play next. While Lee explains what he wants to play by throwing in some rather unspecific words, the piano player responds with a chord played in a soft mode which Lee reacts to approvingly. Without any further verbal explanation, they simultaneously start off playing together, accompanied also by some percussion. This interlude demonstrates an important part of Nathan 'Flutebox' Lee's sound practices of liveness and jamming and relates them to a specific production culture.

The analysis of Dusk + Blackdown's sound practices showed how sound becomes an agent in the transcultural re-configuration of bass materialism. Concerning their track 'Kuri Pataka', it was demonstrated how a Bollywood string section becomes a key sound in an instance of sonic and cultural transformation. The analysis concentrated here on a string section sampled from a Bollywood tune. The strings were pitched down with the help of equalizers until they reached the sub-bass level. Being pitched down in such a radical way, the strings are no longer identifiable as strings, but sound much more like a synthesized sub-bass. The underlying Bollywood tune that was used as the raw material for this sound practice becomes audible only a few bars later in the track, when the bass frequencies are decreased again and the strings are levelled out on their characteristic pitch. Only when the pitch is gradually reconstructed, the sound regains its recognizability as Bollywood key sound. What is significant about this sound practice is that the shift from Bollywood to dubstep and back is staged in a seamless way – the exact moment when Bollywood key sounds become dubstep key sounds is hardly detectable. Listening to the track in this way, the idea of 'bass materialism' (Goodman 2010) becomes tangible as the core principle of electronic urban dance music such as drum'n'bass, grime and dubstep (to name just a few particular styles). The way in which the Bollywood sample is manipulated and refashioned in 'Kuri Pataka' demonstrates the musical engagement with the sample as sonic raw material, rather than an engagement with a particular Indian musical tradition. As shown in my analysis, Dusk + Blackdown's sound practices need to be carefully regarded in the context of many musical productions of non-Asian musicians and producers which have drawn from South Asian sonic repertoires, some of which have clearly capitalized on the 'exotic' markers under which these sounds are often perceived. However, coming to their rescue, the British artists Dusk + Blackdown have also collaborated closely with Black British and British Asian musicians and see their own musical and production practice firmly based in the British 'hardcore continuum', as once defined by Simon Reynolds in 2009 as 'a musical tradition/subcultural tribe that's managed to hold it together for nearly 20 years now, negotiating drastic stylistic shifts and significant changes in technology, drugs, and the social/racial composition of its own population' Reynolds 2013 [2009]. Dusk + Blackdown see their album as one of the outcomes of this inherently transcultural sonic/technological/social fabric. However, as my analysis detailed, the use of South Asian sounds as sonic raw material in creating new musical tracks also has problematic implications.

The concept of South Asian dance music which is established with regard to the case studies is one which is seen as porous, as dynamic and as 'conflicting' as culture itself. Music and the concrete sound practices were studied here as a field of cultural production that constantly reinvents itself as well as reshapes the cultural forms it creates. The techniques of cutting and pasting, looping, layering and reproducing sounds bear the potential of reshaping ideas of culture. And it is from the vantage point of this multifaceted and transcultural musical output of South Asian dance music that the liminality of some of the popular discourses on music and culture become most apparent (as discussed in Chapter 2, for example) that still try to make sense of culture as compartmentalized forms of ethnic communities or 'world' music. As the case studies have shown, the investigation of transcultural sound practices was useful here to engage with the diverse aspects that link the realms of music and culture such as sampling practices, liveness, globalization, gender, transculturality and transnational connections, margin and centre. Thus, the concept of transcultural sound practices combines approaches from sound studies, popular music studies, cultural studies and postcolonial studies in order to enable a more nuanced and deep listening to the transcultural aspects of South Asian dance music. Transculturality refers to processes of cultural formation that reach beyond the boundaries that are usually drawn between nations, ethnic communities, class or gender identities, and highlights strategies of transgressing these boundaries through aesthetic and social strategies that were found in the cultural productions in the UK that are influenced by various cultural and musical traditions and practices. The concept of transcultural sound practices was established in order to approach these various and multilayered musics without being confined to the grand narrations of musical history, nor by the analytical, and terminological repertoire of classical musicology. To analyse the specific sound practices in South Asian dance music, attention was brought to sound as constitutive element in processes of cultural transformation.

Analysing transcultural sound practices and its resulting sonic fictions challenge listening conventions. While the fact that South Asian sounds such as Bollywood samples or sitar sounds feature in a musical track often nurture the assumption that these sounds are clearly definable ethnic markers that somehow suggest that these ethnic markers signify a direct relation to a traditional Indian cultural identity of the musician, the analyses demonstrated that these apparently direct links between music and stable notions of ethnicity are constantly challenged, transgressed and transformed.

To put sound on the agenda in analysing South Asian dance music, and this might include other contemporary diasporic musics, does not demand yet another neologism such as 'global sound', as mentioned in the introduction. Rather, it demands the ability to listen, to listen attentively and open-mindedly, 'a listening for the background and the half muted' (Back 2007: 8), a listening that challenges a reproduction of ethno-centric discourses.

9

Outlook – On Transcultural Sound Practices beyond Music

Working on a concept of transcultural sound practices, as established throughout this book, was always guided by both my interest in South Asian dance music and sonic culture in the UK and my interest in sonic thinking that reaches beyond music, into the realm of sound and listening in everyday life, the urban space, and in the (sonic) arts and design. The following elaborations therefore emphasize some of the outcomes of my sonic thinking, aspects of which have been mentioned throughout the book, which very often are in relation to postcolonial and transcultural perspectives, and, by pointing out to some examples of my work which exceed the field of music and partly also what has been centrally the scope of this book, sketch out an analytical framework for thinking sound as cultural transformation.

There are several instances in my study in which the urban space is referred to as a particularly productive and vibrant field for the study of sound. The urban space (or particular cities) has been central to the study of sound for scholars from many different and interdisciplinary perspectives, with a special interest in how cities are constructed as a juxtaposition of architectural, infrastructural, institutional and social ideas, techniques and technologies. Urban spaces are in constant reconstruction, and the ways in which people move through the city, how they orient themselves in the city, how they develop tactics and techniques of challenging the often rigid socio-economic, bureaucratic and surveillant paths and imperatives of action can be studied along the sonic (and other sensual) relationships and practices. To cite a passage from the introduction: the specific social or cultural functions of sound in a certain time at a certain place have changed over time. The sound of a church bell in early modern England could serve here as an example as relevant as that of the muzak in a shopping mall or the heavy bass that reverbs from a London underground club. In this respect, a link can be drawn between ubiquitous everyday soundscapes and musical sound. Listening to musical sound is not confined to the musical score, or the musical recording, but extends it – it is cultural praxis: of listening, of feeling, of orientation, of the creation of an individual experience, and of collectivities (Intro. 20–21). Investigating very divergent examples of how the urban space is constituted sonically, this was exactly to show how transcultural sound practices work on very different – historical, situational and aspirational or futuristic – levels. An example which was not mentioned in this book and also exceeds the musical realm is the performative art of skateboarding which I studied as a social practice that challenges and reconfigures urban, cultural and gendered configurations (Maier 2016). The concrete ways in which sound is produced while skateboarding as a way to balance out physical, corporeal and sensual aspects of this complex movement are described in detail and regarding the particular relationship of sound, knowledge and space. Taking as an example the experience of four female skaters skating London's Brick Lane on a Friday night, the sound of skateboarding is explored as a tool for transcultural intervention into gendered urban space and for constructing alternative socialities. Apart from the performative practice of skateboarding, the ways in which people live with functional sounds in everyday life –the designed sounds that are created for all kinds of devices, environments and work and leisure situations – have become a crucial field to critique the mere semiotic functionality of theses sounds and turn to the situative, ambiguous, problematic, or ecstatic characteristics and intensities of these sounds in creating urban social space. How the urban space becomes a sonically and culturally contested space was part of a participant observation/participant listening I conducted at a Turkish wedding in Berlin/Schöneberg. Here, the functional sounds of car horns and engine noises in juxtaposition with the music of the wedding band and the singing and clapping of the wedding crowd resulted in an amplification and complication of ethnic, gendered and classed relationships in the larger cultural and social politics of the urban in the middle of Berlin (Maier and Schulze 2019).

Conceptualizing sound practices in South Asian dance music has led to a more nuanced understanding of the agency of sound in particular settings and situations, for instance in the form of the intensity of bass frequencies that have been used by M.I.A. to both amplify and revoke ethnic and gender stereotypes, or for the creation of an affective force which Asian Dub Foundation uses on stage and in the studio recordings as vehicles for their sonic-political activism and new sonic fiction. In his 2018 book *Sonic Agency*, LaBelle points out some of the questions that have been also driven my research, in and beyond this book:

Is there a potential embedded in sonic thought that may lend itself to contemporary struggles? What particular ethical and agentive positions or tactics might be adopted from the experiences we have of listening and being heard? Might the knowledges nurtured by a culture of sounding practices support us in approaching the conditions of personal and political crisis? (LaBelle 2018: 1)

Rethinking these questions, it seems important to note that not the sound *itself* is political, but the affective dimension of sound does have an impact on how we perceive the world, act within it and make sense of it. Therefore, I have always been interested in the challenge that sound and aurality pose to our habitual perceptions, actions and thinking. Studying South Asian dance music through the particularities of individual musical tracks, this radical particularity also informed my analysis of the performance by Mendi + Keith Obadike with the title *Numbers Station [Furtive Movements]* from 2015, which became part of the already-mentioned collaborative writing on *Sound Works* with Holger Schulze (2019). We were interested in how the artists' sound practices can be interpreted as decolonial practices in their unique way of using the self-reported stop and frisk data of the New York Police Department from over 123 precincts and sonified them. Mendi + Keith Obadike read aloud the number of the quarter and the number of stop requests alternately, underscored by sound generated from the same NYPD database, taking numbers of stops and translating them into frequencies:

> The subject of this performance was the data. However, it was a sonic pattern that resonated underneath, crafted by a humanoid, in a sensitive and somehow loving artistic practice, so that the data could play out its capacity to disrupt and to disturb the well-known stereotypes, the toxic essentialism, and the racial violence of this police activity. '041, 274, 042, 176'. Sonification of data is turned in this case into a decolonizing strategy. A functional sound is not just repurposed, refunctionalized, and thus resignified, but it is through the adding of sound and voice and context with a clearly functional goal that new layers of meaning of the data are revealed resonated underneath, crafted by a humanoid, in a sensitive and somehow loving artistic practice, so that the data could play out its capacity to disrupt and to disturb police activity and become public: a matter to be discussed, to hear, to feel. The sonic presence emphasizes a semiotic absence. '043, 207, 044, 334'. (Maier and Schulze 2019)

How transcultural sound practices become decolonizing practices has become one of the key interests in my current research on *Travelling Sounds*. *Travelling Sounds* is a sensory ethnography of (sonic) art in Copenhagen and

London, incorporating artistic works that are also situated in the Virgin Islands and Greenland. The perspective on transcultural and decolonial sound practices is developed along artistic and activist interventions in the urban public space, shifting the analytical focus on narratives, fictions and ideas of Europe and how it is sonically shaped, and imagined, through its postcolonial condition. One of the works I am looking at is *I Am Queen Mary* by artists LaVaughn Belle and Jeanette Ehlers, a transnational and decolonial commentary on Denmark's (post-)colonial legacies with the Virgin Islands, which is part of my continuous engagement with music, sound art and the urban space in relation to 'contemporary struggles' (as LaBelle has it), and a growing interest in the situativity, materiality and agency of sound. While this is not a piece of sound art, there is a sonic performativity in the references this monument makes, paying tribute to rebel leader of the Fireburn Revolts, Mary Thomas and a number of historical and contemporary resistance movements against colonial and imperialist rule, on the Virgin Islands and in Europe. Returning firmly to the realm of music, and zooming in on Broken Beat and Grime, Stefanie Alisch and I have explored the potentials and limits of 'the sound of afrofuturism' as an analytical and decolonial perspective on UK based Black Atlantic Music (Alisch and Maier 2019). While the ethnography of the present study was mostly concentrated on conducting interviews and participant observations in concert venues and clubs, my expertise in sensory ethnography has become more nuanced while working on a multi-authored book (in preparation) on *Transcultural Materialities*,[1] which is based on a transdisciplinary ethnographic study which compares the transcultural arenas of school and theatre in their dealings and interactions with refugees, migrants and post-migrants. The socio-material and affective aspects of transcultural sonic practices and thinking are investigated here in relation to how difference (in terms of ethnicity, gender, class, age, etc.) is performed, put on stage, mediated and negotiated in formal and informal educational and artistic contexts, and how the transcultural effects of migration and post-migration emerge from the intra-action of bodies, things, sounds and space. Therefore, although the concept of transcultural sound practices was primarily developed in this book as an extended concept for the study of music, it has become, and still is to become, a methodological framework for thinking sound as cultural transformation and decolonial practice beyond music, such as in everyday life, the (sonic) arts and the urban space.

Notes

Introduction

1 In Lipsitz's book with the same title, he defines 'dangerous crossroads' with regard to the creative and conflicting dynamics of migration and transnational music production: 'In our time, social and cultural crises often come to us in the form of struggles over place and displacement, over transformations in our relationship to both physical places and discursive spaces. The relationship between popular music and place offers a way of starting to understand the social world that we are losing – and a key to the one that is being built' (Lipsitz 1994: 3).
2 I use the term 'post-migrant' as defined by Shermin Langhoff, who, as founder of the Ballhaus Naunynstraße in Berlin's Kreuzberg district, made significant contributions to establishing the concept of post-migrant theatre: 'For us, post-migrant means that we critically question the production and reception of stories about migration and about migrants which have been available up to now and that we view and produce these stories anew, inviting anew reception' (Langhoff 2011, cited in Stewart 2017: 153). In the context of my book, my definition of the term 'post-migrant' also resonates with how sociologist Kira Kosnick describes it, 'to refer to an increasing number of people who were born in the country of residence in the second, third etc. generation, but for whom diasporic or transnational affiliations created through family histories of migration still play a significant role in their lives. Neither the term migrant nor the concept of an ethnic minority can adequately describe these circumstances' (Kosnick 2010: 38).

Chapter 1

1 I conceive of cultural formation as an activity, and thus speak of 'formation' in terms of a dynamic and ongoing process rather than a fixed structure or a specific model.
2 I use musics in the plural here to indicate the different aesthetic, stylistic and discursive parameters of the musical examples which I am investigating.
3 For overviews on South Asian cultural production in the UK, see Ali (2006), Hingorani (2010), Dawson (2007).

4   In his 2001 'chicken tikka masala speech', Cook used tikka masala as a metaphor for Britain's history of adapting and appropriating external influences and thus highlighting its cultural diversity.
5   For a more thorough investigation of ethnic commodification, see Hutnyk (2000), Huggan (2001).
6   For a more detailed account of discourses around Britpop music and New Labour politics, see Zuberi (2001), Bennett and Stratton 2010, Huq (2010), Eckstein (2010a).
7   For an account of the controversial discourses that have formed around the term 'diaspora', see Slobin (2003).
8   Simon Frith explains that the making of the world music label has been from the beginning part of a 'commercial process': 'World music is an unusual pop genre in that it has a precise moment of origin. In July 1987 eleven independent record companies concerned with "international pop" began meeting at a London pub, the Empress of Russia, to discuss how best to sell "our kind of material." As a press release at the end of the month explained: "The demand for recordings of Non-Western artists is surely growing [...] the new WORLD MUSIC section will be the first place to look at"' (Frith 2000: 305).
9   For a discussion of The Beatles' 'Norwegian Wood', see Viol (2001).
10 BBC Radio Leicester was established in 1977.
11 Chauhan, Nerm. Interviewed at a bar near his workplace at the BBC, London, UK. November 2008.
12 Kamaljit Singh Jhooti, better known as Jay Sean, is a hip-hop and r'n'b songwriter and beatboxer.
13 Hirani, Ritu. Interviewed at *Club Kali*, London, UK. October 2008.
14 Hirani, Ritu. Interviewed at *Stadtgarten*, Köln, Germany. January 2006.
15 Goodman, Steve. Interviewed at *Clandestino Festival*, Gothenburg, Sweden. June 2009.
16 Two examples for this sound practice are given by Burkhalter who mentions Mazen Kerjaj, a musician from Beirut, who imitates sounds of the war on his trumpet and Raed Yassin, who uses sounds from the Lebanese Civil war in his music (Burkhalter 2010).
17 For an investigation of the emergence of music cultures which are shaped through practices that are intrinsically connected to the internet, see Dhiraj Murthy's article on Pakistani music subculture on the internet (2010).

Chapter 2

1   Schmidt opposes the common view that Aristotle was ignorant of the epistemological relevance of the sense of hearing and states that '[t]he prisoners in Plato's cave, it is easily forgotten, were troubled not only by the flickering images but also by the echoes' (Schmidt 2004: 42).

2   For accounts of how Marshall McLuhan imagines a reversal of the process of rationalization in the age of electronic media, see McLuhan (1962).
3   The original quotation reads: '[W]eg von einem vermeintlichen Gegensatz der visuellen zur akustischen Kommunikation – hin zu einem weiterzielenden Projekt: die gesamte Welt der Artefakte in ihrer Vielfalt sinnlicher Wahrnehmungen als gestaltet zu begreifen.'
4   See e.g. studies which deal with the analysis of film sound and soundtracks, practices of sound design in filmmaking and video games (Altman 1992, Flückiger 2001, Kassabian 2002, Collins 2008); avant-garde music and sound art (Kahn 1999, Cox 2006, LaBelle 2007); historical anthropology of sound (Schulze 2007, 2008); rhythm analysis (Lefebvre 2004); the social dimension of sound and listening practices (Bull and Back 2004, Back 2007, Bull 2007); functional sounds (Langenmaier 1993, Spehr 2009); sonic architecture (Hellström 2003, Blesser 2006).
5   Interestingly, Schafer is said to have been greatly influenced by McLuhan. 'Schafer entered the Royal Conservatory of Music and the University of Toronto in 1952 to study with John Weinzweig. His casual contact with Marshall McLuhan on campus in that period could arguably be singled out as the most lasting influence on his development' (Grey 2005).
6   For studies on the sounds of modernity, see Bijsterveld (2001, 2008).
7   Barry Truax highlights that 'contemporary music also tends to model the characteristics of environmental sound organization, such as foreground, background, ambience, texture, and spatiality, with results that often reflect the contemporary soundscape' (Truax 2001: 53).
8   According to Feld, '[t]he Kaluli are one of four groups of 2000 Bosavi people who live in the tropical rainforest of the Great Papuan Plateau in the Southern Highlands Province of Papua New Guinea' (Feld 2004: 224).
9   For a more detailed account of this study, see Feld (1982).
10 Cf. DeNora 2000.
11 For another study of urban soundscapes, see Tonkiss (2004: 303–309).
12 Bull refers to Marc Augé's notion of the non-place (see Bull 2007: 4–5 and 14–15).
13 For a discussion of the relationship between *roots* and *routes*, see Gilroy (1993).
14 Schafer explains: 'The futurist experimenter Luigi Russolo [...] invented an orchestra of noisemakers, consisting of buzzers, howlers and other gadgets, calculated to introduce modern man to the musical potential of the new world about him. In 1913 Russolo proclaimed the event in his manifesto The Art of Noises (L´Arte dei Rumori)' (Schafer 1994: 110).
15 I say 'musics' here to refer to a range of different musical styles and traditions.
16 Jonathan Sterne in *The Audible Past: Cultural Origins of Sound Reproduction* traces the developments of sound reproduction and its significance for how people have

perceived the world and how culture and society have been fundamentally generated in a process of interaction between human action and audio-technology (Sterne 2003).
17 I therefore use the terms 'technique' and 'technology' in the opposite order from Théberge: technique is the specific use of a technological device, or the playing technique of an instrument; technology is the general performative, or discursive practice.
18 Cf. Frederickson (1989).
19 Cf. Foucault (1980).
20 Théberge mentions Blacking's differentiation of 'means' of production and 'mode' of production to emphasize the latter as being more relevant to analyse the specific use of sounds, instruments and technological devices and their effects on musical practice (Théberge 1997: 158, in reference to Blacking 1977).
21 For other accounts that prefer track rather than song in popular music analysis, see Bonz (2008), Ismaiel-Wendt (2011).
22 The original quotation reads: *'Die von Hawkins ins Spiel gebrachte Vorstellung eines offenen und mehrdimensionalen Klangraums, der eher als ein Set von generativen Prozeduren denn als fixierter Strukturzusammenhang zu verstehen wäre, ist dafür ungemein produktiv und reicht weit über die Frage nach den Möglichkeiten und Grenzen der Notationsverfahren hinaus.'*
23 For questions of copyright in cultural production, see Schumacher (1995).

Chapter 3

1 Steel Pulse is a reggae band from Handsworth that was founded in 1975 and is active to the present day.
2 Conscious reggae or roots reggae refers to a sub-style of reggae that is associated with the music of Bob Marley and Peter Tosh in the 1970s and early 1980s. The lyrics often deal with Rastafarianism and a critique of social and economic injustice.
3 For an overview of UK bhangra music, see Dudrah (2007).
4 'Toasting' is the term for singing lyrics on a reggae beat.
5 Dancehall, or ragga, is a form of reggae which emerged in the late 1980s as a faster and more 'electronic' form of Jamaican roots reggae. The terms 'dancehall' and 'ragga' will be used here more or less interchangeably. While dancehall originally only referred very generally to music that is played in Jamaican dancehalls, ragga does more specifically refer to the beats and vocals characteristic of this form of reggae; however, to talk about the dancehall sound is an equally valid description for the sonic particularities of this style.
6 Tricia Rose's description of flow in rap music can be transferred here to the ragga context: 'The music and vocal rapping in rap music also privileges flow, layering,

and ruptures in line. Rappers speak of flow explicitly in lyrics, referring to an ability to move easily and powerfully through complex lyrics as well as of the flow in the music' (Rose 1994: 39).
7   On constructions of 'black masculinities' in popular magazines, see Bell-Jordan (2011).
8   For a valuable account of the art of turntablism, see Katz (2004).
9   Album version refers to the version of the track that appears on the album *Arranged Marriage*.
10 I refer to a British version of Jamaican patois as street-style patois. It is particularly popular with young people and often functions as a type of street slang outside of Jamaica. Linguist Susanne Mühleisen states with regard to Creole that '[t]he fact that Creole in Britain has been such a prominent part of popular youth culture has the effect that Creole features are employed for prestige in the speech of adolescents of different (non-West Indian) backgrounds' (Mühleisen 2002: 170).

Chapter 4

1   This blurring of the lines between analogue and digital is not constricted to the album *Community Music*. When the band's debut album *Facts and Fictions* was released in 1995, mixing dancehall, jungle, ragga, punk and Asian sounds in such a way was quite unprecedented. Their live shows attributed to their diverse sound practice by combining a rock-band setup with a live DJ adding the electronic music elements and a hip-hop attitude put forward by the vocalist.
2   In spite of the various influences, I refer to the track as a dancehall track because I believe that the dub bass line, the off-beat guitar and the ragga vocals are the dominant key sounds in the track, all of which clearly refer to dancehall.
3   Eight-bit refers to data units that are not more than eight-bit wide.
4   For the use of computer game sounds in pop music, see Collins (2008).
5   Savale, Steve Chandra. *Centralstation*, Darmstadt, Germany. May 2003.
6   For a detailed account on hip-hop as a global phenomenon, see Mitchell (2001).

Chapter 5

1   *SoundCloud* is 'an audio platform that enables anyone to upload, record, promote and share their originally-created sounds across the internet […] SoundCloud allows sound creators anywhere to instantly record audio on the site or via mobile applications and share them publicly or privately; to embed sound across websites, social networks and blogs and receive feedback from the community' (*Soundcloud.com* 2012).

200　　　　　　　　　　　　　　Notes

2   For discussions about transnational piracy and how it shapes public (music) culture and economic life, see Haupt (2008), Sundaram (2010), Eckstein and Schwarz 2014).
3   While one may assume that Arulpragasam is referring to the capital of Sri Lanka, Colombo, *Columbo* [which is also the way she pronounces it] is making reference to an American crime fiction series.
4   In an interview, Arulpragasam explains the linguistic connection between London-based Sri Lankans and Jamaicans:
    The main area where Sri Lankans moved into in London is called Tooting, which was also a real big ragga section,'cause there was loads of Jamaicans there, too. So all the Sri Lankan kids that came over that were slightly a bit on the edge soon adapted ragga culture. If you go to Tooting now, you can still find that – you wouldn't be able to tell a Sri Lankan from a Jamaican. It's really weird – Sri Lankans find coming to England and talking with a Jamaican patois accent is easier than learning the Queen's English. (Manish 2005)
5   In order to provide context for this line, it is useful to consider the possibility of a connection to M.I.A.'s father's activism. The album is dedicated to her father; *Arular* is actually his first name. According to the *Washington Post*'s discussion of this issue: 'M.I.A.'s father, a Sri Lankan intellectual who had moved to London in 1971 to work as an engineer, helped found the Eelam Revolutionary Organization of Students (EROS) in 1975, just three years before she was born Mathangi "Maya" Arulpragasam. EROS was one of the first Tamil political organizations – Tamil Hindus being the ethnic minority in Sinhalese Buddhist-dominated Sri Lanka – to seek the creation of an independent state (Tamil Eelam), and it evolved into one of several militant groups engaged in a civil war now into its third decade (the most notorious group being the Liberation Tigers of Tamil Eelam) [...] A.R. Arulpragasam [M.I.A.'s father] reportedly trained in Lebanon with Palestinian militants' (Harrington 2005).
6   For details on M.I.A.'s visa issue, see her appearance on the TV show *The Hour* with George Stroumboulopoulos (2007).
7   The original quotation reads: '*Die anfängliche Kriminalisierung des Funk in Rio de Janeiro war nur ein Symptom dieser Angst vor dem sozialen und kulturellen Aufstieg der Gruppen von jungen Menschen aus der Peripherie, die den Markt eroberten. Der Erfolg dieser Bewegungen des Funk und Hiphop führte dazu, dass die beständig vermittelte unkritische und entkontextualisierte Beziehung zwischen Verbrechen, Armut und Gewalt bestätigt wurde.*'
8   Downbeat (or downtempo) refers to fewer beats per minute than in an average dance music track. While 'Paper Planes' has 86 beats per minute; a modern uptempo dance track would have around 126 beats per minute.
9   As if it would be acceptable for the blue in a painting to be toned down before

it was put in an exhibition, because it was too blue and thus didn't fit the artistic profile of the gallery. In this example, the picture would simply not have been exhibited.
10 Newspaper articles insisted on M.I.A.'s decline as a credible artist for living in the United States with Benjamin Bronfman, son of the CEO of the Warner Music group (cf. Hirschberg 2010).
11 For a more detailed critical investigation of the controversial press coverage of M.I.A.'s 'Born Free' video, see Eckstein 2010b.

Chapter 6

1 Burtner describes various ways in which winds and brass instruments have been applied with extended techniques: 'Extended techniques for winds and brass include disassembling the instrument and playing various parts independently. Mouthpieces can be played alone or tapped like a small percussion instrument. With the mouthpiece alone or with the full instrument, all the extended embouchure effects are available, such as flutter, double, triple, or slap tonguing, a variety of articulations, playing the mouthpiece upside down or biting the mouthpiece and blowing (single reed instruments), bending the pitch with the embouchure, and various vibrato effects such as changing speed or wide vibrato' (Burtner 2005).
2 Lee, Nathan. Musician. Interviewed in Brixton, London, UK. 27 November 2008.

Chapter 7

1 Goodman, Steve. Interviewed at *University of East London,* London, UK. November 2008.
2 Some of the more popular members are Wiley, Skepta, as well as the former member Dizzee Rascal.
3 Sarah Thornton uses the term 'subcultural capital' in reference to Bourdieu's (1984) notion of cultural capital in order to depict those 'in the know' about the 'values and hierarchies of club culture' (Thornton 1995: 11).
4 Actually, the title 'Kuri Pataka' is the original title of the Hindi tune which is the basis of Dusk + Blackdown's track; 'The firecracker girl' is the translation of the Hindi title.
5 A tabla break is a short beat pattern played with tablas which often features in bhangra songs. According to Clark, the sampled tabla breaks in 'Kuri Pataka' are

classic Punjabi breaks, which were drawn from sound compilations that can be bought on CDs which include many different samples of tabla breaks and other percussion.

6   A tumbi is a high-pitched, single-stringed wooden instrument which is derived from the Punjab region of North India. The tumbi was played by Asian-American Kush Arora, an electronic music producer from San Francisco and connoisseur of both tumbi and algoze flute (Nachmann 2009). The tumbi was recorded with Dusk + Blackdown who then sampled and rearranged the recorded footage that features on several tracks of the album.

7   'Drum'n'bass' is used here as an umbrella term for electronic dance music tracks which are based on drums and bass, because the track cannot be clearly related to a specific musical style.

8   For an account of copyright legislation and practices in India, see Manuel (1993).

9   Jarral is referring to a sruti box.

10 There is an intertextual reference here to the fifth chapter of Salman Rushdie's *The Satanic Verses* (1988) called 'A City Visible but Unseen', which deals with the protagonist Gibreel Farishta's troublesome journey through London.

Chapter 9

1   This book is written in the context of the research project 'Transcultural Practices in Postmigrant Theatre and in School' (2016–2019), based at Leuphana University Luneburg and (currently) Kunstakademie Düsseldorf. See trakubi.com.

References

Abdellatif, Farah. 'Definition of Beat Box'. *Farah-Beat-Box.* 22 January 2009. Web. 24 June 2012. http://www.facebook.com/pages/Farah-Beat-Box/45573902276?sk=info.
Adam [last name not mentioned]. 'Origins of Funk Carioca'. *Eyes on Brazil.* 7 August 2008. Web. 17 March 2012. http://eyesonbrazil.com/2008/08/07/origins-of-funk-carioca.
ADF. *asiandubfoundation.* 'About'. 2008. Web. 14 June 2008. http://asiandubfoundation.com/about.
Ali, N. et al., eds. *A Postcolonial People: South Asians in Britain.* London: Hurst, 2006.
Altman, Rick. *Sound Theory, Sound Practice.* New York: Routledge, 1992.
Anderson, Benedict. *Imagined Communities: Reflections on the Origin and Spread of Nationalism.* London: Verso, 1991 [first published 1983].
Appadurai, Arjun. 'Disjuncture and Difference in the Global Cultural Economy'. *Public Culture* 2.2 (1990): 1–24. Rpt. in *Modernity at Large: Cultural Dimensions of Globalization.* Ed. Arjun Appadurai. Minneapolis: University of Minnesota Press, 1996. 27–47.
Attali, Jaques. *Noise: The Political Economy of Music.* Minneapolis: University of Minnesota Press, 2006 [first published 1977].
Back, Les. *The Art of Listening.* Oxford: Berg, 2007.
Back, Les. *New Ethnicities and Urban Culture: Racisms and Multiculture in Young Lives.* Oxon: Routledge, 1996.
Bakrania, Falu. *Bhangra and Asian Underground: South Asian Music and the Politics of Belonging in Britain.* Durham and London: Duke University Press, 2013.
Bauman, Gerd. *Contesting Culture: Discourses of Identity in Multi-Ethnic London.* Cambridge: Cambridge University Press, 1996.
Beck, Ulrich. 'Wie wird Demokratie im Zeitalter der Globalisierung möglich? Eine Einleitung'. *Politik der Globalisierung.* Ed. Ulrich Beck. Frankfurt/M: Suhrkamp, 1998. 7–66.
Bell-Jordan, Katrina E. 'Still Subscribing to Stereotypes: Constructions of Black Masculinities in Popular Magazines'. *Masculinity in the Black Imagination.* Ed. Ronald L. Jackson et al. New York: Peter Lang, 2011. 129–146.
Bennett, Andy and Jon Stratton, eds. *Britpop and the English Music Tradition.* Farnham: Ashgate, 2010.
Bennett, Andy. *Popular Music and Youth Culture: Music, Identity and Place.* London: Macmillan, 2000.
Bentes, Ivana. 'Das Copyright des Elends und das Bild als Kapital'. *City of Coop: Ersatzökonomien und städtische Bewegungen in Rio de Janeiro und Buenos Aires.* Ed. Stephan Lanz. Berlin: b_books, 2004. 75–89.

Bhaba, Homi. *The Location of Culture*. New York: Routledge, 1994.

Bijsterveld, Karin. *Mechanical Sound. Technology, Culture and Public Problems of Noise in the Twentieth Century*. Cambridge: MIT, 2008.

Bijsterveld, Karin. 'The Diabolical Symphony of the Mechanical Age'. *Social Studies of Science* 31.1 (2001): 37–70.

Blacking, John. 'Towards an Anthropology of the Body'. *The Anthropology of the Body*. Ed. John Blacking. London: Academic Press, 1977. 1–28.

Blesser, Barry and Linda-Ruth Salter. *Spaces Speak, Are You Listening? Experiencing Aural Architecture*. Cambridge: MIT, 2006.

Bolter, David J. and Richard Grusin. *Remediation: Understanding New Media*. Cambridge: MIT, 1999.

Bonz, Jochen. *Subjekte des Tracks: Ethnografie einer Postmodernen/Anderen Subkultur*. Berlin: Kulturverlag Kadmos, 2008.

Born, Georgina and David Hesmondalgh. 'Othering, Hybridity, and Fusion in Transnational Popular Musics'. *Western Music and Its Others: Difference, Representation, and Appropriation in Music*. Ed. Georgina Born and David Hesmondalgh. Berkeley: University of California Press, 2000. 21–37.

Born, Georgina. 'Techniques of the Musical Imaginary'. *Western Music and Its Others: Difference, Representation, and Appropriation in Music*. Ed. Georgina Born and David Hesmondalgh. Berkeley: University of California Press, 2000. 37–47.

Bourdieu, Pierre. *Distinction: A Social Critique of the Judgement of Taste*. Trans. Richard Nice. London: Routledge, 1984 [first published 1979].

Brackett, David. *Interpreting Popular Music*. Cambridge: Cambridge University Press, 1995.

Bradshaw, Melissa. 'Give Me Your Bits'. *Decks and the City*. 19 August 2008. Web. 10 September 2008. http://melissabradshaw.net/?p=148more-148.

Bull, Michael. *Sound Moves: iPod Culture and Urban Experience*. London: Routledge, 2007.

Bull, Michael, and Back, Les. *The Auditory Culture Reader*. New York: Continuum, 2003.

Bull, Michael and Les Back, eds. *The Auditory Culture Reader*. 2nd edition. New York: Bloomsbury, 2015.

Burkhalter, Thomas. 'World Music 2.0: Between Fun and Protest Culture'. *NearEastQuarterly*. 28 November 2010. Web. 2 Febuary 2011. http://www.neareastquarterly.com/index.php/2010/11/28/world-music-2-0-between-fun-and-protest-culture.

Burtner, Matthew. 'Making Noise: Extended Techniques after Experimentalism'. *NewMusicBox*. 1 March 2005. Web. 21 November 2011. http://www.newmusicbox.org/articles/Making-Noise-Extended-Techniques-after-Experimentalism.

Butler, Mark J. *Unlocking the Groove: Rhythm, Meter, and Musical Design in Electronic Dance Music*. Bloomington: Indiana University Press, 2006.

Castells, Manuel. *The Information Age: Economy, Society, and Culture*. Vol. 1: *The Rise of the Network Society*. Oxford: Blackwell, 2000.

Chakrabarty, Dipesh. *Provincializing Europe: Postcolonial Thought and Historical Difference*. New Jersey: Princeton University Press, 2000.

Chatterjee, Anirvan. 'Suman Chatterjee and the Asian Dub Foundation: New Models of Hybrid Bengali Identity'. *Diasporic Tendencies*. 2000. Web. 11 July 2011. http://www.diasporic.com/articles/suman_adf.

Clayton, Jace. 'Through the Wires'. *The National*. 31 December 2009. Web. 7 March 2012. http://www.thenational.ae/arts-culture/music/through-the-wires.

Clifford, James. *Routes: Travel and Translation in the Late Twentieth Century*. Cambridge, MA: Harvard University Press, 1997.

Clifford, James. *The Predicament of Culture: Twentieth-Century Ethnography, Literature and Art*. Cambridge, MA: Harvard University Press, 1988.

Clifford, James. 'Traveling Cultures'. *Cultural Studies*. Ed. Lawrence Grossberg et al. New York: Routledge, 1992. 96–116.

Collins, Karen. *Game Sound: An Introduction to the History, Theory, and Practice of Video Game Music and Sound Design*. Cambridge: MIT, 2008.

Cook, Robin. 'Robin Cook's Chicken Tikka Masala Speech: Extracts from a Speech by the Foreign Secretary to the Social Market Foundation in London'. *Guardian*. 19 April 2001. Web. 17 February 2012. http://www.guardian.co.uk/world/2001/apr/19/race.britishidentity.

Cooper, Caroline. *Noises in the Blood: Orality, Gender, and the 'Vulgar' Body of Jamaican Popular Culture*. Durham: Duke University Press, 1995.

Cooper, Caroline. *Sound Clash: Jamaican Dancehall Culture at Large*. Basingstoke: Palgrave Macmillan, 2004.

Corbin, Alain. 'The Auditory Markers of the Village'. *The Auditory Culture Reader*. Ed. Michael Bull and Les Back. Oxford: Berg, 2004. 117–125. Reproduced with permission from: Corbin, Alain. *Village Bells: Sound and Meaning in the Nineteenth Century French Countryside*. New York: Columbia University Press, 1998. 95–101.

Cox, Christoph and Daniel Warner, eds. *Audio Culture: Readings in Modern Music*. New York: Continuum, 2006.

Dawson, Ashley. *Mongrel Nation: Diasporic Culture and the Making of Postcolonial Britain*. Ann Arbor: University of Michigan Press, 2007.

DeNora, Tia. 'Culture and Music'. *The SAGE Handbook of Cultural Analysis*. Ed. Tony Bennett and John Frow. Los Angeles: Sage, 2008.

DeNora, Tia. 'Music As a Technology of Self'. *Music in Everyday Life*. Cambridge: Cambridge University Press, 2000. 46–63.

Dery, Mark. 'Black to the Future'. *Flame Wars: The Discourse of Cyberculture*. Ed. Mark Dery. Durham: Duke University Press, 1994. 179–222.

Derrida, J., & Klein. 'Economimesis'. *Diacritics* 11.2 (1981): 3–25.

Drobnick, Jim. 'Listening Awry'. *Aural Cultures*. Ed. Jim Drobnick. Toronto: YYZ Books, 2004. 9–15.

Dudrah, Rajinder. 'Introduction: Drum "n" Dhol'. *Bhangra: Birmingham and Beyond*. Ed. Rajinder Dudrah. Birmingham: Birmingham Library Services, 2007. 12–43.

Dutta, Madhumita. 'Wind Instruments'. *Music and Musical Instruments of India*. London: ibs Books, 2008.

Eckstein, Lars. *Reading Song Lyrics*. Amsterdam: Rodopi, 2010a.

Eckstein, Lars. 'M.I.A.'s "Born Free" and the Ambivalent Politics of Authenticity and Provocation'. *Hard Times* 88.2 (2010b): 34–37.

Eckstein, Lars and Anja Schwarz (eds.). *postcolonial Piracy: Media Distribution and Cultural Production in the Global South*. London: Bloomsbury, 2014.

Erlmann, Veit, ed. *Hearing Cultures. Essays on Sound, Listening and Modernity*. Oxford: Berg, 2004.

Erlmann, Veit. *Reason and Resonance: A History of Modern Aurality*. New York: Zone Books, 2010.

Eshun, Kodwo. *More Brilliant Than the Sun: Adventures in Sonic Fiction*. London: Quartet Books, 1998.

Featherstone, Mike et al., eds. *Global Modernities*. London: Sage, 1995.

Feld, Steven. 'A Rainforest Acoustemology'. *The Auditory Culture Reader*. 1st edition. Ed. Michael Bull and Les Back. Oxford: Berg, 2004. 223–239. An earlier version of this article appeared as part of the article 'Sound Worlds' in *Sound*. Ed. Patricia Kruth and Henry Stobart. Cambridge: Cambridge University Press, 2000. 173–200.

Feld, Steven. *Sound and Sentiment: Birds, Weeping, Poetics, and Song in Kaluli Expression*. Philadelphia: University of Pennsylvania Press, 1982.

Flores, Juan. Foreword. *Reggaeton*. Ed. Raquel Rivera Z. et al. Durham: Duke University Press, 2009. ix–xii.

Flückiger, Barbara. *Sounddesign: Die virtuelle Klangwelt des Films*. Marburg: Schüren, 2001.

Foucault, Michel. *The History of Sexuality. Vol. 1: An Introduction*. Trans. Robert Hurley. New York: Vintage, 1980.

Frederickson, Jon. 'Technology and Music Performance in the Age of Mechanical Reproduction'. *International Review of the Aesthetics and Sociology of Music* 20.1 (1989): 193–220.

Frith, Simon. 'The Discourse of World Music'. *Western Music and Its Others: Difference, Representation, and Appropriation in Music*. Ed. Georgina Born and David Hesmondalgh. Berkeley: University of California Press, 2000. 305–322.

Frith, Simon. 'Music and Identity'. *Questions of Cultural Identity*. Ed. Stuart Hall and Paul Du Gay. London: Sage, 1996. 108–127.

Gajaweera, Nalika. 'The Discontents of the Hyphenated Identity: Second Generation British Asian Youth Culture and Fusion Music'. Occidental College. 2005. Web. 1 February 2012. http://www.focusanthro.org/essays0405/nalikagajaweera0405.htm.

Gatsas, Georg. 'From The Epicentre Of The Bass Quake'. *WoZ* 41 (2009). Web. 14 March 2012. http://www.georggatsas.com/serieswork/signal-the-future.html.

Giddens, Anthony. *Runaway World: How Globalization Is Reshaping Our Lives*. London: Profile, 1999.

Gill, Andy. 'Album: M.I.A'. *Independent*. 22 April 2005.
Gilroy, Paul. *There Ain't No Black in the Union Jack: The Cultural Politics of Race and Nation*. Chicago: University of Chicago Press, 1991.
Gilroy, Paul. *The Black Atlantic: Modernity and Double Consciousness*. London: Verso, 1993.
Glick-Schiller, Nina. 'From Immigrant to Transmigrant: Theorizing Transnational Migration'. *Anthropological Quarterly* 68.1 (1995): 48–63.
Goodman, Steve. *Sonic Warfare: Sound, Affect, and the Ecology of Fear*. Cambridge: MIT, 2010.
Grey, John S., Rev. 'R. Murray Schafer'. *Canadian Music Centre*. Reproduced with the permission of the *Encyclopedia of Music in Canada*. National Library of Canada, 2005. Web. 22 January 2011. http://www.musiccentre.ca/apps/index.cfm?fuseaction=composer.FA_dsp_biography&authpeopleid=1916&by=S.
Großmann, Rolf. 'Reproduktionsmusik und Remix-Culture'. *Mind the Gap: Medienkonstellationen zwischen zeitgenössischer Musik und Klangkunst*. Ed. Marion Saxer. Saarbrücken: Pfau, 2011. 116–127.
Gupta, Akhil and James Ferguson. 'Beyond "Culture": Space, Identity, and the Politics of Difference'. *Cultural Anthropology* 7.1 (1992): 6–23.
Hall, Stuart. 'New Ethnicities'. *'Race', Culture and Difference*. Ed. James Donald and Ali Rattansi. London: Sage, 1992. 252–259.
Hannerz, Ulf. *Transnational Connections: Culture, People, Places*. London: Routledge, 1996.
Hanrahan, Nancy Weiss. *Difference in Time: A Critical Theory of Culture*. Westport: Praeger Publishers, 2000.
Hardt, Michael and Negri, Antonio. *Empire*. Cambridge, Massachusetts: Harvard University Press, 2000.
Harrington, Richard. 'M.I.A., No Loss for Words'. *The Washington Post*. 16 September 2005. Web. 3 March 2012. http://www.washingtonpost.com/wp-dyn/content/article/2005/09/15/AR2005091500697.html.
Haupt, Adam. *Stealing Empire: P2P, Intellectual Property and Hip-Hop Subversion*. Cape Town: HSRC, 2008.
Hawkins, Stan. *Settling the Pop Score. Pop Texts and Identity Politics*. Aldershot: Ashgate, 2002.
Hebblethwaite, Phil. 'Why did these 8 musicians decline a British honour?' *BBC*. 2018. Web. 7 October 2019. https://www.bbc.co.uk/music/articles/e477656b-eed1-470c-ad56-3e06fa50901a.
Hebdige, Dick. *Cut'n'mix: Culture, Identity, and Caribbean Music*. London: Routledge, 2000 [first published 1987].
Hellström, Björn. *Noise Design: Architectural Modeling and the Aesthetics of Urban Acoustic Space*. Gothenburg: Bo Ejeby, 2003.
Henriques, Julian. *Sonic Bodies: Reggae Soundsystems, Performance Techniques and Ways of Knowing*. New York: Continuum, 2011.

Henriques, Julian. 'Sonic Dominance and the Reggae Sound System Session'. *The Auditory Culture Reader*. Ed. Michael Bull and Les Back. Oxford: Berg, 2004. 451–480.

Hesmondalgh, David. 'International Times: Fusion, Exoticism, and Antiracism in Electronic Dance Music'. In: Born, Georgina and Hesmondalgh, David. *Western Music and its 'Others': Difference, Representation, and Appropriation in* Music. Berkeley, Los Angeles: University of California Press, 2000. 280–304.

Hesmondhalgh, David and Caspar Melville. 'Urban Breakbeat Culture: Repercussions of Hip-Hop in the United Kingdom'. *Global Noise: Rap and Hip-Hop Outside the USA*. Ed. Tony Mitchell. Middletown: Wesleyan University Press, 2001. 86–110.

Hingorani, Dominic. *British Asian Theatre: Dramaturgy, Process and Performance*. Basingstoke: Palgrave Macmillan, 2010.

Hirani, Ritu. 'Asian Underground'. *The Rough Guide to Asian Underground*. London: Rough Trade, 2003. CD booklet.

Hirschberg, Lynn. 'M.I.A.'s Agitprop Pop'. *New York Times*. 25 May 2010. Web. 8 March 2012. http://www.nytimes.com/2010/05/30/magazine/30mia-t.html?pagewanted=all.

Hope, Donna. 'The British Link-Up Crew: Consumption Masquerading as Masculinity in the Dancehall'. *Interventions* 6.1 (2004): 101–117.

Howes, David. *Empire of the Senses: The Sensual Culture Reader*. Oxford: Berg, 2005.

Huggan, Graham. 'Derailing the "Trans"? Postcolonial Studies and the Negative Effects of Speed'. *Inter-und Transkulturelle Studien: Theoretische Grundlagen und interdisziplinäre Praxis*. Ed. Heinz Antor. Heidelberg: Winter, 2006. 55–61.

Huggan, Graham. *The Postcolonial Exotic: Marketing the Margins*. London: Routledge, 2001.

Huq, Rupa. 'Asian Kool? Bhangra and Beyond'. *Dis-Orienting Rhythms: The Politics of the New Asian Dance Music*. Ed. Sanjay Sharma et al. London: Zed Books, 1996. 61–80.

Huq, Rupa. 'Labouring the Point? The Politics of Britpop in "New Britain"'. *Britpop and the English Music Tradition*. Ed. Andy Bennett and Jon Stratton. Farnham: Ashgate, 2010. 89–102.

Hutnyk, John. *Critique of Exotica: Music, Politics, and the Culture Industry*. London: Pluto, 2000.

Hutnyk, John. 'Poetry after Guantanamo: M.I.A.' trinketization. 2 Febuary 2012. Web. 27 June 2012. http://hutnyk.files.wordpress.com/2012/02/poetry-after-guantanamofinal draftsocialidentities.pdf.

Ismaiel-Wendt, Johannes. *Tracks 'n' Treks: Populäre Musik und Postkoloniale Analyse*. Münster: Unrast, 2011.

Jazeel, Tariq. 'The World Is Sound? Geography, Musicology, and British-Asian Soundscapes'. *Area* 37.3 (2005): 233–241.

Jenks, Chris. 'The Centrality of the Eye in Western Culture: An Introduction'. *Visual Culture*. Ed. Chris Jenks. London: Routledge, 1995. 1–25.

Jonze, Spike. 'M.I.A'. *Time* Magazine. 30 April 2009. Web. 7 March 2012. http://www.time.com/time/specials/packages/article/0,28804,1894410_1893836_1894427,00.html.

Kahn, Douglas. *Noise, Water, Meat: A History of Sound in the Arts*. Cambridge: MIT, 1999.

Kalra, Virinder S. et al. 'Introduction'. *Diaspora and Hybridity*. Ed. Virinder S. Kalra et al. London: Sage, 2005. 1–7.

Kalra, Virinder S. et al. 'Re-Sounding (Anti)Racism, or Concordant Politics: Revolutionary Antecedents'. *Dis-Orienting Rhythms: The Politics of the New Asian Dance Music*. Ed. Sanjay Sharma et al. London: Zed Books, 1996. 15–31.

Kassabian, Anahid. 'Ubiquitous Listening'. *Popular Music Studies*. Ed. David Hesmondalgh and Keith Negus. London: Arnold, 2002. 131–142.

Katz, Mark. *Capturing Sound: How Technology Has Changed Music*. Berkeley: University of California Press, 2004.

Kim, Helen. *Making Diaspora in a Global City: South Asian Youth Cultures in London*. New York: Routledge, 2014.

Kosnick, Kira. 'Migrant Publics: Mass Media and Stranger-Relationality in Urban Space'. *Revue Européenne des Migrations Internationales* 26.1 (2010): 37–55.

LaBelle, Brandon. *Sonic Agency: Sound and Emergent Forms of Resistance*. London: Goldsmiths Press, 2018.

LaBelle, Brandon. *Acoustic Territories: Sound Culture and Everyday Life*. New York: Continuum, 2010.

LaBelle, Brandon. *Background Noise: Perspectives on Sound Art*. New York: Continuum, 2007.

Lamb, Bill. 'Gunshots as Music in a Pop Song? The M.I.A. "Paper Planes" Controversy'. *About.com*. 7 August 2008. Web. 2 June 2012. http://top40.about.com/b/2008/08/07/gunshots-as-music-in-a-pop-song-the-mia-paper-planes-controversy.htm.

Langenmaier, Amica-Verena, ed. *Der Klang der Dinge*. München: Design Zentrum München, 1993.

Lefebvre, Henri. *Rhythmanalysis: Space, Time, and Everyday Life*. London: Continuum, 2004.

Lester, Paul. 'Rappers with a Cause'. *Guardian*. 24 January 2003. Web. 12 May 2011. http://www.guardian.co.uk/music/2003/jan/24/artsfeatures.

Lipsitz, George. *Dangerous Crossroads: Popular Music, Postmodernism, and the Poetics of Place*. London: Verso, 1994.

Maier, Carla J. and Holger Schulze (2019). 'Living with Sound: The Semiotics and Mediology of Sonic Signs'. *Sound Works: A Cultural Theory of Sound Design*. Ed. Holger Schulze. New York: Bloomsbury.

Maier, Carla J. and Stefanie Alisch. 'The Sound of Afrofuturism'. *We Travel the Space Ways: Black Imagination, Fragments, and Diffractions*. Ed. Henriette Gunkel and kara lynch. Heidelberg: transcript, 2019.

Maier, Carla J. 'The Sound of Skateboarding: Aspects of a Transcultural Anthropology of Sound'. *The Senses and Society* 11.1 (2016): 24–35.

Manuel, Peter. 'Music as Symbol, Music as Simulacrum: Postmodern, Pre-Modern, and Modern Aesthetics in Subcultural Popular Musics'. *Popular Music* 14 (1995): 227–239.

Manuel, Peter. *Cassette Culture: Popular Music and Technology in North India*. Chicago: University of Chicago Press, 1993.

Marshall, Wayne. 'A Whole Nu World?' *wayne&wax*. 1 November 2010. Web. 2 March 2012. http://wayneandwax.com/?p=4568.

Marshall, Wayne et al. 'Introduction: Reggaeton's Socio-Sonic Circuitry'. *Reggaeton*. Ed. Raquel Z. Rivera et al. Durham: Duke University Press, 2009. 1–16.

Macpherson, Alex. 'Ikonika: The Woman Pushing Dubstep Forward'. *The Guardian*. 8 April 2010. Web. 24 March 2012. http://www.guardian.co.uk/music/2010/apr/08/dubstep-ikonika-hyperdub-electronic-music.

Manish. 'M.I.A., Fashion Victim'. *sepia Mutiny*. 5 May 2005. Web. 24 May 2012. Orig. published by *pitchfork* (2005). http://blog.teawithtanya.com/2005/05/05/mia_fashion_vic.

McLuhan, Marshall. *The Gutenberg Galaxy: The Making of Typographic Man*. Toronto: University of Toronto Press, 1962.

Mercer, Kobena. 1994. *Welcome to the Jungle: New Positions in Black Cultural Studies*. New York, London: Routledge.

Mignolo, Walter D. *Local Histories/Global Designs: Coloniality, Subaltern Knowledges, and Border Thinking*. New Jersey: Princeton University Press, 2000.

Mirzoeff, Nicholas, ed. *The Visual Culture Reader*. London: Routledge, 1998.

Mitchell, Tony, ed. *Global Noise: Rap and Hip-Hop outside the USA*. Middletown: Wesleyan University Press. 2001.

Mitchell, Timothy. 'Orientalism and the Exhibitionary Order'. *Colonialism and Culture*. Ed. Nicholas Dirks. Ann Arbor: University of Michigan Press, 1992. 289–318.

Mühleisen, Susanne. 'From Speech Community to Discourse Communities. Changing Creole Representations in the Urban Diaspora'. *Creole Discourse. Exploring Prestige Formation and Change across Caribbean English-lexicon Creoles*. Ed. Susanne Mühleisen. Amsterdam: John Benjamins, 2002. 135–80.

Murthy, Dhiraj. 'Muslim Punks Online: A Diasporic Pakistani Music Subculture on the Internet'. *South Asian Popular Culture* 8.2 (2010): 181–194.

Nachmann, Ron. 'Kush Arora's Sonic Conflicts'. *San Francisco Weekly*. 7 October 2009. Web. 1 October 2011. http://www.sfweekly.com/2009-10-07/music/kush-arora-s-sonic-conflicts.

NWA. 'Biography'. *nwaworld*. 2007. Web. 2 April 2010. http://www.nwaworld.com/biography.php.

Ong, Aihwa. 'Introduction'. *Flexible Citizenship: The Cultural Logics of Transnationality*. Ed. Aihwa Ong. Durham: Duke University Press, 1999. 1–28.

Oxford English Dictionary (OED). Entry: 'ghetto fabulous'. Second Edition, 1989. Online Version 2011. Last retrieved Oct 7, 2019.

Pennycook, Alastair. 'Hip Hop Be Connectin'. *Global Englishes and Transcultural Flows*. London: Routledge, 2007. 1–16.

Picker, J. *Victorian Soundscapes*. Oxford: Oxford University Press, 2003.

Pinch, Trevor and Karin Bijsterveld. *The Oxford Handbook of Sound Studies*. New York: Oxford University Press, 2012.

Reynolds, Simon. 'The Wire 300: Simon Reynolds on the Hardcore Continuum: Introduction'. *The Wire*. 2013 [2009]. Web. 7 July 2019. https://www.thewire.co.uk/in-writing/essays/the-wire-300_simon-reynolds-on-the-hardcore-continuum_introduction.

Robinson, Knox. 'Now Thing'. *Fader*. 1 June 2006. Web. 30 May 2012. http://www.thefader.com/2006/01/06/ya-ya-heeeeeeey.

Rose, Tricia. *Black Noise: Rap Music and Black Culture in Contemporary America*. Hanover: Wesleyan University Press, 1994.

Sanio, Sabine. 'Aspekte einer Theorie der auditiven Kultur: Ästhetische Praxis zwischen Kunst und Wissenschaft'. *kunsttexte.de, Auditive Pers-pektiven* 1 (2010): 1–14. Web. 1 February 2012. http://edoc.hu-berlin.de/kunsttexte/2010-4/sanio-sabine-2/PDF/sanio.pdf.

Sayyid, S. 'Introduction: BrAsians: Postcolonial People, Ironic Citizens'. *A Postcolonial People: South Asians in Britain*. Ed. N. Ali et al. London: Hurst, 2006. 1–10.

Saha, Anamik. 'Negotiating the Third Space: British Asian Independent Record Labels and the Cultural Politics of Difference'. *Popular Music and Society* 34.4 (2011): 437–454.

Schafer, R. Murray. *The Soundscape: Our Sonic Environment and the Tuning of the World*. Rochester: Destiny Books, 1994.

Schulze, Holger, ed. *Sound Studies: Traditionen – Methoden – Desiderate: Eine Einführung*. Bielefeld: transcript, 2008.

Schulze, Holger and Christoph Wulf, eds. *Klanganthropologie: Performativität – Imagination – Narration. Paragrana: Internationale Zeitschrift für Historische Anthropologie* 16.2 (2007).

Schulze-Engler, Frank and Sissy Helff, eds. *Transcultural English Studies: Theories, Fictions, Realities*. Amsterdam: Rodopi, 2009.

Schulze-Engler, Frank. 'From Postcolonial to Preglobal: Transnational Culture and the Resurgent Project of Modernity'. *Towards a Transcultural Future: Literature and Society in a 'Post'-Colonial World*. Ed. G. V. Davis et al. *Cross/Cultures* 77, ASNEL Papers 9.1. Amsterdam: Rodopi, 2004. 49–64.

Schulze-Engler, Frank. 'Von "Inter" zu "Trans": Gesellschaftliche, kulturelle und literarische Übergänge'. *Inter-und Transkulturelle Studien: Theoretische Grundlagen und interdisziplinäre Praxis*. Ed. Heinz Antor. Heidelberg: Winter, 2006. 41–53.

Schmidt, Leigh Eric. 'Hearing Loss'. *The Auditory Culture Reader*. Ed. Michael Bull and Les Back. Oxford: Berg, 2004. 41–59.

Schumacher, Thomas G. '"This Is a Sampling Sport": Digital Sampling, Rap Music and the Law in Cultural Production'. *Media, Culture and Society* 17.2 (1995): 253–273.

Senekowitsch, Susanne. '"Traficando Cultura": Funk aus Rio de Janeiro im Spannungsfeld zwischen lokaler Identität und globalisierter Jugend-kultur'. Dipl. thesis. University of Wien, 2010. Web. 12 August 2010. http://othes.univie.ac.at/8558/1/2010-02-18_9502022.pdf.

Sharma, Ashwani. 'Sounds Oriental: The (Im)possibility of Theorizing Asian Musical Cultures'. *Dis-Orienting Rhythms: The Politics of the New Asian Dance Music*. Ed. Sanjay Sharma et al. London: Zed Books, 1996. 15–31.

Sharma, Sanjay. 'Telling Stories about Bhangra: A Short Review of the Soho Road to the Punjab Exhibition'. *anti-babel*. 4 October 2007. Web. 10 April 2009. http://antibabel.wordpress.com/2007/10/04/telling-stories-about-bhangra-a-short-review-of-the-soho-road-to-the-punjab-exhibition.

Sharma, Sanjay. 'Asian Sounds'. *A Postcolonial People: South Asians in Britain*. Ed. N. Ali et al. London: Hurst, 2006. 1–10.

Sharma, Sanjay et al. 'Introduction'. *Dis-Orienting Rhythms: The Politics of the New Asian Dance Music*. Ed. Sanjay Sharma et al. London: Zed Books, 1996. 1–11.

Sharma, Sanjay. 'Noisy Asians or "Asian Noise"?' *Dis-Orienting Rhythms: The Politics of the New Asian Dance Music*. Ed. Sanjay Sharma et al. London: Zed Books, 1996. 32–57.

Sharma, Sanjay. 'The Sounds of Alterity'. *The Auditory Culture Reader*. Ed. Michael Bull and Les Back. Oxford: Berg, 2004. 409–418.

Shusterman, Richard. *Performing Live: Aesthetic Alternatives for the Ends of Art*. Ithaka: Cornell Univeristy Press, 2000.

Slobin, Mark. 'The Destiny of "Diaspora" in Ethnomusicology'. *The Cultural Study of Music: A Critical Introduction*. Ed. Martin Clayton et al. New York: Routledge, 2003. 284–296.

Smith, Bruce R. 'Tuning Into London c.1600'. *The Auditory Culture Reader*. Ed. Michael Bull and Les Back. Oxford: Berg, 2004. 127–135.

Spehr, Georg, ed. *Funktionale Klänge. Hörbare Daten, klingende Geräte und gestaltete Hörerfahrungen*. Sound Studies Series 1. Bielefeld: transcript, 2009.

Sterne, Jonathan. *The Audible Past: Cultural Origins of Sound Reproduction*. Durham: Duke University Press, 2003.

Sterne, Jonathan, ed. *The Sound Studies Reader*. New York: Routledge, 2012.

Stewart, Lizzie. 'Postmigrant theatre: the Ballhaus Naunynstraße takes on sexual nationalism'. *Journal of Aesthetics and Culture* 9.2 (2017): 56–68.

Stokes, Martin. 'Globalization and the Politics of World Music'. *The Cultural Study of Music: A Critical Introduction*. Ed. Martin Clayton et al. New York: Routledge, 2003. 297–308.

Stowell, Dan and Mark D. Plumbley. 'Characteristics of the Beatboxing Vocal Style'. University Paper. University of London, 2008. Web. 1 March 2012. http://goblin.elec.qmul.ac.uk/people/markp/2008/StowellPlumbley08-tr0801.pdf.

Stroumboulopoulos, George. 'M.I.A. Interview'. *The Hour. CBC/Radio-Canada.* 15 October 2007. Web. 24 May 2012. http://www.youtube.com/watch?v=bfhEQL6b_7o.

Sundaram, Ravi. *Pirate Modernity: Delhi's Media Urbanism.* New York: Routledge, 2010.

Taylor, Timothy D. 'Anglo-Asian Self-Fashioning'. *Global Pop: World Music, World Markets.* New York: Routledge. 1997. 147–172.

Théberge, Paul. *Any Sound You Can Imagine: Making Music / Consuming Technology.* Hanover: Wesleyan University Press, 1997.

Thompson, Paul. 'M.I.A. Confronts the Haters'. *Pitchfork.* 3 August 2007. Web. 2 March 2012. http://pitchfork.com/news/27349-mia-confronts-the-haters.

Thornton, Sarah. *Club Cultures: Music, Media and Subcultural Capital.* Cambridge: Polity, 1995.

Tonkiss, Fran. 'Aural Postcards. Sound, Memory and the City'. *The Auditory Culture Reader.* Ed. Michael Bull and Les Back. Oxford, New York: Berg, 2004. 303–309.

Truax, Barry. *Acoustic Communication.* Westport: Greenwood, 2001 [first published 1985].

TyTe and Defenicial. 'The Real History of Beatboxing: Part 1'. *humanbeatbox.* 2010. Web. 12 August 2011. http://www.humanbeatbox.com/history/p2_articleid/27.

Urry, John. *Sociology Beyond Societies: Mobilities for the Twenty-First Century.* London: Routledge, 2000.

Viol, Claus-Ulrich. 'Br-Asian Overground: Marginal Mainstream, Mixing, and the Role of Memory in British Asian Popular Music'. *Journal for the Study of British Cultures* 8.1 (2001): 73–90.

Walser, Robert. *Running with the Devil: Power, Gender, and Madness in Heavy Metal Music.* Middletown: Wesleyan University Press, 1993.

Watkins, Lee. 'Rapp"in" the Cape: Style and Memory, Power in Community'. *Music, Space and Place: Popular Music and Cultural Identity.* Ed. Sheila Whiteley et al. Aldershot: Ashgate, 2004. 124–146.

Weheliye, Alexander G. *Phonographies: Grooves in Sonic Afro-Modernity.* Durham: Duke University Press, 2005.

Welsch, Wolfgang. 'Transculturality – the Puzzling Form of Cultures Today'. *Spaces of Culture: City, Nation, World.* Ed. Mike Featherstone and Scott Lash. London: Sage, 1999. 194–213.

Welz, Gisela. 'Multiple Modernities: The Transnationalization of Cultures'. *Transcultural English Studies: Theories, Fictions, Realities.* Ed. Frank Schulze-Engler and Sissy Helff. Amsterdam: Rodopi, 2009. 37–57.

Welz, Gisela. 'Transnational Cultures and Multiple Modernities: Anthropology's Encounter with Globalization'. *'Between Worlds': The Legacy of Edward Said.* Ed. Günter H. Lenz et al. *ZAA Quarterly* 52.4 (2004): 409–422.

Wheaton, RJ. 'Profile of M.I.A.' *RJ Wheaton.* 2015. Web. 22 May 2017. http://www.rjwheaton.com/blog/2005/5/6/profile-of-mia.html.

Whiteley, Sheila and Andy Bennett. 'Introduction'. Music, *Space and Place: Popular Music and Cultural Identity*. Ed. Sheila Whiteley et al. Aldershot: Ashgate, 2004. 1–21.

Wicke, Peter. 'The Art of Phonography: Sound, Technology and Music'. *The Ashgate Research Companion to Popular Musicology*. Ed. Derek B. Scott. Farnham: Ashgate, 2009. 147–168.

Wicke, Peter. 'Popmusik in der Analyse'. *Acta Musicologica* LXXV (2003): 107–115.

Zuberi, Nabeel. *Sounds English: Transnational Popular Music*. Chicago: University of Illinois Press, 2001.

Discography

Apache Indian. 'Arranged Marriage'. *No Reservations*. London: Island Records, 1992. CD.

Apache Indian. 'Arranged Marriage (Indian Wedding Anthem Mix)'. *Arranged Marriage*. London: Island Records, 1992. CD single.

Apache Indian. 'Arranged Marriage (Ragga Mix)'. *Arranged Marriage*. London: Island Records, 1992. CD single.

Apache Indian. 'Calling Out to Jah (feat Luciano)'. *No Reservations*. London: Island Records, 1992. CD.

Apache Indian. 'Movie Over India'. *No Reservations*. London: Island Records, 1992. CD.

'Arkanoid Sound'. *Arkanoid: The Revenge of DOH*. Dev. Taito. Torrance: Romstar Inc., 1986. Computer game.

Asian Dub Foundation. *A History of Now*. Tokyo: Beat Records, 2011. CD.

Asian Dub Foundation. 'Collective Mode'. *Community Music*. London: London Records, 2000. CD.

Asian Dub Foundation. 'Naxalite'. *Naxalite Culture Move*. London: London Records, 1998. CD.

Asian Dub Foundation. 'Rebel Warrior'. *Facts and Fictions*. London: Nation Records, 1995. CD.

The Beatles. 'Norwegian Wood (This Bird Has Flown)'. *Rubber Soul*. London: EMI, 1965. Vinyl.

Bill Conti. 'Gonna Fly Now'. *Gonna Fly Now*. Los Angeles: United Artists Records, 1976. Vinyl single.

The Clash. 'Straight to Hell'. *Combat Rock*. London: CBS, 1982. Vinyl.

Deize Tigrona. 'Injeção'. *Slum Dunk Presents Funk Carioca*. Brighton: Mr Bongo, 2004. CD.

DJ Wonder. 'Asia'. B-side. *What*. London: Dump Valve Recordings, 2004. Vinyl single.

Dr. Alimantado. 'Poison Flour'. *Poison Flour*. Kingston: Ital Sounds, 1978. Vinyl single.

Dr. Buzzard's Original Savannah Band. 'Sunshower'. B-Side. *Cherchez La Femme*. New York: RCA, 1976. Vinyl single.

Dusk + Blackdown. 'Darker Than East'. *Margins Music*. London: Keysound Recordings, 2008. CD.
Dusk + Blackdown. 'Kuri Pataka (The Firecracker Girl)'. *Margins Music*. London: Keysound Recordings, 2008. CD.
Dusk + Blackdown. 'Rolling Raj Deep'. *Margins Music*. London: Keysound Recordings, 2008. CD.
Eminem. 'One Shot 2 Shot'. *Encore*. Santa Monica: Interscope, 2004. CD.
Horsepower Productions. 'Sholay (Epic Mix)'. *To The Rescue*. London: Tempa, 2004. CD.
Kode 9. 'Sub-Kontinent'. *Grime 2* (Compilation). Redruth: Rephlex, 2004. CD.
Kode 9 and the Spaceape. 'Fukkaz'. London: Hyperdub, 2006. MP3.
Loefa. 'Indian Dub'. *Jungle Infiltrator*. London: Big Apple Records, 2004. Vinyl.
M.I.A. *MAYA*. London: XL Recordings/N.E.E.T., 2010. CD.
M.I.A. 'Born Free'. Dir. Roman Gavras, 2011. Music video.
M.I.A. 'Bucky Done Gun'. *Arular*. London: XL Recordings, 2005. CD.
M.I.A. 'Bucky Done Gun'. Dir. Anthony Mandler, 2005. Music video.
M.I.A. 'Galang'. *Arular*. London: XL Recordings, 2005. CD.
M.I.A. 'Sunshowers'. *Arular*. London: XL Recordings, 2005. CD.
M.I.A. 'Sunshowers (Diplo Mix)'. *Piracy Funds Terrorism*. Not on Label (M.I.A. Self-released), 2004. CD-R.
M.I.A. 'Paper Planes'. *Late Show with David Letterman*. New York: CBS, 2008. Music video.
M.I.A. 'Paper Planes'. *Kala*. London: XL Recordings, 2007. CD.
Nathan 'Flutebox' Lee. Concert. Queen Elisabeth Hall, 2010. Live Performance.
Nathan 'Flutebox' Lee. 'Dog'. *Flutebox*. London: Swaraj Music, 2010. CD.
Nathan 'Flutebox' Lee. 'Interlude'. *Flutebox*. London: Swaraj Music, 2010. CD.
Nathan 'Flutebox' Lee. 'Intro'. *Flutebox*. London: Swaraj Music, 2010. CD.
Vybz Kartel. 'Gun Session'. *J.M.T.* Greensleeves Records, 2005. CD.
Wreckx-N-Effect. 'Rump Shaker'. *Rump Shaker*. Chicago: MCA Records, 1992. Vinyl single.
Yellowman. 'Zungu Zungu Zungu Zeng'. *Zungu Zungu Zungu Zeng*. Kingston: Volcano, 1982 Vinyl single.

Index

The ABC music shop 172
Abdel-Hamid, Sara. *See* Ikonika (Abdel-Hamid, Sara)
Abdellatif, Farah 147
acid house 40, 169
ADF. *See* Asian Dub Foundation (ADF)
Afrika Bambaataa 45
Afro-Caribbean music 29, 40, 43, 90, 92, 98, 104, 109, 116–17, 160
Afro-diasporic music 62, 161
Afrofuturism 40–1
Alaap (band) 33
Alchemy Festival 2011 70
Ali, N. 21
Anderson, Benedict 18
Anokha (club night) 36–7
anti-racist activism 10, 114
Any Sound You Can Imagine (Théberge) 70, 148
Apache Indian 6, 8–10, 29, 38, 89, 91–103, 120, 156, 170, 181–4
Appadurai, Arjun 24, 28
Aristotle 50–1, 196 n.1
Arkanoid sound 109–10, 118, 184
Arora, Kush 171, 202 n.6
'Arranged Marriage' (track) 10, 92–3, 181–2, 184, 199 n.9
analysis of 93–104
The Art of Noises 197 n.14
Arular (2005) 1, 4, 10, 30, 126, 132, 134–5
Arulpragasam, Mathangi. *See* M.I.A. (Arulpragasam, Mathangi)
'Asia' (2004) 160
Asian Dub Foundation (ADF) 4, 6, 9–10, 16, 20, 29, 36, 38, 68, 105–6, 119–20, 183–5, 192
   Arkanoid sound 109–10
   Bollywood sample 107–9
   ethnic identity 114–16
   lyrics 110–13, 116–18
Asian Kool 33–4
Asianness 10, 21, 34, 38, 91, 113, 119, 161

'Asian Noise' 109
Asian Underground 29, 34, 36–8, 40, 45, 67
Atari 109
Attakkalari Centre for Movement Arts 70
Attali, Jaques 49, 63, 79
The Audible Past: Cultural Origins of Sound Reproduction (Sterne) 197 n.16
auditory culture 53, 60–1, 80, 143
The Auditory Culture Reader (Bull and Back) 55
Augé, Marc 197 n.12

Ballhaus Naunynstraße 195 n.2
bamboo flute 146
Bangladeshi identities 114
basic beat pattern 126–8, 139
bass materialism 166–8, 188
BBC Radio Leicester 196 n.10
beat-boxing 10, 72, 144, 147–50, 153, 157, 186–7
Beatles 31, 168
Belle, LaVaughn 194
Bengali identity 114–16
Bentes, Ivana 133
Berger, Harris M. 116
'bhangramuffin' 29, 89–91
bhangra music, UK 7, 9–11, 15, 25–6, 29–36, 45, 67–8, 74, 89–92, 94–5, 98–9, 101–5, 108, 116, 120, 161, 171–2, 181–2, 201 n.5
'Bidrohi' (Bengali poem) 114
Billboard Hot 100 136
binarisms 2, 25, 53, 89
Black, Don 39
Black Atlantic (Gilroy) 16
Blacking, John 148
black masculinities 199 n.7
Blair, Tony 19
Bollywood music 26, 32–3, 39, 45, 85, 104, 107–10, 118, 161, 166, 168–72, 174, 183–5, 188–9

Bolter, Jay David 103, 107
bongos/tablas 83
  key sound 139
'Boom-Shak-a-lak' (song) 92
Born, Georgina 74–5
Bourdieu, Pierre 201 n.3
Brackett, David 96
Bradshaw, Melissa 172
BrAsian (British Asian) 21–2, 25, 30–9, 42, 45–6, 92, 98, 103–6, 111–13, 160
'British-Asian Soundscapes' 67
Britishness 21–2, 31, 34, 38, 75, 85, 96, 168
Britpop music 196 n.6
'Bucky Done Gun' (track) 126, 132–5, 139–40, 170, 185–6
Bull, Michael 8, 59–61, 197 n.12
Burkhalter, Thomas 42, 124, 196 n.16
Burtner, Matthew 146, 201 n.1
Butler, Mark 82–3, 145

Cage, John 64–5
'Calling Out to Jah' (track) 93
Capturing Sound (Katz) 68, 76, 139
Cartridge Music 65
cash register sound 137–8
CBS 138
CCCS. *See* Centre for Contemporary Cultural Studies (CCCS)
Centre for Contemporary Cultural Studies (CCCS) 53
Chandola, Ash 36
Chatterjee, Anirvan 114–15
Chuck D 116
A City Visible but Unseen 202 n.10
Clandestino Festival 40
Clark, Martin 11, 159, 161, 168–9, 171–2, 174, 201 n.5
The Clash 135–7
classical music 58, 72, 147, 187
  European 187
  Indian 31, 102, 105, 108, 120, 143, 145–6, 149, 156, 172, 187
  Western 146, 149
Clayton, Jace 41, 125
'Collective Mode' (track) 105–7, 111, 118, 120, 183–4
colonialism 17, 21, 51, 113–14
Combat Rock (1982) 135

Community Music (2000) 10, 105–6, 199 n.1
concrete sound practices 5, 74–5, 83, 109, 119, 160–1, 180, 189
'Con/Fusion' (track) 172
connotations 10, 27, 52, 55, 82, 85, 95, 97, 101, 121–2, 124–5, 129, 133–4, 138, 141–2, 155–7, 166, 168–9, 173, 185
Conti, Bill 132, 139–40, 185–6
Cook, Norman 77–8, 196 n.4
copyright practices 79, 198 n.23
Corbin, Alain 56
Cubase 83
cultural analysis, of musical sound 5, 8–9, 54–5, 75, 84, 104, 119, 140, 144–5, 157, 180
cultural formation 7, 15–18, 23–4, 31, 33, 50, 53, 55–66, 74, 81–2, 104, 120, 189, 195 n.1
cultural identity(ies) 15, 17–18, 23, 25, 32, 56, 67, 75, 85, 101, 103, 111, 115–16, 119–20, 140, 181, 183, 189
cultural politics, of music 3, 6–7, 19–20, 25–30, 33, 52, 73–4, 117, 124, 168
cultural practice 15, 20, 24–5, 46, 49, 53–4, 57–8, 74–5, 81–2, 119, 182
cultural production 6, 16, 19–24, 30, 32–4, 37–8, 54, 76, 81, 125, 189, 195 n.3, 198 n.23
cultural racism 19
cultural technology 8, 68
cultural transformation 7, 11, 39, 109, 188–9, 191, 194

dancehall/ragga (Jamaican) 2, 9–10, 29, 36, 40, 61–2, 89–90, 93–5, 97–9, 101–2, 104–5, 108, 110–11, 118, 120–1, 128, 133, 156, 160, 181–4, 198 n.5, 199 n.1, 199 n.2
Dangerous Crossroads: Popular Music, Postmodernism and the Poetics of Place (Lipsitz) 17, 23, 92
'Darker Than East' (track) 77, 161–5, 168, 175
Das, Aniruddha (Dr Das) 105, 109, 114
Davis, Mike 122
Dawson, Ashley 19–21, 29
Deeder Zaman 106, 114, 116–17
DeNora, Tia 149, 151

Derrida, Jacques 103
Dery, Mark 40
dhol drum (double-barrelled drum) 30, 33, 94, 99, 169, 181
diasporic dance music production 6–8, 15–16, 18–24, 28, 34, 39–40, 42–3, 46, 50, 55, 62, 82, 91–2, 104, 106, 113–15, 161, 179, 190, 195 n.2
dichotomization 25–6, 69
difference, sound 80
digital media technologies 18, 41–2, 66, 68–9, 83, 91–2, 122
digital sampling 7, 9–10, 39, 68, 71, 73, 76–81, 104, 106–9, 118–19, 150, 163, 168, 183
Diplo. *See* Pentz, Thomas Wesley (Diplo)
disco 33, 130, 185
discontinuities 79
Dis-orienting Rhythms: The Politics of the New Asian Dance Music (Sharma, Hutnyk and Sharma) 26, 67, 105, 112–13
dissonance 79, 95
distractions 79
Dizzee Rascal 201 n.2
DJ Target 162
DJ Wonder 160
'Dog' (track) 152–4, 187
Dorian scale 108
downbeat 200 n.8
Dr. Buzzard's Original Savannah Band 130, 185
Drobnick, Jim 54
drum'n'bass 9, 36, 40, 72, 79, 85, 98, 104, 127, 149, 160, 170, 188, 202 n.7
'dub materialism' 160, 166–7, 170
dubstep 9, 11, 25, 30, 40, 79, 104, 159–62, 166–70, 172, 188
Dudrah, Rajinder 30
Dusk + Blackdown/Dusk & Blackdown 6, 9, 11, 29–30, 61, 77–8, 188, 201 n.4, 202 n.6
  'Darker Than East' (track) 161–5
  description 159–61
  'Kuri Pataka' (The Firecracker Girl)' (track) 165–8
  poetics and politics of place 170–3
  'Rolling Raj Deep' (track) 169–70

visual and textual conception of *Margins Music* 173–6

Eazy-E 44
Eckstein, Lars 3, 118
EDM. *See* electronic dance music (EDM)
Eelam Revolutionary Organization of Students (EROS) 200 n.5
Ehlers, Jeanette 194
electric guitar 90, 108–9
electronic dance music (EDM) 2, 25, 36–7, 77, 79, 82–4, 121, 136, 145, 152, 156, 170–1, 173, 202 n.7
electronic music 15, 36, 42, 62, 65, 72, 79, 83, 90–1, 106, 124–5, 157, 171, 199 n.1, 202 n.6
Emerging Artist in Residence (EAR) 11
entangled histories 16
EROS. *See* Eelam Revolutionary Organization of Students (EROS)
Eshun, Kodwo 5, 40–1
ethnicity/ethnic identity 10, 15, 18, 22, 24, 27–8, 82, 99, 104–5, 114–16, 120, 129–30, 173, 175, 179, 183, 189, 196 n.5
ethnoscapes 24, 28
European classical music 187
everyday sounds and music 55–66, 77
extended playing technique 146–8, 201 n.1

Facts and Fictions (1995) 105, 114, 199 n.1
fat beats 67
Feld, Steven 59, 197 n.8
'Fight the Power' 76, 78
figure and ground 58, 80
fingo 129
Fireburn Revolts 194
Flexible Citizenship (Ong) 22
Flores, Juan 43
Flutebox EP (2010) 10, 144–5, 151–3, 155–7, 187
flutebox technology 145–51, 153–4, 186
folk music 26, 70
Foucault, Michel 71
Frampton, Dan 11, 159, 174
Frankie Paul 90
Frederickson, Jon 71
Frith, Simon 119, 196 n.8

'Fukkaz' (2006) 160
Fun^da^mental/Fun-Da-Mental 16, 20, 22, 36, 106, 113, 116
funk carioca 2, 27, 43–5, 77–9, 121, 125–6, 132–4, 185–6
Funky 160
fusion, musical 27, 31, 34, 108, 179

Gajaweera, Nalika 36
'Galang' (track) 4, 135
gangsta rap 44
Gatsas, Georg 160
Gavras, Romain 3, 141
ghetto fabulous 123–4, 134, 136, 139, 141–2
Gilroy, Paul 16, 28, 95
Glick-Schiller, Nina 20
global fusion 2
global ghettotech 42–3, 121–5, 141–2, 179
globalization 18, 23, 75, 122
global pop. *See* pop music
Global Pop, Local Language (Berger) 116
global sound 1–2, 190
global South 123–4, 126
global village 122
'Gonna Fly Now' (track) 132, 139–40, 170, 185–6
Goodman, Steve 40–1, 62, 121, 125, 160, 166
Gosh, Arun 34
grime pattern 154, 164, 160, 166
Großmann, Rolf 66
Grusin, Richard 103, 107
The Guardian 161
guitar music 72
gunshot sound 137–8

Handel 63
'handmade' instrumental music 70
hardcore continuum 188
Harrison, George 31
Hawkins, Stan 72–3
H-Dhami 34
'Hearing Loss' 50
Hebdige, Dick 15
Heera (band) 33
Henriques, Julian 8, 61–2, 95
Hesmondalgh, David 74, 78, 117

Hindi music 11, 32, 91, 99–103, 107–8, 119, 165–71, 182
Hindustani music 146
hip-hop 2, 9, 28–9, 44, 62, 66, 72, 78, 90, 100, 103–4, 107–8, 111, 117, 120–1, 123, 126, 129, 133–6, 141, 144, 146–9, 152, 155, 157, 167, 172, 179, 187, 196 n.12, 199 n.1, 199 n.6
Hirani, Ritu/DJ Ritu 34–7
A History of Now 105
Horsepower 160
hot rhythms 67
The Hour 200 n.6
Huggan, Graham 23
Huq, Rupa 105
Hustlers HC 36, 106, 113
Hutnyk, John 5, 15, 67
hypermediacy 107, 183–4

I Am Queen Mary 194
Ice Cube 44
ideoscapes 24
i-D magazine 89
Ikonika (Abdel-Hamid, Sara) 161
Imagined Communities (Anderson) 18
immediacy 144–5
imperialism 17, 19, 75
The Independent 1
Indian classical music 31, 102, 105, 108, 120, 143, 145–6, 149, 156, 172
'Indian Dub' (2004) 160
Indian folk dance 30
Indianness 31, 75, 85, 91, 96, 102, 150, 156–7, 167–8, 182–3
Indi-Pop 67
Indo-Jazz 34
'Injeçao' (track) 132–4, 139–40, 185
instrumentation 2, 30, 33, 39, 90, 115–16, 185
intensity 144–6
'Interlude' (track) 154–5, 187
Interpreting Popular Music (Brackett) 96
iPod culture 8, 59–61
'Iqbal's Groove' (track) 172
Islam, Kazi Nazrul 114
Islamophobia 20
Island Records 92
Ismaiel-Wendt, Johannes 39

Jamaican reggae. *See* dancehall/ragga (Jamaican)
Jarral, Farrah 167, 172, 174, 202 n.9
Jazeel, Tariq 67–8, 73–4
jazz music 147–9, 154–5, 187
    drum kit 152
    fusion 27
Jhooti, Kamaljit Singh (Jay Sean) 196 n.12
jungle breaks 30, 36, 40, 72, 105, 108, 120, 149, 199 n.1

Kala (2007) 1, 126, 131, 135, 137
Kaliphz 106
Kalra, Virinder S. 15, 21
Kaluli people 8, 59
Kapur, Steven. *See* Apache Indian
Katz, Mark 68–9, 76–8, 118, 139, 163
Kaur, Raminder 15
Kerjaj, Mazen 196 n.16
key sounds/keynote sounds 9, 57, 76, 84–5, 94, 99, 106, 108, 136, 139, 166, 169–72, 175, 181, 183–5, 188
Khan, Hanif 151
Kim, Helen 35
knowledge production 50–2, 164
Kode 9 160
Kosnick, Kira 195 n.2
KRS1 116
'Kuri Pataka' (The Firecracker Girl)' (track) 165–8, 171–2, 174–5, 188, 201 n.4, 201 n.5
kwaito 2, 121, 125

LaBelle, Brandon 65, 192
Langhoff, Shermin 195 n.2
language choice 116–17
Lansky, Paul 76
Late Show with David Letterman (TV show) 138
layering of sounds 39, 84, 106, 162, 181, 189, 198 n.6
Lebanese Civil war 196 n.16
Lee, Nathan ('Flutebox') 6, 9–10, 29–30, 34, 72, 77, 186–7
    Cover art 155–6
    'Dog' (track) 152–4
    flutebox technology 145–51
    'Interlude' (track) 154–5

liveness 144–5, 151–2
live performance 143–4
and recorded music 151–2
Liberation Tigers of Tamil Eelam (LTTE) 3
Limehouse 162–4, 175
Lipsitz, George 17–18, 23–4, 92, 164, 195 n.1
liveness 144–5, 151–2, 163
live performance 143–4, 159
Loefa 160
Logic Pro 83
London underground 8, 49, 191
LTTE. *See* Liberation Tigers of Tamil Eelam (LTTE)
lyrical performance 7, 10, 74, 82, 89, 95–8, 104, 106, 110–13, 116–18, 126, 128–9, 131, 139–40, 156, 181–3

machine technologies 71
McClymont, Jepther (Luciano) 93
McLuhan, Marshall 52–3, 122, 197 n.2, 197 n.5
Manuel, Peter 90–1, 93, 98–9, 101–2
Margins Music (2008) 11, 30, 61, 159, 161, 171–3
    visual and textual conception of 173–6
Marley, Bob 198 n.2
Marshall, Wayne 42, 125
Maxi Priest 90, 92
MAYA (2010) 3
MBE award 3–4
MCing 150–2, 187
Member of the British Empire Award 113
Mendi + Keith Obadike 193
Mercer, Kobena 26
M.I.A. (Arulpragasam, Mathangi) 1–6, 9–10, 29–30, 42–3, 120, 140–1, 185–6, 192, 200 n.5, 200 n.6, 201 n.10, 201 n.11
    'Bucky Done Gun' (track) 126, 132–5, 139–40, 170
    description 121–6
    'Paper Planes' (track) 135–40
    'Sunshowers' (track) 126–32, 139–40
Miami bass 44–5, 132
MIDI. *See* Musical Instrument Digital Interface (MIDI)
migration 17, 20

Mirzoeff, Nicholas 51–3
Missy Elliot 130
Mitchell, Timothy 51
'modes of production' 148
Mongrel Nation (Dawson) 19, 29
'Movie over India' (track) 93
MTV 131, 138, 149
muffled background rhythm 107–8
Mühleisen, Susanne 199 n.10
multiple modernities 16
Mumford, Lewis 64
musical analysis 9, 27, 42, 58, 68, 73–4, 96
musical creation 28, 61, 65, 69, 76, 83, 187
musical/cultural identity(ies) 15, 17–18, 23, 25, 32, 56, 67, 75, 85, 101, 103, 111, 115–16, 119–20, 140, 181, 183, 189
musical fusion 27, 31, 34, 108, 179
Musical Instrument Digital Interface (MIDI) 83
musicality 74
musical practices 6–7, 15, 28, 46, 59, 64–5, 67–9, 84, 198 n.20
musical sounds 7–8, 49. *See also* sound practice(s), transcultural
 cultural analysis of 5, 8–9, 54–5, 75, 84, 104, 119, 140, 144–5, 157, 180
 qualities of 8
 and transcultural formation 55–66
musical styles 2, 7, 9, 11, 15, 25–7, 29–33, 31, 35–7, 40–4, 67–8, 71, 73, 81–2, 85, 90, 102–3, 105–6, 125–6, 132, 147–9, 153–4, 157, 161, 179, 187, 197 n.15, 202 n.7
musical technologies. *See* technology/ technologies, sound
'Music as a Technology of Self' 149
music's 'otherness' 26, 32, 175
musique concrete 65–6
Mystro (Amarfio, Kevin) 151–2

national identity 19–21, 24–5, 46
nationalism/nationality 15, 18, 21, 23, 35, 37, 39, 41, 114
Nation Records (music label) 36, 38
nation states 16–17, 20, 23, 26
Naxalite Culture Move (1998) 114
'Naxalite' (song) 114
Nerm 33, 39

New Asian Dance Music 36
New Asian Kool 27, 113
New Labour 19, 196 n.6
New York Police Department 193
Nike 131
Noise: The Political Economy of Music (Attali) 49
noise and music 79
No Reservations (1992) 10, 92–3, 102–3
'Notjustmoreidlechatter' 76
Numbers Station [Furtive Movements] (2015) 193
N.W.A. (Niggaz With Attitude) 44

off-beat reggae rhythm 89, 94, 96, 98, 118, 127
Ong, Aiwha 22–3
ornamental effect 102, 108, 156, 170, 182–4
'otherness,' music's 26, 32, 175
Outcaste (music label) 36

Palazhy, Jayachandran 70
Pandit, John 4, 113
'Paper Planes' (track) 126, 135–40, 142, 200 n.8
'Parental Advisory: Explicit Content' stamp 155
Patois 128
Pennycook, Alastair 79
Pentz, Thomas Wesley (Diplo) 125
percussion instruments 67
performative spaces 39
perreo (doggy style) 126
'Peter und der Wolf' 146
phonograph effect 68–9
Phonographies (Weheliye) 71
physicality 144–5
Piracy Funds Terrorism 129
Pitchfork (music magazine) 134
Planet of Slums (Davis) 121–2
playing technique, of flute 146, 153
poetics of place 17, 24, 164, 168, 170–3
'Poison Flour' (1978) 94
politicized lyrics 133, 135
politics of place 11, 17, 23, 159, 165, 170–3
pop music 1, 3–4, 10, 18, 26–7, 29–31, 34, 40, 66–7, 73, 80, 90, 92, 102, 123,

131, 133–4, 141, 147, 170, 179, 196 n.8, 199 n.4
popular music 17, 66, 72, 83
post-bhangra music styles 7, 90
postcolonial ear training 39
A Postcolonial People: South Asians in Britain (Ali, Kalra and Sayyid) 21–2
post-migrant theatre 10, 25, 31, 106, 194, 195 n.2
post-2000 UK, dance music in 29, 38–47
'Praise You' (song) 77
production culture 98, 119, 150, 166, 168, 170, 173, 182–4, 187, 198 n.20
Prokofjew, Sergei 146
Public Enemy 44, 76, 78–9, 117
'Pump Me Up' (song) 78
Punjabi lyrics 89–90, 93, 96–7, 120, 182
punk music/punk guitars 29, 36, 66, 105, 108, 120, 130, 135–6, 171, 183, 186, 199 n.1
'Push It' 129

Queen Elisabeth Hall 143–4, 149

racism 20
ragga/reggae. *See* dancehall/ragga (Jamaican)
Rahman, A. R. 39
'Rainforest Acoustemology' 59
rap music 4, 17, 36, 44, 66, 79, 91, 105, 112, 114–18, 120, 123, 128–30, 132, 134–6, 138, 152, 154, 183, 198 n.6
Rastafarianism 93, 103, 198 n.2
rave 40
'Rebel Warrior' (track) 114
received pronunciation (RP) 116
recontextualization 9, 68, 77–8, 80, 82, 94, 104, 106, 109, 114–15, 118, 126, 130, 132, 163–4, 169–70, 181, 185
recorded performance 96
recorded sound 10, 69, 73, 159
recording technology 68–9, 76, 78, 107, 151–2
re-fusing bhangra 104
reggaeton 2, 43, 121, 125–6, 125–8, 130, 185
repertoires 5, 10, 30, 55, 58, 102, 137, 139, 146–8, 157, 169–71, 184–5, 187–9

rewind 118, 184
Reynolds, Simon 188
rhythm/rhythmic patterns 11, 66, 84, 99, 107–8, 110, 128, 130, 132, 136–7, 147, 152, 154, 167, 169, 184
Richi Rich 34
r'n'b vocal feature 34, 100, 130
Robinson, Knox 127
rock music 27, 66, 83, 105–6, 108, 199 n.1
Rocky theme 132, 139–40, 170, 185–6
Roland MC-505 drum machine 127
Roll Deep 161, 165
'Rolling Raj Deep' (track) 169–71, 175
Rose, Tricia 198 n.6
RP. *See* received pronunciation (RP)
'Rump Shaker' (track) 135–7, 141
Rushdie, Salman 202 n.10
Russolo, Luigi 64, 197 n.14

Sagoo, Bally 37
Saha, Anamik 37
Salt'n'Pepa 129–30
samplers 67, 76
sampling technology 7, 9–10, 39, 68–9, 71, 73, 76–81, 104, 106–9, 118–19, 150, 163, 168, 183
The Satanic Verses (Rushdie) 202 n.10
Savale, Steve Chandra 112–13, 119
Sawhney, Nitin 4, 22, 34, 37
Sayyid, S. 21–2
scatting 148
Schafer, R. Murray 8–9, 55–8, 63–4, 80, 84, 197 n.5, 197 n.14
Schmidt, Eric Leigh 50–1, 196 n.1
Schulze, Holger 54, 193
scratching noise 131
Sean, Jay 34
2nd Generation Magazine 37–8
semiotic strategy 76–7
Senekowitsch, Susanne 132–3
sequencers 76
sexually charged lyrics 132–3, 186
sexy sounds 67
Shankar, Ravi 31
Sharma, Ashwani 26, 67
Sharma, Sanjay 22, 31–4, 36, 67, 109, 117, 119
Shiva Soundsystem 39–40
'Sholay (Epic Mix)' (2004) 160

Singh, Mona 34
Singh, Talvin 22, 36–7
Sister India 36, 106
sitar 108, 181
Skepta 201 n.2
Skrein 151, 154
The Slits 130, 186
Smith, Bruce R. 59
social politics 6, 192
social technology 70
'Soho Road to the Punjab' 31
son clave pattern 127–8
Sonic Agency (LaBelle) 65, 192
Sonic Bodies (Henriques) 95
sonic constellations 9, 17, 50, 59, 71–2, 80, 82, 85, 101, 119, 135, 144, 150–1, 153–4, 181, 183
sonic ecology 56
sonic fictions 6, 10, 40, 84, 126, 131, 135, 137, 140–1, 168, 172–3, 181, 185–7, 189, 192
sonic ornament 182
sonic perception 66
sonic production 3, 55, 72
sonic recontextualization 77–8, 80, 94, 118, 130, 163–4, 170, 185
sonic re-embodiment 65–6
sonic repertoires 5, 10, 30, 55, 58, 102, 137, 139, 146–8, 157, 169–71, 184–5, 187–9
sonic turn 54
Sonic Warfare (Goodman) 62, 166
sonological competence 55
SoundCloud 199 n.1
sound collage 77, 162, 164
soundmarks 57–9
Sound Moves (Bull) 59
sound practice(s), transcultural 27, 180. See *also* musical sounds
  of ADF (*see* Asian Dub Foundation (ADF))
  analysis of South Asian dance music 81–5
  digital sampling as 76–81
  everyday sounds 55–66
  of Lee (*see* Lee, Nathan ('Flutebox'))
  of M.I.A. (*see* M.I.A. (Arulpragasam, Mathangi))

recontextualization 9, 68, 77–8, 80, 82, 94, 104, 106, 109, 114–15, 118, 126, 130, 132, 163–4, 169–70, 181, 185
  techniques and technologies 66–76
  and visual culture/visuality 50–5
sound reproduction 6–7, 11, 66, 83, 144, 197 n.16
soundscapes 55–8, 60, 63, 77, 197 n.11
Soundscapes: The Tuning of the World (Schafer) 8, 55–6
Sounds English (Zuberi) 89
sound signal 57
sound systems 61–2
soundtracks 11, 60–1, 73, 172–3, 197 n.4
Sound Works (Schulze) 193
'Southall sound' 171
South Asian dance music 3, 5–6, 11, 15, 24, 62, 67–9, 73, 79, 91–2, 159, 179–81, 189–93
  of ADF (*see* Asian Dub Foundation (ADF))
  aesthetics and ethics in 159
  analysis of 81–5
  Asian Underground 36–8
  bhangra 29–36
  cultural politics of 25–30
  diasporic production 18–24
  in post-2000 UK 29, 38–47
Spaceape 160
speaker stacks 62
sruti box 202 n.9
Steel Pulse 198 n.1
Sterne, Jonathan 197 n.16
'Straight to Hell' (song) 135–6
street crier 58
street-style patois 94, 96, 102, 110, 116, 199 n.10
Stroumboulopoulos, George 200 n.6
Strummer, Joe 136
sub-bass sounds 40, 79, 84, 127, 154, 160–2, 166, 169, 175, 188
subcultural capital 201 n.3
'Sub-Kontinent' (2004) 160
Sunrise Radio 33, 171
'Sunshowers' (track) 126–32, 139–40, 185
Supercat 90
surrendo 129
Swaraj (club night) 36, 38–9

syncopated beat patterns/syncopation 5, 11, 45, 79, 85, 100, 108, 111, 127–8, 130–2, 139, 143, 154, 165, 167, 185
synthesised post-bhangra music styles 7
synthesizer-sounds 33, 76, 96, 118, 127–8, 136, 139, 152, 188

tablas 83, 94, 96–7, 99, 169, 202 n.5
Tagore, Rabindranath 4
'Take Yo' Praise' (soul/funk song) 77
Taylor, Timothy D. 100–1
technology/technologies, sound
   cultural 8, 68
   digital media 18, 41–2, 66, 68–9, 83, 91–2
   digital sampling 7, 9–10, 39, 68, 71, 73, 76–81, 104, 106–9, 118–19, 150, 163, 168, 183
   flutebox 145–51
   machine 71
   recording 68–9, 76, 78, 107, 151–2
   social 70
   techniques and 66–76
   and tribalism 8
technoscapes 24
Teji 167, 171
territorialism/territorialization 15, 38–9, 56, 93, 179
textual conception 173–6
Théberge, Paul 70–2, 148, 198 n.17, 198 n.20
There Ain't No Black in the Union Jack (Gilroy) 95
Thomas, Mary 194
Thornton, Sarah 201 n.3
Tigrona, Deize 132–4, 140, 170, 185–6
Timbaland 172
toasting 91, 94, 97, 181, 198 n.4
Tosh, Peter 198 n.2
transculturality 6–7, 17–18, 23–4, 104, 189
Transcultural Materialities 194
transnational entanglements 7, 18, 23, 42
transnationality 23, 46
Travelling Sounds 193
tribalism, and technology 8
Trouble Funk 78–9
Truax, Barry 9, 56, 197 n.7
Tuff Gong Studios 92
tumbi sound 98–9, 101, 165, 171, 202 n.6

'Tuning into London c.1600' 59
turntablism 69, 100, 131, 150, 199 n.8
12×12 guitar box 67
2livecrew 45

Unlocking the Groove (Butler) 82
urban dance music 1, 9, 11, 15, 25, 29–30, 36, 38, 42–4, 46–7, 49–50, 55, 58, 62–3, 68, 72, 126, 139, 147–8, 150, 160–1, 165, 168, 179–80, 188
urban spaces 8, 11, 27–9, 42, 59, 61–3, 160, 191–2, 194

vibrant microeconomics 124
vibrato' 69
Vietnam War 136
vinyl record 107
viola 153
VIP records 171
visual and textual conception 173–6
The Visual Culture Reader (Mirzoeff) 51, 53
visual culture/visuality 50–5, 80, 123
vocal introduction 94
vocal sample 36, 78, 108, 128, 165–6, 168

Walser, Robert 72
Wandan 151
Washington Post 200 n.5
Watkins, Lee 28
'Wedding Anthem mix' 101
Weheliye, Alexander 71
Welsch, Wolfgang 24
Western classical music 146, 149
Western Music and Its Others (Born and Hesmondalgh) 74
Whiteley, Sheila 27–8
Wicke, Peter 72, 159
'Wild Apache' 90
Wilehouse 162–5
Wiley 201 n.2
Womad 26
world fusion 1, 25–6
'The World Is Sound? Geography, Musicology and British-Asian Soundscapes' 73
world music 1–2, 4, 10, 25–7, 33, 42, 53, 112, 121, 124–5, 179, 189, 196 n.8
2.0 1, 42

'World Soundscape Project' 9, 56, 84
World Trade Organisation (WTO) 124
worldtronica 1
Wreckx-N-Effect 135–7, 141
WTO. *See* World Trade Organisation (WTO)

XL Recordings 126
X-Ray-Spex 130

Yarbrough, Camille 77
Yassin, Raed 196 n.16
Yellowman 94

Zuberi, Nabeel 38, 42–3, 89
'Zungu Zungu Zungu Zeng' (1982) 94

www.ingramcontent.com/pod-product-compliance
Lightning Source LLC
Chambersburg PA
CBHW052037300426
44117CB00012B/1858